What Your Colleagues Are Sayin

Beyond Crises is the humanizing, empowering book we need ~~...~~ *...for a compelling vision and action steps to move beyond crisis and create the interconnected schools and communities our multilingual learners deserve.*

Tonya Ward Singer
Consultant and author of *EL Excellence Every Day*
and *Opening Doors to Equity*

By using voices from communities, schools, and classrooms, Beyond Crises *re-envisions how systems can move away from deficit-based paradigms. The practical and new ways of reimagining presented in this book highlight and inspire a call to action that encourages strengths-based partnerships to acknowledge assets and competencies within systems.* Beyond Crises *is a relevant and responsive book that motivates hope and empathy to address polarizing and chaotic times in our nation.*

Ivannia Soto
Professor of Education, Whittier College,
and Author of *Shadowing Multilingual Learners* (2nd ed.)

Beyond Crises: Overcoming Linguistic and Cultural Inequities in Communities, Schools, and Classrooms *is just the resource administrators, instructional leaders, and educators in all walks of life need! This timely book by the powerful trio Debbie Zacarian, Margarita Calderón, and Margo Gottlieb is destined to pave the way for imagining and reimagining our communities, schools, and classrooms in a postcrisis world. Their unapologetic call for action is to overturn racial, cultural, and linguistic inequities—this book will show you how!*

Andrea Honigsfeld
Associate Dean and EdD Program Director, Molloy College,
and Author of *Collaborating for English Learners* (2nd ed.)

Through witnessing the pandemic's detrimental effects on English learners, I'm left grasping for a silver lining. I need to know how to make sense of what has happened, to learn from the challenges and heartbreak, and to thoughtfully move forward. Beyond Crises *comes at just the right time. Through compelling student stories, anecdotes from fierce advocates, and spot-on reflection questions and tools, the authors guide us to reimagine education for English learners."*

Diane Staehr Fenner
President of SupportEd Consulting and Author of
Unlocking English Learners' Potential

What a superb and relevant discussion of how we as educators and servants can take our colleagues, our students, and their families to the next level. Debbie, Margarita, and Margo have done a great job combining practical, critical practices and partnerships with perfect examples of why we as educators do what we do. You'll want to buy two, one for yourself and one to share."

Shawn Slakk
CEO and Educational Consultant,
ABCDSS Consulting Consortium

This timely and unique volume from Zacarian, Calderón, and Gottlieb, three of the most renowned masters in the field of teaching culturally and linguistically diverse students, spotlights the critical need for collaborative relationships between communities, schools, and classrooms to engage in advocacy for equitable educational opportunities for all learners. It guides the reader through a journey of reflection by making connections to one's own experiences with relationship building as well as identifying action steps to strengthen partnerships. It also invites the reader to imagine ways to be open to change and make things happen! This book is a must-read for anyone who works with this special student population."

Maria Dove
Professor, School of Education and Human Services, Molloy College,
and Author of *Collaborating for English Learners* (2nd ed.)

Beyond Crises

FROM ALL OF US

Co-writing and collaborating with our editor, Dan, especially during the pandemic, brought us the full steam of a mission-filled project, even during the darkest of days. We dedicate this book to Dan for making this journey possible.

FROM DEBBIE

The best collaboration comes with positive energy, trust, and ideas that challenge and inspire us to do our best work. It also comes from working with experts who cherish the opportunity to work together. Thank you, Margarita and Margo, for being true collaborators!

From our "regularly scheduled" Zoom calls, emails back and forth, writing, and reading each other's contributions, this project came alive from the first day and carried us right through to the end.

I dedicate this book to Margarita and Margo. Margarita for quickly and seamlessly creating an outline that became our beacon throughout. Margo for suggesting that we think "upside down" in ways that not only made sense, but inspired our thinking. It is an honor to be your partner in this collaboration.

FROM MARGARITA

Writing with Debbie and Margo has been one of my most exhilarating experiences with writing! My mind happily woke me up at 4 am with pieces of information I wanted to mention and share with my awesome co-authors. Therefore,

I dedicate this book to Debbie Zacarian for her gentle way of prodding us to think beyond the crises and the chaos to write this tome that connects her views to my lifelong efforts to bring equity for English learners in all schools, and

I dedicate this book to Margo Gottlieb for her way-out-of-the-box ideas that inspired us every inch of the way. Her imagination helped us see things upside down but with a focus in mind.

It all came together very smoothly and lovingly. I will cherish their collaboration with respect and high regard for their talents.

FROM MARGO

Beyond Crises provided me with the opportunity to contribute to the synergy from the visions and perspectives of two amazing experts and professionals. Debbie and Margarita took on the challenge of this fast-paced project and dove right in. Indeed, I am so grateful for their eternal patience and trust in me.

Thank you, Debbie, for your commitment and dedication to our project. You have been remarkable in providing us with resources and many versions to contemplate!

Thank you, Margarita, for your graciousness and sense of humor. You have been a true partner who has pushed us to do our best.

I have thoroughly enjoyed working with you and dedicate this book to you both.

Beyond Crises

Overcoming Linguistic and Cultural Inequities in Communities, Schools, and Classrooms

Debbie Zacarian

Margarita Espino Calderón

Margo Gottlieb

Foreword by Dan Alpert

CORWIN

FOR INFORMATION:

Corwin

A SAGE Company

2455 Teller Road

Thousand Oaks, California 91320

(800) 233–9936

www.corwin.com

SAGE Publications Ltd.

1 Oliver's Yard

55 City Road

London EC1Y 1SP

United Kingdom

SAGE Publications India Pvt. Ltd.

B 1/I 1 Mohan Cooperative Industrial Area

Mathura Road, New Delhi 110 044

India

SAGE Publications Asia-Pacific Pte. Ltd.

18 Cross Street #10–10/11/12

China Square Central

Singapore 048423

Printed in the United States of America

ISBN: 9781071844649 (spiral)

Program Director and Publisher: Dan Alpert

Senior Content Development Editor: Lucas Schleicher

Associate Content
  Development Editor: Mia Rodriguez

Production Editor: Tori Mirsadjadi

Copy Editor: Sarah J. Duffy

Typesetter: C&M Digitals (P) Ltd.

Proofreader: Dennis W. Webb

Indexer: Integra

Cover Designer: Gail Buschman

Marketing Managers: Maura Sullivan and Sharon Pendergast

This book is printed on acid-free paper.

21 22 23 24 25 10 9 8 7 6 5 4 3 2 1

Contents

PART I: IMAGINING COMMUNITIES

Chapter 9: Striving for Interconnections Among Communities, Schools, and Classrooms 199

Visit the companion website at
resources.corwin.com/BeyondCrises
for downloadable versions of this book's Reflection and
Imagine activities.

List of Figures and Resources

CHAPTER 7

CHAPTER 8

CHAPTER 9

Foreword
by Dan Alpert

How will the year 2020 be remembered in our history books? It's a question that has surfaced with some regularity in our social media, national news, and the plethora of Zoom gatherings that have consumed our workdays. Like most juicy questions it elicits a range of opinions, but I think we can all agree on some very basic truths:

1. Those who are reading this book have endured a pandemic that resulted in the loss of hundreds of thousands of lives.

2. The collateral damage caused by the pandemic included economic instability, massive job loss, social isolation, disruption of K–12 and higher education, and increased incidences of trauma, mental illness, and substance abuse.

3. Some groups experienced disproportionate harm (e.g., higher infection and mortality rates) as a result of the pandemic. These groups included the elderly, those with preexisting conditions, low-income families, and people of color.

4. Similarly, some populations of K–12 students (low income as well as Black and Brown children) experienced disproportionate levels of harm, including loss and illness of family members; severe learning loss caused, in part, by the digital divide and lack of available parental supports (many of their parents served as frontline workers); and higher rates of anxiety and trauma. Among those who experienced the highest degree of harm are our nation's multilingual learners.

5. As the pandemic shed light on a broad range of structural inequities that were present well before its onset, a heightened awareness of racial injustice was amplified by tragic episodes of police brutality that were captured on video and covered by the media. In response, a protest movement coalesced and enacted demonstrations and marches in cities and towns across the country.

As I compose this prologue, my beautiful Northern California sky has been disfigured by haze and smoke from surrounding wildfires. COVID-19 infection rates are on the rise in a number of states. Our nation is increasingly polarized and many of us live in fear of losing our fundamental civil rights. We are consumed by malaise, an existential grief.

And yet, there are days when I feel something resembling hope. And I know I'm not alone in feeling this way.

K–12 educators are among the most hopeful people I know. Despite the challenges of teaching in what feels like a dystopian landscape, we are energized by the hopefulness that brought us into our profession in the first place. The prospect of helping children build on their unique assets and cultivate their inner brilliance is enlivening. The prospect of facilitating learning, both within our students and within ourselves, is intoxicating. And the prospect of imagining a better world will carry us through these dark days.

The authors of this powerful book embody hopefulness on a grand scale. They have captured and responded to many of the critical lessons we learned over the course of 2020. When our schools shut down, we attended to the daunting challenge of ensuring that our students had access to basic nutrition and health services. We learned that, in moments of crisis, attending to students' psychosocial needs took precedence over raising test scores. (Recall the mantra *Maslow before Bloom*.) We learned that forming effective partnerships with families and communities was essential to the health and well-being of our students. And we were offered a blunt reminder that a system that was designed to serve the interests of a privileged few was destined to fail our historically underserved students—including the millions of multilingual learners who populate our nation's schools. Above all, we learned that the "normal" that many of us yearned for was never good enough for large numbers of children and families.

Beyond the Crises envisions a better world in which educators, students, families, and communities work in partnership to ensure that multilingual-multicultural learners can grow into their best selves. Informed by an assets-based framework, the book envisions communities, schools, and classrooms working together in the manner of a "whole-child ecosystem" that values students' identities, home languages, and cultures. The authors open the book with a section on how to enact school/home/community partnerships in a manner that promotes students' physical, social-emotional, and intellectual growth. The whole-school domain—the subject matter of the second section of the book—is envisioned as a community in which every teacher and administrator is dedicated to the well-being and success of multilingual learners. Finally, the third section is devoted to classrooms (both virtual and face-to-face) that function as warm and welcoming refuges. Imagine a counternarrative to the traditional disconnect between the languages and cultures of classrooms and those of homes and communities, in which classrooms serve as *extensions* of homes and communities with a common goal of linguistic and cultural sustainability!

Challenging deficit mindsets and dismantling inequitable systems necessitates a shared commitment to common objectives across the ecosystem. We are called upon to critically examine practices and policies that failed to serve the interests of students of color and multilingual learners across many generations. Above all, such change requires new learning on the part of education professionals, families, and other members of the community. The pandemic surfaced a disquieting truth—that most of us were ill prepared for the adaptive challenges that emerge in times of crisis. For this reason, the authors stress the importance of professional learning across all spheres of the ecosystem. Our future depends on empowering teachers and administrators to give voice to multilingual-multicultural learners who can then claim their own power to serve the greater good.

Finally, we can't enact such conditions in the traditional silos that divide us. Systems can only be transformed when we come together, in the manner of a collective, in the interest of the whole child, driven by our commitment to overcoming systemic linguicism and racism and other formidable barriers to equity.

We can gain resilience by leveraging hope and acting on our capacity for empathy and our infinite capacity for creativity. Remember that we have it within us to move beyond the crises, the barriers to equity, the failure of imagination that brought us to this moment in history, as long as we continue to learn together.

Acknowledgments

We gratefully acknowledge and offer our thanks to the following educators for lending their voices to this book. Each brings to life the great flexibility, resilience, and courage that we have seen in educators worldwide. Each brings to life the ideals of moving beyond crises to overcome inequities and making education work—even in the most challenging of times.

Ysidro Abreu, Principal, Middle School #319, New York, NY

Caroline Carter Curtice, ESOL Teacher, Charleston County Public School District, Charleston, SC

Mark Gaither, Principal, Wolfe Street Academy, Baltimore, MD

Jennifer Hunter, English Language Acquisition Coach, Brockton Public Schools, Brockton, MA

Kellie Jones, English Language Learners Coordinator, Brockton Public Schools, Brockton, MA

Giuliana Jahnsen Lewis, Seventh-Grade Dean, Sterling Middle School, Loudoun County, VA

Herman Mizell, Principal, Sterling Middle School, Loudoun County, VA

Amal Qayed, Site-Based Coordinator, Salina Elementary School, Dearborn, MI

Carlos Ramírez, Principal, Randolph Elementary School, Arlington, VA

Jennifer Iamele Savage, Literacy Coach, James Simons Montessori, Charleston, SC

Michael Silverstone, Teacher, Massachusetts

Susan Stanley, Principal, Salina Elementary School, Dearborn, MI

Lisa Tartaglia, Reading Specialist, Loudoun County High School, Leesburg, VA

Michael P. Thomas, Superintendent, Brockton Public Schools, Brockton, MA

Dr. Eric Williams, Superintendent, Loudoun County Public Schools, Leesburg, VA

About the Authors

Dr. Debbie Zacarian, founder of Zacarian & Associates, provides professional development, strategic planning, and technical assistance for K–16 educators of culturally and linguistically diverse populations. Focusing on strengths-based leadership, instructional practices, and school-family-community partnerships, she has served as an expert consultant for school districts, universities, and organizations including the Massachusetts Parent Information Resource Center, Federation for Children with Special Needs, and Colorín Colorado, a premier national website serving educators and families of English learners.

Debbie served on the faculty of University of Massachusetts-Amherst, where she supported the professional preparation of educators of English learners and designed and taught courses on culturally responsive practices and multilingual education. She served as a program director at the Collaborative for Educational Services, where she provided professional development for thousands of educators, partnered with Fitchburg State University in co-writing a National Professional Development grant initiative that supported STEM education of multilingual learners, and wrote the English learner policies for numerous rural, suburban, and urban districts. Debbie also directed the Amherst Public Schools bilingual and English learner programming, where she and the district received state and national honors.

The author of more than 100 publications, her most recent professional books include *Responsive Schooling for Culturally and Linguistically Diverse Students*; *Teaching to Empower: Taking Action to Foster Student Agency, Self-Confidence and Collaboration*; and *Teaching to Strengths: Supporting Students Living With Trauma, Violence, and Chronic Stress*.

Debbie can be contacted at debbie@zacarianconsulting.com, www.zacarianconsulting.com, and @debbiezacarian.

Dr. Margarita Espino Calderón is Professor Emerita/senior research scientist at Johns Hopkins University. She has worked on numerous research and development projects focusing on reading for English learners funded by the U.S. Department of Education Institute of Education Sciences and the U.S. Department of Labor, and she has collaborated with Harvard University and the Center for Applied Linguistics on a longitudinal study funded by the National Institute of Child Health and Human Development.

The Carnegie Corporation of New York funded her five-year empirical study to develop Expediting Comprehension for English Language Learners (ExC-ELL), a comprehensive professional development model for math, science, social studies, language arts, ESL, and special education teachers that integrates language, literacy, and content. She also developed two other effective evidence-based programs: Reading Instructional Goals for Older Readers (RIGOR) for Newcomers with Interrupted Formal Education and the Bilingual Cooperative Integrated Reading and Composition (BCIRC) program, which was developed for dual language instruction and is listed in the What Works Clearinghouse.

Currently, Margarita collaborates with George Washington University on a Title III five-year grant to implement and further study A Whole-School Approach to Professional Development with ExC-ELL in Virginia school districts.

She is a consultant for the U.S. Department of Justice Office of Civil Rights. She has served on national language and literacy research panels. Margarita is also president/CEO of Margarita Calderón and Associates. She and her team of ten associates conduct ExC-ELL comprehensive multiyear professional development and on-site coaching in schools, districts, statewide and international institutes. She has over 100 publications on language and literacy for English learners.

Margarita can be contacted at mecalde@gmail.com, www.exc-ell.com, and @calderonexc.

Dr. Margo Gottlieb is co-founder and lead developer for WIDA (a consortium of 41 states, territories, and federal agencies along with the international consortium of 500 schools) housed at the Wisconsin Center for Education Research, University of Wisconsin-Madison. For years she was director of assessment and evaluation for the Illinois Resource Center, an arm of the Illinois State Board of Education.

Starting her career as a teacher and bilingual coordinator, Margo has been devoted to the education and equity of multilingual learners. She served as a Fulbright Senior Specialist in Chile, was appointed to the U.S. Department of Education's Inaugural National Technical Advisory Council, and was honored by TESOL International Association in 2016 for her significant contribution to the TESOL profession. Recently, Margo's scholarship has focused on designing language development standards frameworks, promoting student agency through assessment *as, for,* and *of* learning; evaluating language education policy; and designing linguistically and culturally sustainable curriculum.

Margo has keynoted, presented, and consulted in over 20 countries and almost every U.S. state, providing technical assistance to school districts, universities, governments, publishers, and organizations. She has published over 90 articles, monographs, guides, encyclopedia entries, and chapters as well as authored, co-authored, or co-edited over 20 books, including *Classroom Assessment in Multiple Languages: A Handbook for Teachers, Assessing Multilingual Learners: A Month-by-Month Guide, Language Power: Key Uses for Accessing Content* (with M. Castro), and *Assessing English Language Learners: Bridges to Equity* (2nd ed.).

Margo can be contacted at margogottlieb@gmail.com.

Introduction

In this book, we argue that partnerships among communities, schools, and classrooms are essential if we are ever to imagine students truly thriving in school and in their lives.

We see these crises stemming from the pandemic, racial injustices, and natural disasters as fueling our renewal, our restart, our transformational imaginings of what can be done, what is possible, and what is being done when we band together to enhance and support each other's lives. Students and family, classroom, school, and local communities are not silos unto themselves. They are part of a larger whole that is interrelated, interconnected, and even interdependent. And that's good! By forming alliances among communities, schools, and classrooms—the BIG three as we see them—we see the power that can be realized by truly working, socializing, and flourishing together.

In this book, we bring the big three together to demonstrate a new beginning beyond crises to overcome the inequities that have been occurring and continue to occur. We look at how local communities are our partners, how families are engaged, and how educators are advocates who continuously hone their professional craft so that students are empowered as learners and community members. We show how we can create conditions in which our students and families feel safe, included, and valued only when we come together in a comprehensive ecosystem that encompasses the classroom, school, and local community.

With voices from the field, we show how local, school, and classroom communities are working together in places such as Brockton, Massachusetts; Loudon County Virginia; New York City; Dearborn, Michigan; Baltimore, Maryland; and Charleston, South Carolina. With schools in these locales as our partners in imagining beyond crises, we show new concepts for organizing and creating structures for interconnected collaborations in online, in-person, and hybrid formats. We also show how professional development can support us in our effort to look beyond crises to overcome inequities.

Our book has three parts: Imagining Communities, Imagining Schools, and Imagining Classrooms. Each includes three chapters on designing and enacting strengths-based approaches, sustaining momentum and growth, and striving for interdependent interconnections. We illustrate the experience of Álvaro, a seventh grader, and his second-grade sister Inés, who have come to the United States with their mother, Mrs. Pérez, from Guatemala after experiencing the tragic losses of their father and sister. We also meet some members of their local community and the two schools the children attend, specifically, Dr. Cestari, a local optometrist; Ms. James, a school principal; Mrs. Morales, a family–community liaison; Ms. Rozier, an ESL teacher; and Ms. Ortega-Miller, a second-grade teacher. We do this to show how we can powerfully take actions to design and implement in-person, online, and hybrid teaching and learning.

We also use varied terminology, as many in our professional field do, to describe many students, including *English learners, multilingual learners, long-term English learners (LTEL), newcomers,* and *students with interrupted formal education (SIFE).* In addition, we use a variety of terms to describe the school-based professionals whose role is to bring family, individual, agency and organizational, school, and classroom communities together, such as *coordinator, liaison, outreach worker, family resource coordinator, community relations facilitator,* and *parent advocate.* We are delighted to have co-written this book, bringing decades of professional experience and passion in working toward overcoming linguistic and cultural inequities.

In our spirit of collaborating, working interdependently, and being interconnected, we begin Part I by exploring the rationale for designing and enacting strengths-based family and community partnerships. We look closely at the importance of identifying, valuing, and acknowledging the assets and competencies of all students and their families while taking time to understand how crises amplify the tremendous struggles of some Latinx, Black, and indigenous Americans as well as students and families living in poverty and the epic number who have been affected by adversity. We share how federal, state, local, district, school, and classroom roles can be enacted for the benefit of students' academic and social-emotional success.

Part I explores how we can create and sustain an ecosystem to enhance students' assets and address challenges to complement our goal of using a strengths-based approach with children and families. We provide examples from several districts and exemplary professionals who engage in family and community partnerships.

Additionally, we look more closely at ways that we can intentionally build sustained interwoven partnerships with various sectors of family and community partners. We discuss how to talk to partners about raising awareness of our students' interests, desires, and needs; ensuring that students' medical health, well-being, and social-emotional and intellectual growth are supported; and addressing challenges and overcoming barriers by using an asset-based ideology.

Once we take a deep dive into learning about our local communities, in Part II we turn to our schools and the policies, structures, and now irrelevant ways of schooling that call for change. We share how English learner (EL) specialists have become a pivotal part of the leadership team and family connections. Two amazing teacher leaders share all that they and their colleagues do to engage ELs and attempt to create success within all these constraints.

Part II details how ESL and core content teachers are reinventing co-teaching to be more effective, efficient in delivering hybrid instruction, and inclusive. They give us some examples of their turn taking in teaching academic language, reading comprehension, and writing. We also share a form that includes planning, who delivers what part of the lesson, assessment and monitoring turns, and communication with students and families.

Since professional development also has to be reconfigured, we go back to the basics by (1) identifying the outcomes we want; (2) selecting the processes that work and the trends that don't; (3) applying the features that create growth for multilingual learners, their peers, and their teachers and administrators; and (4) forecasting transfer from training. We provide tools for each decision.

Finally, principals from three schools bring all these pieces together as they describe what they are doing and even how they are holding up their staff and themselves. The three principals are implementing a whole-school approach to professional development on EL success. The Virginia and New York principals found that implementing key instructional strategies is resulting in ELs and all other students showing great growth. Loudoun County Public Schools shares their comprehensive professional development model focused on preparing all core content teachers, instructional coaches, school-site administrators, and central district office specialists on integrating language, literacy, and core content into every lesson in every classroom to better reach their ELs.

In Part III, we turn to the inner workings of classrooms, where we see teachers' extraordinary efforts to optimize opportunities for all students—particularly minoritized students—to grow cognitively, linguistically, and social-emotionally. The focus on multilingual learners and their peers accentuates their talents in knowing and using multiple languages and in being encouraged to interact in their preferred language in linguistically and culturally sustainable environments. As a result, students are gaining confidence, growing into agents of learning in their own right, and becoming empowered to make a difference.

We applaud teachers during these times of crisis for being so nimble, flexible, and innovative while simultaneously having to cope with and endure their own stressors. What we present are continued opportunities for teachers and all their partners to engage in collaboration, to take advantage of this upheaval, and to make it a time to change the educational system. As teachers are the lifeblood of schools and are directly connected to families, we envision how we might co-construct a future through the lens of equity.

It might seem strange to readers that our book closes with Imagining Classrooms. However, we purposefully wanted to reverse the usual organization of books representing K–12 settings to envision education from the outside-in prior to viewing it from the inside-out. In doing so, we accentuate the important presence and influence of communities on schools and, consequently, the impact of schools on classrooms. The inverse order allows us to imagine the potential synergy that can be created and maintained on an ongoing basis.

In depicting the interdependence and interconnections among three ecosystems (community, school, and classroom), our intent is to touch a broad array of stakeholders and to illustrate their interrelationships. The primary audience for this book includes everyone affiliated with elementary, middle, and secondary schools and their spheres of influence—ESL and core content teachers, coaches, community liaisons, and principals, to name a few. Each person makes a unique contribution, and we would like to acknowledge everyone who touches the lives of children and youth.

As we have been navigating unique times, *Beyond Crises* has tried to capture this most unusual point in our history with several distinct features. Understanding the stress and distress that everyone has been facing, we confront challenges head on and imagine what the educational world might look like if and when we can overcome its inequities. We invite you in partnership to also make postcrisis predictions in a series of colorful boxes where we pose questions for you to reflect on and contemplate with others. In addition, we offer checklists, tools, and resources for you to use in learning communities or during ongoing professional development and coaching.

Beyond Crises contributes to the K–12 landscape by infusing much-needed empathy, hope, and inspiration into discussion of the people in our communities, schools, and classrooms. We see these three intertwined ecosystems as foundational to optimize conditions for teaching and learning. Working together as committed partners, we can overturn persistent linguistic and cultural inequities and achieve what is possible by embracing these ideals together.

IMAGINING COMMUNITIES

Designing and Enacting Strengths-Based Communities

When I play soccer, my mind is able to stop swirling around. I'm able to concentrate on the game I love and feel free as I run.

—Álvaro, Seventh-Grade Student

Imagine being this student, Álvaro Pérez. In the fall of 2019, you come to the United States from Guatemala after experiencing the terror of Volcano de Fuego the year prior. How might you feel leaving your homeland after experiencing the trauma and crisis of this natural disaster where you, your mother, and younger sister watched your father and older sister perish and you have been struggling since? As you imagine yourself as this student, respond to the following reflection question:

> ## IMAGINE
>
> What would you want your new local community to provide you so that you feel safe and that you belong, are valued, and are seen as competent in your new community?
>
> _____
>
> _____
>
> _____
>
> _____
>
> _____
>
> _____

online resources — Available for download from **resources.corwin.com/BeyondCrises**.

Now, imagine that you work for the school or district in which Álvaro enrolls. He and his mother come to your school accompanied by his younger sister Inés and are welcomed to a multilingual-multicultural environment that honors and values their identity and supports Álvaro wholly to feel safe, welcome, and competent. Mrs. Morales, a Spanish-English bilingual-bicultural family–community liaison from your school takes time to meet with Álvaro and his mother as he enrolls in his new school. She learns about Álvaro's prior schooling and his personal, cultural, social, and life experiences including the tragedy that he, his mother, and his younger sister experienced. For example, Álvaro shares how much he enjoys math and that it is his favorite subject. Mrs. Morales also learns from Mrs. Pérez that Álvaro was traumatized by the volcano, is afraid to fall asleep at night, and has been having trouble eating. As the meeting unfolds, imagine Mrs. Morales telling them about a school partner that they work with, a community bilingual-bicultural therapist, who supports students that have had traumatic losses such as Álvaro's.

Mrs. Morales was born and reared in this metropolitan suburb, learned to speak Spanish at home, and identifies with her families' Puerto Rican roots. While she is not from Guatemala and has not experienced significant adversity, she is a caring, curious, empathetic professional who has participated in many professional development experiences to raise her level of awareness and consciousness about students from other countries, learning a new language, and living with adversity. She takes time to support Álvaro to feel welcomed at his new school. She asks about the activities he enjoys doing outside of school. When Álvaro and his mother share that he loves to play soccer, imagine Mrs. Morales contacting the local soccer club to ensure that he joins the program. And imagine the community partner reaching out to Álvaro and his mother and arranging to take them to that soccer program. Imagine that the soccer program partners know to provide supports such as Spanish-speaking translators so that they can engage in a free flow of communication with Álvaro and his mother.

Additionally, imagine Mrs. Morales asking Mrs. Pérez how she was involved in Álvaro's prior schooling. She learns that Mrs. Pérez engaged in daily conversations with his teacher as she dropped off her son at school and often supported his teacher as she planned various school activities such as serving meals or making costumes for school plays. Imagine that after learning this information, Mrs. Morales tells Mrs. Pérez about the outreach program coordinated by families that provides buddies for parents/guardians who are new to the community to support them in becoming acquainted with the various activities that parents/guardians engage in at the middle school. Imagine Mrs. Morales even saying, "It's one of the best activities that our middle school offers!"

After the interview with Álvaro and his mother, imagine Mrs. Morales excitedly sharing information about the new student and his family with his classroom and specialist teachers so that they can prepare for his entry and his mother's participation at the school.

REFLECTION

How does this experience relate to what you have experienced in your local community as a student, parent/guardian, educator, and/or member of a program such as a soccer club?

_____

_____

_____

_____

_____

_____

online resources Available for download from **resources.corwin.com/BeyondCrises**.

Imagine that when Álvaro has trouble reading the board and seeing the soccer field, his school's child study team alerts Mrs. Morales, who seamlessly supports Álvaro and his mother in working with one of the district's community partners, Dr. Cestari, an optometrist. Further, during the eye exam, Dr. Cestari takes an interest and the time to converse with Álvaro and his mother. Dr. Cestari asks him questions about his interests and his hopes and dreams. Further, she takes time to learn about his life experiences in Guatemala, the tragedy he experienced during the volcano, and the fears that Álvaro has about moving to the United States, where he fears reprisals for being from Guatemala.

REFLECTION

How does this experience relate to what you have experienced as an advocate for students and families from multilingual-multicultural experiences in your work context?

_____

_____

_____

_____

_____

_____

online resources Available for download from **resources.corwin.com/BeyondCrises**.

In class, Álvaro's ESL teacher, Ms. Rozier, knows about his interests in soccer as well as the trauma he experienced living through the volcano in Guatemala. With support from the school's counselor, Mrs. Morales, and the professional development experiences that she has had on trauma-sensitive practices, Ms. Rozier feels more secure in using strengths-based practices for students who are experiencing or have experienced adversity. And as COVID-19 forced the district's schools to close, Álvaro's school and their community partners worked to ensure that he, his younger sister, and his mother are safe and that they fully understand how to access the food, medical, school, and housing supports that they might need. Most importantly, they also ensure that they are full contributing members of their community's COVID-19 efforts. For example, Álvaro's mother has become part of the support initiatives to help other families during the crisis to obtain health, cultural, social supports, and other services.

IMAGINE

Drawing from the responses you have written thus far in this chapter (and in the Reflection box that follows), imagine the themes that are emerging in the ways that students such as Álvaro and his mother are being welcomed:

Into their new local community

_____

_____

_____

_____

_____

Into their new school community

_____

_____

_____

_____

_____

_____

Into their new classroom community

_____

_____

_____

_____

_____

_____

REFLECTION

What are two to three key features of community partnerships that are present in your school or work context?

_____

_____

_____

_____

_____

What actions do you believe would strengthen the school–community partnerships in your school or work context?

_____

_____

_____

_____

_____

_____

_____

online resources   Available for download from **resources.corwin.com/BeyondCrises**.

In this chapter of our book, we explore the importance of designing and enacting strengths-based partnerships among communities, schools, and classrooms as these are critical for us to strategically enact the types of interactive supports and contributions that will amplify the assets, interests, and ever-changing needs of students and their families.

We use the terms *multilingual, multicultural, multiethnic,* and *multiracial* to describe the diversity of students and families whose personal, social, linguistic, cultural, racial, and ethnic experiences are distinct from those of white middle-class groups who speak the formal language of school and commonly (and evaluatively) referred to as standard American English.

We also want to set the stage for the suburban community in which Álvaro and his family live. It looks like many metropolitan suburbs in the United States—more like a sprawling city than a grassy suburb of the 1960s, and its population has become more economically, racially, culturally, linguistically, and ethnically diverse during the past decade (Kotok & Frankenberg, 2017). Álvaro, a seventh grader, is joining Kennedy Middle School, a public school of about 650 students, and Inés is entering Sally Ride Elementary School, a public school of about 400 children spanning Grades K–5. Like at most schools across the nation, the teachers and administrators in the two schools and their respective district are mostly white (Kotok & Frankenberg, 2017). At Kennedy and Ride, the most common language spoken by their multilingual learners is Spanish, followed by Haitian Creole, Arabic, Vietnamese, and, in small numbers, by twenty additional languages. While most of the schools' multilingual students are from Central America and the Caribbean, there are also students from a range of countries in Africa, South America, Southeast Asia, the Middle East, and Europe, not to mention the United States. With this as our demographic background, let's look at what we mean by designing and enacting strengths-based partnerships as we begin the first chapter of our book.

Designing and Enacting Strengths-Based Communities

Moving From Deficits to Assets

As educators, we have a tendency to focus on what we perceive is missing or lacking in the lives of our students. Examples include making deficit-based statements such as these:

- ✓ They don't know English.
- ✓ They have been in the English learning program forever.
- ✓ They have not gone to school.
- ✓ They are too poor to help.
- ✓ They live in a shelter.
- ✓ Their life is too chaotic for us to help them.
- ✓ Their parents aren't literate.
- ✓ Their parents don't know how to help their child in school.
- ✓ Their parents don't care about their child's school.

This deficit lens can unfortunately contribute to predictable odds of failure for historically marginalized students, especially during the many crises that we have encountered. When we focus exclusively on what we perceive as weaknesses, we fail to see the inherent strengths (and there are many to be found!) that our students bring to our schools and classrooms. And if we do this often enough, it becomes our modus operandi rather than focusing our attention where it should be—cultivating and building on students' existing and developing assets.

Indeed, research points to the essential relationship between acknowledging students' personal, social, cultural, and academic assets and their growth and greater academic and social-emotional success (Biswas-Dienera, Kashdan, & Gurpal, 2011). Similarly, applying such a strengths-based lens to our students and their families enables us to form more effective partnership with families. One of the few silver linings of the COVID-19 pandemic has been the manner in which educators responded with a renewed sense of purpose around partnering with and caring for multilingual-multicultural families. Indeed, many of the educators we work with ask us how they can be more supportive and involved with families during the pandemic. And, just as importantly, they also ask how they can work more closely with their local community and beyond to provide comprehensive (often referred to as *wraparound*) supports for students and families. In this section of our book, we take the step of working with the community further. As shown in Figure 1.1, we look at how we can overcome inequities by building on and from the strengths and assets of each of our unique communities (i.e., our students and families as well as individuals, organizations, agencies, and institutions), schools, and classrooms.

Figure 1.1 • Whole Community, Whole District, Whole School, Whole Classroom

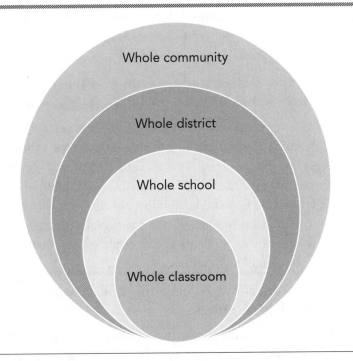

A Whole Community, District, School, Classroom Approach!

A whole-classroom, whole-school, whole-district, whole-community assets-based perspective requires that we, as educators and members of a school, district, and local community, do the following:

✓ **Recognize students' strengths.**

For example, our focal student, Álvaro, speaks Spanish, loves mathematics, and plays and is passionate about soccer. In addition, he also witnessed his father and sister's death, experienced an active volcano, and, at the same time, mustered the strength and courage to move to the United States and enroll in a new school, where he is acquiring an additional language in which to communicate. Each of these individual attributes and characteristics can be described and seen as an important strength that Álvaro possesses when they are coupled with our acknowledgment of and value for them.

✓ **Recognize parents'/guardians' strengths.**

These include the various strengths and attributes, which often go unseen, that parents/guardians use to support their child's education (Gonzalez, Moll, & Amanti, 2005; Zacarian, Alvarez-Ortiz, & Haynes, 2017; Zacarian & Silverstone, 2015). For example, Álvaro's mother, Mrs. Pérez, attends his soccer games to show her support for him engaging in this activity. She also drops him off at school so that she may engage in a conversation with his teacher to show support and gratitude for what the teacher is doing. Mrs. Perez is also a highly skilled seamstress who is keenly aware of the importance of many competencies including the mathematic skills needed to design clothing. Álvaro has observed her seamstress work for as long as he can remember and has helped her in a variety of tasks including helping her measure and create clothing patterns.

✓ **Be curious and caring, and take time to learn about the many skills and assets that students and parents/guardians possess.**

An assets-based approach shines a light on the importance of taking a genuine interest in learning about students and parents/guardians that moves beyond collecting required information. It is focused on learning about the personal, cultural, social, linguistic, and life experiences of children and their families so that we may infuse these understandings in our work with them. Further, it involves our willingness to share our own personal, cultural, social, linguistic, and life experiences with students and families so that they may know us as equal partners who embrace connection.

✓ **Invest time and effort in creating and sustaining meaningful partnerships with families.**

Building partnerships with multilingual-multicultural families should be foundational to what we do. Doing so can greatly increase the amount of meaningful interactions that our students engage in to support their social-emotional and academic growth. These partnerships are also wonderful supports for deepening our awareness of and connection to our students.

✓ **Build and advance school–parent/guardian partnerships with the support of bilingual-bicultural communication.**

In addition to the federal requirement that parents meaningfully understand their child's programming (U.S. Department of Education [USDOE] & U.S. Department of Justice [USDOJ], 2015) and any state requirements regarding family engagement, bilingual-bicultural administrators, staff, specialists, and translators can greatly help parents/guardians and schools have meaningful back-and-forth communication that is essential for the overall goal of working closely as partners together.

✓ **Recruit, select, and sustain community partners who believe in the same assets-based ideology as we do.**

Community partnerships with individuals, agencies, organizations, and institutions are essential for enhancing students' and families' interests, hopes, and dreams and addressing their needs. As important as it is to develop partnerships, it is essential that our partners operate from the same assets-based philosophy as we and others are advocating. Doing this requires that every partner

- sees the importance of working collaboratively with parents/guardians by building trusting reciprocal relationships,
- unconditionally accepts and welcomes students and parents/guardians for who they are, and
- believes that our students will be successful in school and beyond and that their parents will be active, meaningful, and purposeful partners with us.

Figure 1.2 presents a way of considering our work in classrooms, schools, districts, and communities using a partnership ideology.

Figure 1.2 • Community Partner Ideology

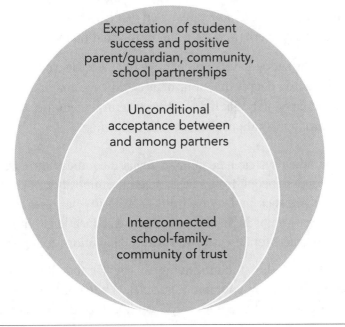

IMAGINE

Think about the ways you might continuously learn about and draw from the skills and assets of students and families. How would your school or district incorporate an assets-based approach as part of its efforts?

_____

_____

_____

_____

_____

_____

online resources ⏷   Available for download from **resources.corwin.com/BeyondCrises**.

Shining a Light on Inequities

We are in a time of dramatic changes in education. While the pandemic has affected every classroom across the globe, it has also amplified the tremendous struggles of some Latinx, Black, and Indigenous Americans as well as students and families living in poverty and the millions who have been affected by trauma, violence, and chronic stress in the United States and elsewhere. Additionally, millions of people in the United States and across the globe live in fear of, have been infected by, or have died from COVID-19. Further, against the backdrop of the pandemic are multiple other crises including fires that have ravaged the West Coast, floods that have severely impacted states in the South, and the largest civil rights' protests in our nation's history in the wake of police-involved deaths. These crises and others have brought widespread concerns about the inequities that many people face every day.

Moreover, while the sudden and drastic move to remote learning required that we all use technologies to a degree that none of us could have imagined or anticipated, it also shone a very stark and bright light on the structural inequities that are occurring in our schools and in the nation. Consider the following:

✓ "Long-standing systemic health and social inequities have disproportionly placed groups of people from racial and ethnic minority groups at an increased risk of getting sick and dying from COVID-19" because of discrimination against these groups in "health care, housing, education, criminal justice, and finance" (Centers for Disease Control and Prevention, 2020, paras. 1, 4).

✓ Almost half of the students living in the United States live in poverty (Southern Education Foundation, 2020). While multilingual learners are a rapidly growing and tremendously diverse group (Bethell, Davis, Gombojav,

Stumbo, & Powers, 2017), 60 percent of their families' incomes are 185% below poverty level (Grantmakers for Education, 2013).

✓ Almost half of U.S. students have experienced or are experiencing significant adversity (Bethell et al., 2017; Child and Adolescent Health Measurement Initiative, 2013) in the form of abuse, neglect, parental loss, or mental illness. In addition to the multilingual-multicultural learners who have experienced these phenomena, many have also experienced living in war or conflict zones and being persecuted, displaced, and living in constant fear of being deported or becoming homeless.

✓ "Suburban schools are rapidly becoming more culturally, economically, linguistically, and racially diverse, yet these diverse groups are still likely to live in neighborhoods where they are isolated from whites, regardless of income" (Edwards, Domke, & White, 2017, p. 109).

✓ It is more likely for teachers to represent cultures, speak languages, and live in communities that are a distance from and different than their students and have few natural, everyday conversations with parents (Edwards & White, 2018, pp. 6–7).

✓ The disproportionate graduation rates among students from various groups, as depicted in Figure 1.3, continues to be an enduring fixture of U.S. public school education.

Figure 1.3 • 2017–18 U.S. Graduation Rates of Public School Students

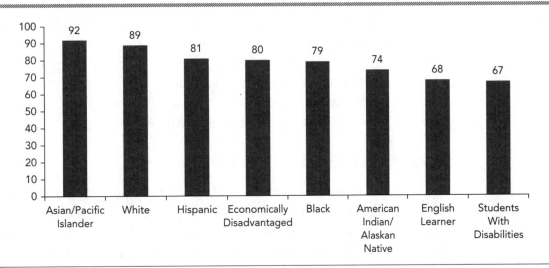

Source: National Center for Education Statistics (2019).

Listening, Really Listening!

While the pandemic and other crises are challenging educators and communities in unprecedented ways, this does not diminish our need to listen, really listen closely, to the different perspectives and experiences of our dynamically changing student and family populations. In this way,

We have to be willing to embrace the diversity that is occurring in our communities, schools, and classrooms.

we position ourselves to ensure that our students' assets and interests are honored, valued, and acknowledged and, as just importantly, that their needs are fulfilled. And it doesn't stop with students. We also must strive to support families in ways that honor and acknowledge their various assets and competencies as foundational to what we do.

For example, Mrs. Morales, the family–community liaison that we presented earlier, asked Álvaro's mother how she had been involved in her son's previous school. Mrs. Pérez shared that she had supported her son and daughter by dropping them off at school and visiting with their teachers and the other parents each day. Some of us might describe this drop-off activity as a time for parents/guardians to quickly say hello to us and for them to then make as quick an exit as they can so that we may begin our "real" day with our students. However, this mother and many parents/guardians see and value that before- and after-school drop-off ritual as the social glue that maintains their connectivity to their child's school.

Moving Away From Using Too Much Information

Many multilingual-multicultural families come from collectivist cultures that place high value on relationships, belonging, and cohesion (Hofstede, 2011; Hofstede & Hofstede, 2005). The type of social gathering described above represents a collectivist cultural way of being when Álvaro and his mother visit the seventh-grade teacher before school each morning. While many of us, as school staff, seem to spend an inordinate amount of time trying to fill parents/guardians with information (i.e., what we believe is missing or broken in the lives of families)—from enrollment forms, to regularly pouring information into a child's backpack, to holding Back to School nights in order to recite what we believe parents need to know about what their child is learning—we often do so at the expense of relationality. Rather than relying on this typical hyper-focus on sharing information, how might we humbly show and share our respect and value of the assets that students and families have to offer?

Cultivating a Collaborative Culture

It's important to show respect for a family's cultural ways of being and acting. In addition, over the past decades, research has helped us better identify best practices in terms of what and how we teach, how children learn, how learning is measured, and how we should work together and align our resources to support improvements (Ramirez, 2010). However, the one area that has seemed to elude us is how we can collaborate best with diverse families (Ramirez, 2010). It requires two conditions:

- ✓ We challenge, question, and move beyond traditional beliefs about parent involvement.

- ✓ We value parents' role as their child's teacher (it's not ours alone!).

Let's look at what we mean by challenging and questioning traditional beliefs about parent involvement. Earlier, we stated that Mrs. Pérez visits her children's teachers as she drops them off and picks them up at school and expects to use this time to chat with the teachers and fellow parents as she did in Guatemala. If we value Mrs. Pérez's actions, we might learn that she engages in this activity to show her love and support for her children and respect for their teachers. That calls for us to challenge and question what we might assume about our traditional values around U.S. public schooling, namely that parents/guardians should drop off and pick up their children as quickly as possible without disturbing teachers and other children, children are expected to arrive on time and be ready to learn, and parents should make appointments if they want to meet with their child's teacher. When we solicit and are open to various types of parent/guardian involvement, when we look for a variety of perspectives and understandings, we show that our classrooms and schools value all multilingual, multiracial, multicultural, multiethnic, and multi-economic families.

IMAGINE

What would being more open to various types of parent involvement look like in person and remotely?

_____

_____

_____

_____

_____

_____

---

online resources — Available for download from **resources.corwin.com/BeyondCrises**.

Learning Lessons From Crises

If we look closely at what we have learned from the pandemic and other crises that millions have also been facing, it is that many of us have drawn great comfort from

- ✓ reaching out to families to see how they are doing,

- ✓ banding together with community partners to best ensure that students and families receive the services that they need and to which they are entitled, and

- ✓ learning from mistakes made along the way to keep us from reverting back to seeing deficits instead of the many assets that all students and families possess.

In a great sense, what we have discovered during the pandemic mirrors what research from many fields has affirmed: the importance of using an assets-based approach as opposed to a deficits-based one in supporting the success of our students. That is, when we focus on students', families', and our own strengths, we have a much better chance of supporting positive outcomes for students because we are intentionally focusing on strengths as opposed to weaknesses (Biswas-Dienera et al., 2011).

Identifying Strengths, Interests, and Needs

When we take time to identify students', families', and our own strengths; when we take time to honor, value, and acknowledge these in others and ourselves; and when we work together to fully support students in recognizing their strengths, we can create networks that boost our students' social ties and interactions. This positive assets-based stance was first introduced by Maslow (1999). He used the term *positive psychology* to reflect the human potential that can be realized when we focus on the positive attributes and dispositions that empower people. Expert scholars and researchers in equity, linguistics, and diversity, González et al. (2005) used the term *funds of knowledge* to describe the assets and strengths that all humans possess. They also urge us, as educators, to take time to identify, acknowledge, and value these as we work with our diverse learning communities.

One reason for taking an assets-based stance with everyone we work with is the positive effect that it can have on students and families, particularly those who might perceive themselves to be in a racial, linguistic, economic, cultural, ethnic, or other group that is not perceived positively, or what Steele (2010) refers to as perception of stereotype threat. For example, Álvaro fears reprisals for being from Guatemala. It is urgent that we create an environment where he and all students feel safe and that they are active participating members of their classroom, school, and local communities and beyond. These conditions of safety, inclusive membership, value, and competence are what we want all students to feel in our efforts to overcome inequities.

We can create conditions in which our students and families feel safe, included, and valued only when we come together to form a comprehensive ecosystem that encompasses the classroom, school, and local community. In addition to identifying students' and parents' assets and strengths, it is imperative that we help address families' needs so that their children can be physically, socially, and emotionally healthy and successful in school and beyond. After all, if a family is hungry, it is likely that their child is hungry, and if a family is unable to receive much-needed health care, it is likely that the same holds true for their child. At the same time, true partnerships must be built from mutual trust and respect as well as an interest in coming together.

Envisioning Strengths-Based Roles

A whole-child, whole-school, whole-district, whole-community approach involves envisioning roles that embrace collaboration and an assets-based stance.

The Role of the State

The state's primary role is to ensure that federal laws regarding English learners are followed, including that each district

> must take affirmative steps to ensure that students with limited English proficiency (LEP) can meaningfully participate in their educational programs and services. . . . Congress enacted the Equal Educational Opportunities Act (EEOA), which confirmed that public schools and State educational agencies (SEAs) must act to overcome language barriers that impede equal participation by students in their instructional programs. (*Lau v. Nichols*, 1974)

Regulations from the USDOE and USDOJ (2015) state that districts are under "Federal obligation to ensure that LEP parents and guardians have meaningful access to district and school-related information" (p. 2). Further, the same governing bodies provide the following guidelines for schools to avoid failure in meeting compliance:

> Some examples of when the Departments have found [a lack of] compliance issues regarding communication with LEP parents include when school districts: (1) rely on students, siblings, friends, or untrained school staff to translate or interpret for parents; (2) fail to provide translation or an interpreter at IEP meetings, parent-teacher conferences, enrollment or career fairs, or disciplinary proceedings; (3) fail to provide information notifying LEP parents about a school's programs, services, and activities in a language the parents can understand; or (4) fail to identify LEP parents. (p. 11)

In their investigations, the USDOE and USDOJ (2015) consider, among other things, whether

- ✓ SEAs and school districts develop and implement a process for determining whether parents are LEP, and evaluate the language needs of these LEP parents;

- ✓ SEAs and school districts provide language assistance to parents or guardians who indicate they require such assistance;

- ✓ SEAs and school districts ensure that LEP parents have adequate notice of and meaningful access to information about all school district or SEA programs, services, and activities; and

- ✓ SEAs and school districts provide free qualified language assistance services to LEP parents. (pp. 39–40)

While each state's department of education ensures that federal laws are enacted, it is critical that they also support an ideology that families and their communities are foundational influencers of a child's academic success—including that they are the primary providers of children's security, emotional connection, and well-being. To that end, most states have "enacted laws calling for family engagement policies in public schools . . . although these vary greatly across jurisdictions" (Belway, Durán, & Spielberg, 2015, p. 15). California's school funding formula, for example, demands that a certain percentage of local education budgets be invested in parent engagement (Families in Schools, n.d.). Additionally, schools that receive grant funding under the English Language Acquisition and Language Enhancement Act must "promote parental, family, and community participation in language instruction education programs for the parents, families and communities of English learners" (USDOE, n.d., p. 2).

Regardless of the range of activities or regulations, the intent of all family engagement initiatives is "to create policies, strategies, and practices that build on the strengths and wisdom of families to support their child's learning and improve student achievement (Belway et al., 2015, p. 15).

In addition to ensuring the federal and state laws and regulations are adhered to, a state's role should be to encourage and provide supports for collaborative partnerships among schools, families, individuals, agencies, and organizations from the community. A state engaging in the following actions works on behalf of students' social-emotional and academic development by ensuring that students are engaged, attend, and perform successfully in school as well as in their lives:

- ✓ Encourage all school personnel to work closely with families and their community on behalf of students.

- ✓ Provide schools with professional growth trainings and strategies for involving parents/guardians of multilingual-multicultural students as active members with parent advisory and classroom councils.

- ✓ Provide school personnel with information and helpful strategies for communicating with parents/guardians about their child's language learning program and how they can get involved with their child's education.

- ✓ Provide schools with professional growth information about how to recruit and sustain community partners to support students' and families' assets, interests, and needs.

The Role of District Personnel

- ✓ Ensure that the district is in compliance with the law and regulations governing the education of English learners.

- ✓ Provide continuous supports including professional development, community resources, and flexible organizational structures and supports for schools to engage in community partnerships that will enhance the strengths, interests, and needs of its specific and unique multilingual-multicultural communities.

- ✓ Use a systems approach to map out the positive possibilities of inter- and intraschool and community partnerships without creating a one-size-fits-all approach.

The Role of the School Principal

✓ Ensure that federal, state, and district regulations and guidelines are followed.

✓ Implement and enact an assets-based approach with all school personnel.

✓ Assign a school liaison to work with teachers, the school community, and community partners.

✓ Work closely with school personnel and the school liaison to ensure that all partners are using an assets-based approach that acknowledges and honors the assets and interests of students and families and addresses their needs. In Part II of our book, we show how to ensure that professional development takes root and these positive outcomes are attained.

The Role of a Site Coordinator

This position is also referred to as community liaison, family and community outreach worker, community relations facilitator, and parent and community advocates. We use these terms interchangeably to refer to a point person who

✓ works closely with students and families at enrollment and throughout the school year to learn about their personal, cultural, social, and life experiences;

✓ shares information with classroom teachers and other school personnel to ensure that everyone is infusing the assets and interests of students;

✓ recruits, enacts, and sustains assets-based partnerships with individuals, institutions, agencies, and organizations from the community to support students' and families' assets, interests, and needs.

The Role of Classroom and Specialist Teachers

✓ Use an assets-based approach that supports students in developing the skills, competencies, and confidence to be active learners, independent and critical thinkers, and contributing members of their learning community. A helpful means for engaging students in these learning experiences is to learn as much as we can about our students' prior experiences from school liaisons and other school community personnel as well as from students and families.

✓ Provide a variety of opportunities for students to be empowered to have a voice and choice in their learning.

✓ Connect the curriculum to students' personal, social, cultural, and life experiences.

The Role of Bilingual-Bicultural Translators

The primary role of bilingual-bicultural translators is to support us in overcoming barriers to students' access to learning and engagement and, just as importantly, to support parents/guardians in making informed decisions about their child's education as well as partnering and fully engaging with us on behalf of their child's social-emotional and academic development and a school's overall success with its multilingual learners. As such, translators

✓ honor and value the linguistic and cultural identities of students and families;

✓ support meaningful communication between and among community, school, and classroom members;

✓ use an assets-based approach to support students and families to feel safe, a sense of belonging, value, and competence;

✓ support families in making informed decisions about the programming provided for their child; and

✓ support students and their families in overcoming language and cultural barriers.

Once we have developed a deeper understanding about the importance of using a strengths-based approach to amplify the interests and ever-changing needs of students and families and the enacted roles that will support us in this process, our next step is to plan ways to sustain a whole-child ecosystem that seamlessly works together as a whole community to build momentum on behalf of students' academic, physical, and social-emotional development. We discuss this concept of an ecosystem in our next chapter.

Sustaining a Whole-Child Ecosystem

2

It takes a forest to create a microclimate for tree growth and sustenance. So it's not surprising that isolated trees have far shorter lives than those living connected together in forests.

—Tim Flannery (2016)

Forests occupy a vast amount of our globe. They need air, water, and sun to grow. They also exist cooperatively and have vast ways of communicating below the ground (Grant, 2018). While all of these characteristics are important to consider, every tree needs an "additional element, a sustainable 'ecosystem' not just to survive but to flourish" (Zacarian & Silverstone, 2020). The same holds true for every one of our students. That is, we don't want them just to get by or survive a crisis, whatever it might be; we want them to be successful in school and in their lives. Moreover, that takes all of us working together just as trees in the forest do.

To work together, it's helpful to consider the mantra that many sports coaches use: *There is no I in Team.* Look to a winning player, and it's likely that they might say something like, "I couldn't have done it without our team." In reality, there are too many children who are that *I*, alone, without a comprehensive whole ecosystem, such as our forest example. That ecosystem comes from their family, classmates, schoolmates, and community working, learning, and socializing together.

In this chapter, we look more closely at sustaining a whole child ecosystem to enhance students' assets and address challenges in a comprehensive way. This is important for engaging community partners to enact practices that complement our goal of using a strengths-based approach with children and their families.

Being In It Together

While the realities of any crises, including COVID-19, drive many educators and other stakeholders who work on behalf of children to have a renewed sense of purpose and commitment to their professions, they also highlight how much we want to support students and families. And crises such as the pandemic show us that this support is much more possible when we have a school- or district-based team *and* partnerships in place with individuals, institutions, organizations, and agencies from our local communities that we can readily call on when needed. Let's look at an example of a district-based team that launched a rapid response during the pandemic.

Example of Partnership Approach During the Pandemic

Brockton Public Schools, Brockton, Massachusetts

During the onset of the COVID-19 pandemic, the city of Brockton had one of the highest rates of occurrence of the virus in Massachusetts. Since the economic collapse in 2008, it had undergone significant budget cuts year after year. A top priority of its superintendent, Michael P. Thomas, has been to support the physical and social-emotional well-being of students (Brockton Public Schools, 2020) including the district's English learners, representing thirty-two languages, of which Cape Verdean, Portuguese, Haitian Creole, French, Spanish, Chinese, Hmong, Laotian, and Thai are the most common. A team of bilingual and bilingual-bicultural community relations facilitators, school adjustment counselors, parent advocates, and paraprofessionals provides a range of services to ensure that all of the district's students feel safe, valued, and competent and know that they are members of their classroom and school communities by building partnerships with families, community service, and faith-based groups. In March 2020, when the governor of Massachusetts ordered all public and residential schools be closed due to the pandemic, the team engaged in a number of activities to support its community:

✓ It purchased smartphones for its bilingual-bicultural team so that they could continue the type of personal one-to-one family contacts that had worked successfully before the pandemic.

✓ It ensured the seamless continuation of the universal free breakfast and lunch program. During the spring and summer, meals were prepared in one central area and distributed to ten locations, and the bilingual-bicultural team ensured that families were aware of where and when the food distribution occurred. As the 2020 school year opened remotely, the district looked to its districtwide systems approach to address how the one half hour that students are allotted for their mid-day meal could best occur.

✓ It created a small-group summer outdoor program for some students that would continue as an after-school offering during the school year.

✓ It implemented a family–school phone call center and texts with adjustment counselors, nurses, parent advocates, bilingual community relations facilitators, principals, and other key personnel to ensure families were aware of district and community services including health, food, and work-related assistance and offering its services to school staff.

✓ It created and launched multilingual training videos to support families' and students' use of technology.

✓ It provided a call center with multilingual staff to support student learning and address parent questions.

As the district got ready to reopen its schools remotely in the fall of 2020, it expanded its instructional, social-emotional learning, communications, operations, and resources teams from thirty-five to seventy people. Further, each of the five teams included representatives from the district's bilingual department. During the summer months, the teams worked feverishly to reopen school remotely:

✓ It purchased laptops for all of the district's students as well as Wi-Fi hot spots for 3,000 families through grant funds.

✓ It supported the district's full-time parent engagement specialists in providing thrice daily Zoom meetings with families in Haitian and French.

✓ It sought new ways to ensure that students could receive lunches during the allotted lunch time.

✓ It provided one-to-one personal bilingual-bicultural translation services, through grant funding, in the most common languages spoken by the district's students and families. It also provided phone translation (through a contracted service) for students and families from low-incidence groups.

Figure 2.1 • Superintendent Michael P. Thomas, Brockton Public Schools

(Continued)

PART I • COMMUNITIES

(Continued)

Figure 2.2 • Michael P. Thomas, Superintendent of Schools, and Kellie Jones, Director of Bilingual Education, Brockton Public Schools

Figure 2.3 • Brockton Public Schools Team of Bilingual and Bilingual-Bicultural Community Relations Facilitators, Parent Advocates, English Language Acquisition Coaches, and Teachers at a Weekend Parent Event

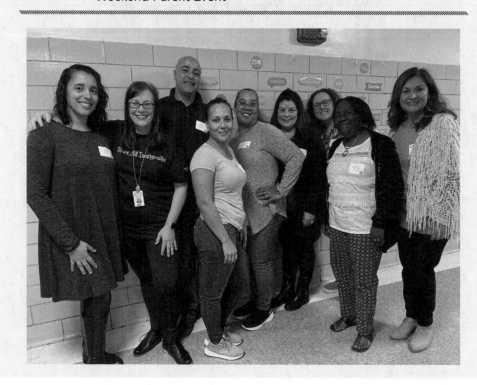

REFLECTION

Compare the similarities and differences between your school and district and the actions taken by the Brockton Public Schools at the onset of COVID-19.

_____

_____

_____

_____

_____

_____

_____

online resources   Available for download from **resources.corwin.com/BeyondCrises**.

Indeed, it is much more possible to create the type of partnerships that support and boost students' social ties and networks when we fully shift from working in isolation to being in it together.

An example of an isolated and siloed response is a teacher who observes one of her students holding his mouth while grimacing in pain during a Zoom breakout session. Being the kind and caring teacher that she is, she calls her dentist and arranges for the student to be seen during COVID-19. Accompanied by his parents, the student is seen by the teacher's dentist and given the dental care that he needs.

While none of us would fault this teacher for taking time to care for her student, it's critical that every school and district has built community partnerships that address and can respond to the ever-changing assets, interests, and needs of our multilingual-multicultural students and families. For example, with support of the family liaison, our focal student Álvaro and his sister Inés went to a local dentist that used the same ideology of caring, curiosity, and interest that responsive school–community partners employ.

Strategically Building External Partners

In order to provide multilingual-multicultural students and families with the types of comprehensive whole-child, whole-family, whole-community experiences in which all should engage, we must

- ✓ strategically plan how we will identify the assets, interests, and needs of our multilingual-multicultural students and families and

- ✓ build community partnerships that will help us do this.

Engaging in these essential activities helps us achieve several positive outcomes:

1. Becoming more aware of the positive possibilities of community partners

2. Expanding our partnerships, as needed—all to respond to our dynamically changing multilingual-multicultural student and family populations

3. Infusing seamless pairings of students and families with community partners, such as Álvaro with the local soccer club program and optometrist

Further, all of these essential actions lead to a fourth outcome:

4. Continuously building interconnected interactions among our students, parents/guardians, families, classrooms, schools, and local community partners and beyond

Let's look at an example from the field of these ideas in action.

Example of Partnership-Building

Wolfe Street Academy, Baltimore, Maryland

An example of the type of essential activities that we are describing is Wolfe Street Academy, a Baltimore Curriculum Project school and key advocate of community school policies enacted in 2016 (Baltimore City Board of School Commissioners, 2016). Part of the Baltimore City Public Schools, it is a preK–5 school of about 270 students; over 80 percent of its families are Spanish-speaking, 55 percent of its students are learning English as a new language, and the majority of students and families live in poverty.

According to its principal, Mark Gaither, "COVID magnified the economic hardship, the lack of basic needs like food, healthcare, and housing, that our community particularly suffers because of a variety of social issues that scare them [away] from the normal avenues of many public assistance programs."

Despite these challenges, what makes Wolfe Street an important school to consider is the great means by which it strategically recruits, sustains, and builds enduring community partnerships.

According to Mr. Gaither, "Each year, Wolfe Street Academy identifies its needs and its site coordinator finds resources and sets up systems to address them. We always use a proactive system to address our needs instead of a reactive, 'this-family-is-hungry-today-let's-feed-them' program. The flexibility that this builds in allows us to respond to needs as they change. In the early years, the need was dental work and we set up the partnership with University of Maryland School of Dentistry that still exists today. Last year, particularly with the closure and food scarcity becoming more and more acute, our community school site coordinator set up partnerships with two or three organizations who made regular donations of food."

One of the critical positions that is part of the school's staff is a bilingual community site coordinator. This is an employee of the University of Maryland School of Social Work who is assigned to work full time in Wolfe Street's community. According to Mr. Gaither, and as we discuss later in this chapter, the community site coordinator performs a critical role in creating and implementing the types of partnerships that are needed.

In a personal interview about the site coordinator, Mr. Gaither shared the following:

✓ The site coordinator is the primary contact and go-to person for these partnerships. She is the demonstrable evidence that the school values partnership and nonacademic family and community needs. A full-time person (with benefits so that someone can make a career out of it) who has a full seat on the School Leadership Team and a literal seat in the office and is supported by and supports many other folks who help establish these partnerships, nurtures them, and maintains them.

✓ Anyone in our community can suggest needs or partnerships. Those initial contacts might help lead to the development of a response to the need and the development of the partnership along with the community site coordinator.

Figure 2.4 • Mark Gaither, School Principal

Source: Photo by Phil Laubner for Heart of the Schools

Bringing Partners Together

The partnerships that Wolfe Street Academy has forged speak to the possibilities of broadening our work by partnering with agencies, institutions, and organizations as well as individuals in our communities. It affirms the idea that a community school is one that acts as a hub in bringing potential partners together on behalf of addressing students' desires, interests, and needs. In the words of Mr. Gaither, community partnerships help in the following ways:

- ✓ It extends our network of possible connections.

- ✓ It allows us to host two to four interns a year . . . for them to learn (a two-way street of partnerships), and the interns work with everyone—teachers, administrators, neighbors, students, families, and more.

- ✓ Our last two hires over the years as site coordinators have been former interns with us.

- ✓ Further, their efforts have helped to recruit and sustain Wolfe's partnerships between its staff and family communities and partners, such as the University of Maryland (including its Schools of Social Work and Dentistry), Julie Community Center, Johns Hopkins Bayview Medical Center, and Upper Fells Point Neighborhood Association. (personal interview, September 30, 2020)

In speaking about the pandemic and the importance of Wolfe Street's family and community partnerships, Mr. Gaither also shared the importance of moving beyond crises to find essential and even inspiring ways to overcome inequities, even those that seem insurmountable:

In His Own Words

Mark Gaither, Principal, Wolfe Street Academy, Baltimore, Maryland

Mr. Gaither, how has Wolfe Street Academy sustained its partnerships with parents/ guardians during COVID? And what are some lessons you and your staff have learned during the crisis that will support the school now and long after COVID?

It was something like a slow suddenness where it seemed that we saw it coming from a mile away, but on March 13, when they closed schools, it felt like it ambushed us. We all went into crisis mode as we learned about the restrictions and limitations that various levels of leadership were putting on our usual systems. There were limits of who could do home visits, how many hours an intern or social worker could be at a building, who was allowed in the building and when. All of these realities changed moment to moment, and we had to come up with solutions.

We have talked about the idea of the "next best plan" for years. It is basically the idea that we never come up with the best plan. We come up with the next best plan together, implement it, watch what happens, realize that two-thirds of it failed (sometimes), come back together, come up with the next best plan, and the whole cycle starts over again. During this ongoing crisis, we have done the same thing.

During COVID-19, After-school programs shut down but community schools ramped up. We had a week of "Spring Break" and then came back virtually in the spring. Families were making connections in any way possible, and teachers were learning the virtual platforms as they were using them. A large focus was put on making connections and not losing kids and the relationship they had with the school. A lot of texting, phone calls to get kids online. We got to about a 75 or 80 percent of our average daily attendance rate and remained in contact—either electronically, online, phone calls, contacts at the food distribution site, or packets—with all of our kids.

✓ Parents were stepping up, getting their children on phones and tablets to get work done and make connections with teachers and the school.

✓ During the first few months, 24,000 pounds of food was collected from neighbors, partners, teachers, and many more and distributed to school and neighborhood families in need.

✓ A Structured Relief Fund was created to organize the eventual $16,000 donated by teachers, staff, families of teachers and staff, Baltimore Curriculum Project (BCP) staff, and a few of our more affluent families for the support of our families in such areas as rent, utilities, and health care support in small grants that continue to this day.

✓ We employed some of our after-school staff to help deliver food, assist with connectivity, provide staffing, food, personal protective equipment, and school supply distribution centers (the primary one at our local Julie Community Center, a long-term partner, because in the beginning we were not allowed to have such distributions at the school). This also allowed us to support our staff in the after-school program who would not otherwise have had income.

✓ In addition to donating food and gift cards, the neighborhood community, including teachers, staff, BCP staff, and neighbors of the school, volunteered to deliver goods to families' homes, especially families of essential workers, vulnerable to the virus, and those that had to quarantine.

✓ After the summer of 2020 and finding nearly $300,000 worth of devices (computers, tablets, and hotspots), hours of training for teachers, planning, hoping, and praying, we are back (100 percent remote at this point) with close to 92 percent attendance. (personal interview, September 30, 2020)

IMAGINE

According to Mr. Gaither, a school is built on its student, family, staff, administrator, and local community partnerships. He described these as "powerful, flexible, and responsive; living breathing things that change each year because its people change, but the structures of relationship-building are what keep it strong."

(Continued)

(Continued)

Imagine you are a teacher assigned to work in a school like the one Mr. Gaither describes. What advantages do you see here for you, your students, and their families?

_____

_____

_____

_____

_____

_____

online resources ↖   Available for download from **resources.corwin.com/BeyondCrises**.

Celebrating Successes of Community Partnerships

One of the unique aspects of comprehensive partnerships is celebrating our collective efforts. At one school, for example, its partnerships were celebrated with weekly volleyball matches between staff, students, families, and community members. While we are not suggesting that every community play volleyball, we do believe that a celebratory activity plays an important role in honoring the successes of our partnerships new and old. For example, one of the key features of Wolfe Street Academy is its opening-of-the-day activity, known as Morning Meeting, an example of which may be viewed at the beginning of this WETA public television feature on Wolfe Street Academy: www.youtube.com/watch?v=0OQ-mZA6hI0&t=2s. While you might imagine this activity as the gathering of students with their teachers, at Wolfe Street, it is an opening-of-the-day ritual where students, staff, and families gather.

In His Own Words About Celebrating Partnerships

Mark Gaither, Principal, Wolfe Street Academy, Baltimore, Maryland

Mr. Gaither, how does Wolfe Street Academy help prevent students and families from feeling and being too isolated during COVID? What are some of the lessons that have been learned that will support the school going forward during and after the pandemic?

A key part of Wolfe community building has always been the Morning Meeting. For the past fifteen years, every morning at 7:50 all the kids, teachers, and about thirty or forty parents and family members would gather in the cafeteria for the pledge, morning announcements, and what I came to think of as the joys and concerns of the school. The meeting allows us to see ourselves as something bigger than just any one part, that we are not just all isolated in our own spaces but part of a team we get to be with each morning and dismiss to classes and a day of learning together.

This fall Ms. Chicas, our front office secretary and all-around great person, and I have been recording a Zoom Morning Meeting and pushing it out through the individual grade-level homeroom Zoom classes, where the teacher can share it with the kids, and on Facebook and YouTube. It's a time to remember a part of our everyday when we were together, a moment to feel a little "normal," and to celebrate the things that we achieve, whether it is the Wolfe Pup award that goes to a student each week who demonstrates one of our virtues [using a list of 100 identified virtues from the Virtues Project: www.virtuesproject. com] or a particular great run of attendance by all our kids. The virtues focus is all about giving the students and adults the language to describe and discuss and identify the characteristics we want to see in ourselves and others. It couples with our mindfulness practices, focused on developing a deep personal reservoir in each of us with which to deal with tough or emotional or stressful situations. And then those sit among our Restorative Practices training that is focused on developing person-to-person relationships in the classroom and throughout the community so that when there is a crisis we can draw on our mindfulness reservoir, describe our needs with our virtues language, and then come together to restore our positive relationships with each other. Of course, all of this also works with positive things and successes where we can deepen our relationships with these same tools. (personal communication, September 30, 2020).

IMAGINE

Think about how you might create a daily activity that includes students, staff, and families. What would it look like?

_____

_____

_____

_____

_____

_____

online resources — Available for download from **resources.corwin.com/BeyondCrises**.

Coordinating Partnership Efforts

Designating a Point Person/Coordinator

All of the partnership activities that we have described thus far are the outcome of an essential role: a point person who facilitates the interconnected partnerships between and among family, school, and local communities. While various titles are used for this role, including coordinator, liaison, and outreach worker, it involves someone who is designated to help families, schools, and communities use their collective assets in the interest of students; this is essential to the success of such interconnected endeavors.

Figure 2.5 illustrates an integrated approach where the designated point person supports these interactions so that

✓ students and parents/guardians actively interact with their classroom, school, and individuals, agencies, institutions, and organizations from their local community;

✓ classroom, school, and community partners engage in a coordinated and integrated effort on behalf of students' success in school and beyond;

✓ students and parents/guardians are honored and valued for the strengths and competencies that they bring to these interactions; and

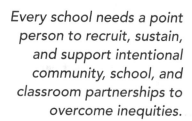

Every school needs a point person to recruit, sustain, and support intentional community, school, and classroom partnerships to overcome inequities.

✓ each person consistently uses a strengths-based approach to support the success and integration of students and families across classroom, school, and local communities.

A powerful example of the type of integrated approach that we are describing, in addition to Brockton Public Schools and Wolfe Street Academy described earlier, is Salina Elementary School. Located in Dearborn, Michigan, Salina is a preK–3 school of about 400 children, 98 percent of whom are Yemeni and 94 percent are English learners. According to school principal Susan Stanley and Communities in Schools of Michigan site

Figure 2.5 • Interconnected School, Classroom, and Local Community Partners

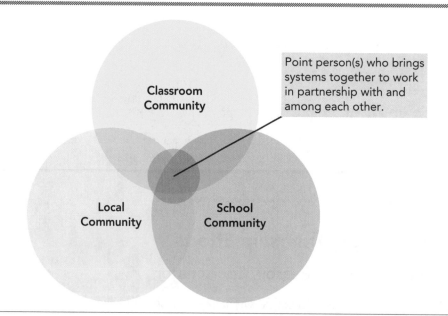

coordinator Amal Qayed, Salina has established partnerships with several community organizations, including the Arab Community Center for Economic and Social Services (ACCESS), Gleaners Community Food Bank, and the Amity Foundation, whose volunteers help with food, supplies, and gift cards for the community. Salina operates as a Communities in Schools (CIS) model, which includes a site-based coordinator who acts as the point person that we described earlier. The liaison role is critical to an integrated community, school, classroom model. The following description of CIS' enactment of the role speaks to the heart of its importance. It is followed by a description of Salina's coordinator, Ms. Qayed.

Description of CIS Site Coordinator

Many students and their families have a hard time accessing and navigating the maze of public and private services. There may be ample resources in a community, but rarely is there someone on the ground who is able to connect these resources with the schools and students that need them most. Through a school-based coordinator, we bring community

Figure 2.6 • Salina Elementary School Site Coordinator Amal Qayed and Principal Susan Stanley

(Continued)

(Continued)

resources into schools to empower success for all students by removing barriers for students at risk of dropping out, keeping kids in schools and on the path to graduation and leveraging evidence, relationships and local resources to drive results (Communities in Schools, 2020, para. 1).

Salina Elementary School's CIS Site Coordinator, Amal Qayed

Salina's CIS site coordinator, Amal Qayed, is fluent in English and Arabic and very nimble and adept working with families and the community, having grown up in Dearborn and attended its public schools. She can best be described as a multitalented, multifaceted, multilingual, multiethnic, multicultural insider—a person who has deep understanding of multilingual families, schools, and individuals, organizations, institutions, and agencies in the school's local and surrounding communities. During a conversation, Mrs. Stanley pointed to Amal and stated, "Amal is the one who makes it happen. We could not do the work we do without Amal" (personal communication, September 2, 2020).

Five Characteristics of a Coordinator

It's helpful to consider the key characteristics of coordinators in multilingual, multicultural, multiracial, multiethnic school settings. This is particularly important as we consider the possibilities for tapping into their unique competencies.

A school may employ one person or a few to enact the point person role of coordinating families, educators, and community members to work together. The five critical characteristics of this role are that the coordinator:

1. is a multilingual-multicultural representative from the community*

2. is deeply familiar with school/district policies and practices

---

*We understand that our linguistically and culturally diverse student and family populations are growing and that it might not be possible, for a variety of compelling reasons (e.g., budgetary constraints, lack of availability), to secure bilingual-bicultural liaisons who represent the same language groups and countries of origin as our students. For example, Mrs. Morales, the family liaison we introduced in Chapter 1, is fluent in Spanish and English, yet she is not from Guatemala and therefore is not familiar with the country Álvaro, our focal student, is from. What is essential for the success of this role is that it be filled by personnel who are

✓ deeply familiar with the local school and district, its multilingual-multicultural families, and local community partners including individuals, agencies and organizations;

✓ proficient in the home language of students and families or supported by bilingual (and where possible) bicultural translators;

✓ trained in using linguistically and culturally responsive practices that wholly support an assets-based approach with students and families living with adversity, who are not fluent in English, and whose personal, cultural, racial, social, and life experiences are distinct from their own; and

✓ trained to work collaboratively with all the teachers (not in isolation).

3. uses an assets-based ideology to train and recruit community partners

4. uses an assets-based ideology to work with school/district partners

5. is a trusted member of the school and family community

The first characteristic is that the coordinator be a familiar and deeply rooted member of the multilingual-multicultural community *and* the school or district community in terms of its practices, policies, and ways of operating and being. Our examples from Brockton Public Schools, Wolfe Street Academy, and Salina Elementary School highlight the importance of the duality of these understandings. For example, Brockton Public Schools deployed its bilingual-bicultural representatives from its Cape Verdean, Portuguese, Haitian, French, Spanish, Chinese, Hmong, Laotian, and Thai communities to create a seamless meal delivery program during the onset of COVID-19. Wolfe Street Academy's trusted coordinator built partnerships with its families, leadership team, and the community. She was seamlessly able to bring together much-needed services during the pandemic. The same holds true at Salina Elementary School, whose school liaison is a bilingual-bicultural representative of the student and family community. The coordinators from these three districts/schools are deeply familiar with their district's/school's policies, practices, and ways of operating. For example, Brockton's liaison personally contacted multilingual-multicultural families about where, how, and when to pick up the meals that were prepared. In addition, all of the liaisons for Brockton Public Schools, Wolfe Street Academy, and Salina Elementary School are able to communicate seamlessly with parent and school communities because they are members of both. They have depth of understanding about what it means to be a student or parent or member of the staff or leadership team. For example, Ms. Qayed knows that most of the parents in her district use WhatsApp as a mode of communicating. When parents requested counseling remotely during COVID-19, she was able to coordinate this service smoothly because she understands parents' preferences.

REFLECTION

Beside what is mentioned above, a liaison actively, collaboratively, and proactively acts as a powerful connector to support community, school, and classroom partnerships.

Which of the key characteristics of this role enactment are apparent in your school/district?

_____

_____

_____

(Continued)

(Continued)

_____

_____

_____

What might you do/suggest for strengthening this role? Share your ideas with colleagues.

_____

_____

_____

_____

_____

_____

online resources   Available for download from **resources.corwin.com/BeyondCrises**.

Identifying Needs, Desires, and Opportunities

One of the key activities that coordinators do is support students, families, and staff in identifying the needs and desires of a school's student and family populations. For example, each year with Ms. Qayed's support, Salina's staff, parents, and students complete a set of surveys to support her in securing community partners that will address the needs and desires identified by the school's staff, parent, and student communities.

Surveys such as the ones used by Salina and other schools and districts generally include three themes:

✓ health and well-being

✓ after- and out-of-school activities

✓ classroom-based supports

They also include critical information about when families are most available to attend school events and meetings, remotely or in person, on behalf of their children. The outcome of activities such as these surveys and Amal's relentless pursuit of this information is a high level of back-and-forth communication among the community, school, and classroom partners.

Examples of Community-Based Activities Facilitated by Site Coordinator Amal Qayed

Before Salina Elementary School opened virtually in the fall of 2020, each student was given a package filled with school supplies. These were donated from local resources that Site Coordinator Amal Qayed collected based on the information she received from families. In addition, from the beginning of the COVID-19 crisis, Amal continuously communicated with families to ensure that they were supported and that she and the school could provide assistance. Through donations from Gleaners Community Food Bank, the Amity Foundation, ACCESS, and local resources, students and families were able to receive much-needed food. Every other week, families drove up to Salina Elementary or other district buildings, opened the trunks of their cars, and received enough food supplies to last two weeks. In addition, using WhatsApp (families' preferred mode of communication), Amal learned that parents wanted to receive counseling to support their children. She secured biweekly multilingual-multicultural counseling, and many families participated in this service. Additionally, families have received free COVID-19 testing—all facilitated by Amal with support from school and community resources.

In a real sense, school and district coordinators/liaisons, such as Ms. Qayed, and bilingual-bicultural support, such as that provided by staff from Brockton Public Schools and Wolfe Street Academy, facilitate the types of interactions that are critical for local community and school and classroom communities to engage in.

Let's participate in one of the survey activities that Ms. Qayed requires of staff. Complete the activity below by responding to the questions according to what you believe about your work site.

Salina Elementary School Staff Needs Assessment

Please select your classification below:

☐ School administrator

☐ School teacher

☐ School support staff (counselor, social worker, custodian, lunch staff, etc.)

☐ Other

Mark what you think are the five most needed services at your school:

☐ After-school clubs and recreational activities

☐ Before-/after-school programs

☐ Classroom conduct incentives

(Continued)

(Continued)

☐ Clothing drives

☐ Cultural/gender/ethnic appreciation

☐ Field trips

☐ First-aid classes

☐ Food drives

☐ Fundraisers for special event funding

☐ Spelling competitions

☐ Other:

_____

_____

_____

_____

_____

REFLECTION

Share what you noted with a few colleagues to get an idea of the five most needed services. Once you have conducted this analysis, describe the steps you might take with a team to ensure that these services are implemented in your workplace.

_____

_____

_____

_____

_____

Key for any family-school-community partnership is to periodically review our capacity to create the type of mutual partnerships that instill family trust: feelings of safety, value, and acknowledgment, and mutually beneficial, valued, and respected dialogue.

PART I • COMMUNITIES

In addition to the activity that we just completed, it is also helpful to identify areas that are successful and those that need strengthening. With this in mind, complete the survey in Figure 2.7. Respond to each question by checking the boxes that most apply to your workplace.

Figure 2.7 Identifying Family-School-Classroom Partnership Areas That Need Strengthening

	A TEENY BIT	SOME OF THE TIME	ALMOST ALL THE TIME	WITH GREAT FREQUENCY
Students and parents/guardians actively interact with the classroom, the school, and individuals, agencies, institutions, and organizations from their local community.	☐	☐	☐	☐
Classroom, school, and community partners engage in coordinated and integrated effort on behalf of students' success in school and beyond.	☐	☐	☐	☐
Students and parents/guardians are honored and valued for the strengths and competencies that they bring to these interactions.	☐	☐	☐	☐
Each person consistently uses a strengths-based approach to support the success and integration of students and families across classroom, school, and local communities.	☐	☐	☐	☐

REFLECTION

Based on your responses, what steps might you take to strengthen the partnerships among communities, parents, and schools in your context?

_____

_____

_____

_____

_____

_____

online resources   Available for download from **resources.corwin.com/BeyondCrises**.

It is essential that our professional development efforts infuse activities such as the ones that we just completed into our collective movement beyond crises to overcome inequities. Part II presents a comprehensive way to engage a whole school in activities such as these. One of the key reasons to engage in professional development is to truly build an empathetic and supportive approach that thoroughly invests wholeheartedly in building reciprocal relationships with students, their families, and our communities. At the center of all of this is the goal of expanding the amount of meaningful interactions that students have with others. This is critical in supporting students' social-emotional, identity, and academic development. Let's take a look at the power of interactions in development.

Understanding Developmental Influences of Interactions

Ever-Expanding Circles of Interactions

It is essential for us to understand that students' identity and understanding of the world around them are drawn from the various communicative interactions they have with others (Gauvain, 2001, 2013). These help us greatly to understand the developmental influences of a child's life, especially as applied to the positive possibilities of what we do as educators. The influence of interactions cannot be underscored enough. Interaction is one of the key foundations of human development. Regardless of where they are born and what language(s) they speak, every child is guided by observing the interactions that occur in their home, school, local community, and more and by engaging in interactions with and across these various groups of people. Our concept of an ecosystem is one in which students are "deeply connected and supported by the people, systems, and ideas around them" for their growth and development (Zacarian & Silverstone, 2020, p. 20).

Consider this way of explaining this connective influence: A child is born. Whether it is to two parents, a single parent, a foster parent, a grandparent, an institutionalized caregiver, individuals who live cooperatively or with extrafamilial supports, these caregivers support that child's physical, nutritional, and emotional needs and continuously and routinely attend to the child. The close interactions that they have with the child are the glue that binds the parent/guardian–child bond. They are included under the label Parents/Guardians in Figure 2.8. In the same figure, we see that these interactive spheres of influence expand between and among a child and their parents/guardians to include their family and their family's community, as they too are key influencers of the child's development. For example, the family's community includes people whom the child sees regularly and consistently through their development, such as their extended family, friends, neighbors, storekeepers, clergy and parishioners where a family worships, and others.

As children grow and become school-age, the interactions they have with others expand to a new circle of influence to include those in their classroom and school communities, including their teachers, peers, school principal, school office staff,

Figure 2.8 • Circles of Interactions

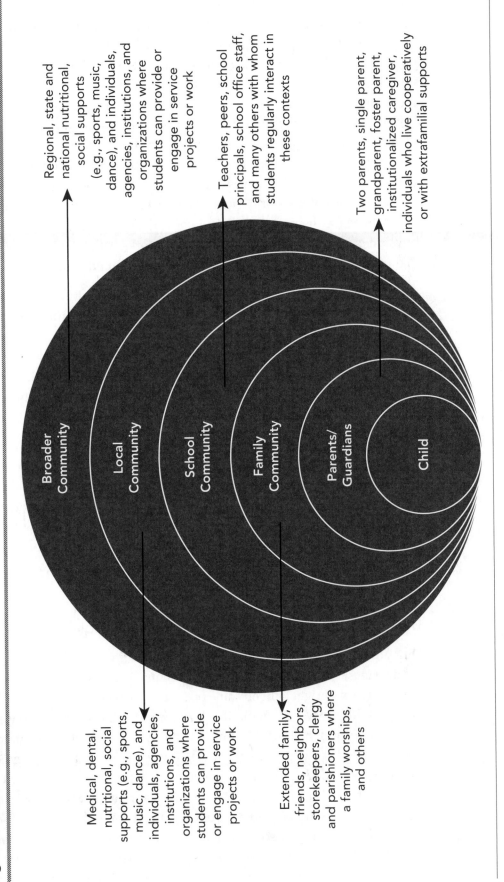

Regional, state and national nutritional, social supports (e.g., sports, music, dance), and individuals, agencies, institutions, and organizations where students can provide or engage in service projects or work

Teachers, peers, school principals, school office staff, and many others with whom students regularly interact in these contexts

Two parents, single parent, grandparent, foster parent, institutionalized caregiver, individuals who live cooperatively or with extrafamilial supports

Broader Community

Local Community

School Community

Family Community

Parents/ Guardians

Child

Medical, dental, nutritional, social supports (e.g., sports, music, dance), and individuals, agencies, institutions, and organizations where students can provide or engage in service projects or work

Extended family, friends, neighbors, storekeepers, clergy and parishioners where a family worships, and others

Source: Adapted from Zacarian, Alvarez-Ortiz, & Haynes (2017).

and many others with whom they regularly interact in these contexts. And, following this train of thought, as children mature, the circles of interactive influence that they have been developing expand to include their local community, such as through local dance, soccer, library, scouting, and community service activities and more, and include a myriad of additional individuals and members of local agencies, communities, and organizations. If we look to the regulations regarding English learners, we see that this is why the U.S. Department of Education and U.S. Department of Justice (2015) require schools to make sure that English learners participate in extracurricular activities such as choir, clubs, sports, and so on. It is these continuous and ever-expanding circles of interactions that support and stretch children's understandings of the world around them and allow for multiple and continuous interactions for them to expand and boost their academic, social-emotional, and physical growth and ties to the various networks with which they communicate. Figure 2.8 illustrates the ever-expanding circles of interaction.

An additional aspect of every child's development is the cultural norms and expectations of the groups in which they are reared. For example, earlier we introduced the idea that many multilingual-multicultural learners are reared in collectivist societies. An expectation for children in such cultures is that they believe strongly in collective relationships versus independent and individual ones. While collectivist cultures represent a wide swath of people from across our globe, including those from Asia, South America, Central America, and Africa, we should not forget that some students are reared in families from a hybrid of both collectivist and individualist groups.

These difference and diversities call for an even greater urgency for our classroom, school, and local communities to be interested, caring, and fully and wholly committed to building partnerships with our dynamically changing student and family populations. We can do this by reviewing the barriers that we know exist and looking closely at how we can work together to eliminate these and build enthusiasm, momentum, and grow together to value and enhance students' assets and address challenges in a comprehensive way.

Barriers, Challenges, and Constraints of Isolation

On April 7, 2020, a few weeks after much of the nation's and globe's schools closed, White House pandemic advisor Dr. Anthony Fauci stated that the pandemic "shine(s) a very bright light on some of the real weaknesses and foibles in our society" (C-SPAN, 2020). Earlier in this book, we used the same lens to view the lives of students and families from multilingual-multicultural homes—namely, that a disproportionate number are at a much higher risk of contracting and dying from the virus because of chronic injustices and inequities that have plagued our county for generations. We also stated that a significant number of English learners, 60 percent, live in extreme poverty. And we highlighted the very stark reality that over half of the nation's students have experienced one or more serious types of adverse childhood experiences. That figure was derived from a survey completed in 2011–2012, well before the COVID-19 pandemic (Child and Adolescent Health Measurement Initiative, 2013) and the massive economic collapse experienced by the United States and other countries. Further, what is missing and important to note about children living with adverse childhood experiences is that the statistics and information on this topic do not include the epic number of students and families who have experienced

✓ living in war or conflict zones;

✓ massive natural disasters;

✓ being persecuted in their home countries;

✓ being displaced;

✓ the long, arduous, and extremely dangerous trip to perceived safety in the United States;

✓ being separated from families;

✓ being inhumanely detained in detention centers;

✓ living in constant fear of being deported; and

✓ becoming homeless.

A way of illustrating some of these complexities is to revisit our circles of interactions to show the isolation that some students and parents/guardians experience in Figure 2.9. According to Yoshikawa (2011), this isolation is not uncommon and reflects the experiences we described.

Figure 2.9 • Barriers, Challenges, and Constraints of Isolation

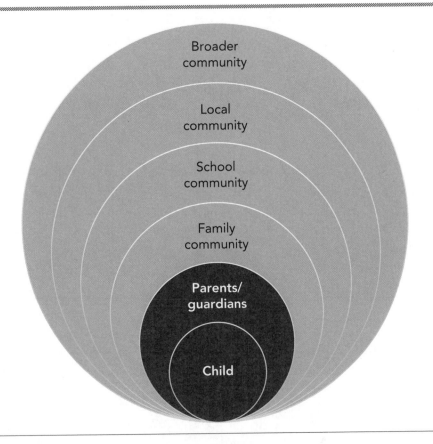

Broader community

Local community

School community

Family community

Parents/ guardians

Child

The compilation and complexities of these factors are urgent to consider as we plan for engaging in deep and meaningful partnerships, especially during the pandemic and going forward, for several reasons. First, it is far too easy to assume that such students' and families' lives are damaged or broken beyond repair. In addition, borrowing from Yoshikawa's (2011) research on undocumented parents and their children, it is also far too easy to fall prey to "policy debates" and think of and label undocumented citizens as "lawbreakers, laborers, or victims—seldom as parents raising children" (p. 2). For far too long, too many students from underrepresented groups and their families have faced far too untenable discrimination due to being stereotyped in the ways that Yoshikawa describes.

While we have all felt isolated during COVID-19, the degree of isolation that many students and families experienced before COVID-19 has been exacerbated to a much more intense degree. Many of the students that we had difficulty reaching or were unable to reach during the spring of 2020, when schools closed, represented those who experience extreme barriers, challenges, and constraints of isolation during COVID-19, as depicted in Figure 2.10. As a result of this isolation, these children were unable to reap the benefits of the holistic, interactive ecosystem that all students need to flourish in school and in their lives. COVID-19 has been a blunt reminder of the urgency for overcoming the inequities that have existed for too long in our communities, schools, and classrooms.

Figure 2.10 • Extreme Barriers, Challenges, and Constraints of Isolation

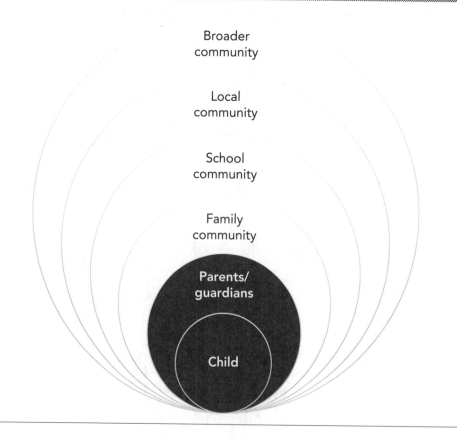

Moving From Isolation to Integration

When we act on these assumptions and stereotypes, we are not operating from the more evidence-based response that tells us that all groups, including undocumented citizens, people living in poverty, and children living with adversity, have strengths and assets that are wholly worth tapping into. Research on partnering with families overwhelmingly points to the importance of using practices that continuously show that we care for and about students and families (Epstein & Associates, 2009). Demonstrating, in our deeds and actions, that we believe in students' inherent strengths, the strengths that they have developed as a result of facing adversity, and the infinite possibilities for their being empowered to be successful in school and their lives greatly supports a much more positive outcome.

To engage in this shift in thinking from deficits to assets requires three actions on the part of all of us. Whether in our everyday practice, reflections on who we teach and what we do or who we work with to teach, or the professional development activities that we engage in (such as the ones included here and throughout Part II), we must do the following:

1.   Believe in the tenets of working from students' and families' strengths to identify and acknowledge the many attributes and competencies that they already possess or can gain from our working together as the strengths-based educators we are. An example is Álvaro in his mathematics class. During the first few weeks of remote school during COVID-19, he never spoke during class. During a one-on-one meeting with his teacher, she commented on his homework. "Álvaro," she said in Spanish, "you show so much passion for math. I appreciate your determination and positive energy. I also see that you learned how to use the Schoolology program to upload assignments. Thank you for taking time to meet with Mr. García and for taking time to learn how to use it. That shows a lot of commitment and determination."

2.   Acknowledge the high value of each student's and family's cultural ways of being and acting, and value these in what we say and do. Let's look at this a little more deeply. According to developmental psychologist Mary Gauvain (2001), children are guided to participate in the world around them both passively (i.e., by observing others such as their parents/guardians speaking with each other) and actively (i.e., interacting with their family, classroom, and school communities). We say this to emphasize that a child's culture is deeply rooted through practicing the same routines and activities over and over again. Let's look at an example of three different children as they accompany their parents/guardians to get food during COVID-19. The first child travels with her parents/guardians to the food distribution center closest to their apartment, where they wait in a seemingly endless line of cars to receive donated cartons of food. The second child and his parents/guardians don masks and walk a few blocks to their local Whole Foods supermarket to purchase items of their choice, including their child's favorite box of graham cracker bunnies. The third child waits by his front door for the Publix

food delivery and yells to his parents/guardians, "Our groceries are here!" when he hears that familiar knock at their door. The three students engage in these routines week after week from March to September. When they begin Kindergarten remotely, their class schedule includes a read-aloud after their morning meeting. The teacher begins by showing her students pictures from the book. She asks them what they see. One of the three students raises his hand on Zoom and is called on. He says, "I see a family going to get groceries at the store. I know what that is! It's what we do every week at Whole Foods!" He does this easily because he has been immersed in the deep cultural way of being and acting month after month. However, let's look at what happens next. His teacher acknowledges him but also discusses that she knows many from the community and her own neighborhood who have gone to the food distribution center to get their groceries, and she tells them about others, including her, who have had food delivered to their home. She then asks, "How many of us know someone who either goes to the market, goes to the food distribution center, or has food delivered?" Every student raises their hand as she has taken time to acknowledge the rich cultural experiences of her students and their families.

3.   Dramatically increase the amount of positive assets-based encounters and interactions within and across all of our classroom, school, and local communities to support our students and families in having lots of connections, interconnections, experiences, and social among those communities. The opening of this segment of our book presented various assets-based interactions that our focal student Álvaro and his mother had with school-based professionals, his and community partners from soccer, and the optometrist. We later read about an interaction that Álvaro had with his mathematics teacher. The common thread among all of these encounters is the positive assets-based language that is used to support students and their families to feel safe; a sense of belonging to and being members of their classroom, school, and local communities; valued; and, just as importantly, competent. More positive interactions across all of these domains lead to more positive outcomes. It is foundational to moving beyond crises and overcoming inequities in our communities, schools, and classrooms.

Engaging in these three actions requires that we move from working in isolated silos to engaging in coordinated, systematic partnership approaches that cannot stand alone or be accomplished by any one person or entity. Rather, it involves creating structures for sustaining and enacting comprehensive classroom, school, and community partnerships. We turn to this topic in the next chapter.

Striving for Interdependent Interconnected Communities

3

We must be the change we seek if we are to effectively demand transformation from others.

—Civil Rights Icon and U.S. Congressman John Lewis (2017)

In the opening chapter of our book, we asked that you imagine being Álvaro, a new seventh grader who had come to a metropolitan suburb in the United States with his mother and sister after they'd experienced the trauma of a volcano in their home country, where Álvaro had horribly seen his father and sister perish. We imagined him enrolling in a school and classroom that wholly supported him and his family to feel safe, a sense of belonging, value, and competence.

In this chapter, we look more closely at ways that we can intentionally strive to build sustained interdependent and interconnected partnerships with various sectors of our family and community partners. We do this to

✓ raise our awareness of the interests, desires, and needs of our students;

✓ ensure students' medical health and well-being, social-emotional and intellectual growth; and

✓ address identified challenges to overcome barriers that do not allow children and families to demonstrate their assets and do not enable children to pursue their interests and desires.

Creating Structures for Community Partnerships

A helpful way to successfully support our transformational efforts to create interconnected assets-based community, school, and classroom partnerships is to look closely at what we (administrators, teachers, staff, and other school employees) are already doing and need to do to draw from

✓ the strengths, interests, and needs of our multilingual students and families, and

✓ the external resources to support these.

The resources found in this chapter are intended for this self and collective assessment. While Part II provides a range of comprehensive activities for schools to engage in, the resources found in this chapter are a complement to support the development of our taking a whole-community, whole-school, whole-classroom stance.

Let's being by completing the survey in Figure 3.1.

Figure 3.1 • Survey Assessing Awareness of Students, Families, and External Partners

I KNOW . . .	NOT AWARE	SOMEWHAT AWARE	AWARE	VERY AWARE
1. that our school routinely engages in identifying the strengths of our multilingual-multicultural student and family populations at enrollment and throughout the school year.				
2. that our school routinely engages in identifying the interests of our multilingual-multicultural student and family populations at enrollment and throughout the school year.				
3. that our school routinely engages in identifying the needs of our multilingual-multicultural student and family populations at enrollment and throughout the school year.				
4. the specific school personnel who engage in the activities listed above.				
5. the process that specific school personnel engage in to secure community partners that will enhance students' and families' interests and desires (e.g., soccer, music, dance).				
6. the specific school personnel who work with community partners to ensure that students' and families' needs are met (e.g., nutritional, housing, medical/dental, counseling).				
7. the specific school personnel who meet with me to support my understanding of students' and families' personal, social, cultural, academic, and linguistic experiences.				

Perhaps you found yourself checking some but not all of the boxes in the Very Aware column, or maybe you didn't check boxes in that column at all. What can you do? Let's start thinking about the steps to take by looking at Figure 3.2. It illustrates what must be done to gain a depth of awareness about our school's community partners.

Consider a new student and their parents/guardians, such as Álvaro and his mother. Many schools may simply require parents/guardians to complete a series of forms (including an emergency contact form, medical history form, and application for free or reduced-priced lunch) that show proof that their child has been immunized and, where available, a child's prior schooling records.

Figure 3.2 • Identifying and Cultivating External Resources

Identifying and cultivating external resources to support the assets, interests, and needs of the students and families in my school

Community resources to support the health and well-being of students and families (e.g., medical, dental, mental, nutritional health, housing)

Community resources to support students' social, academic, and school-college/-to-career development

Schools may assign the person assigned to greet people at the front office to this required document collection task. While the collection of these documents is part of our accountability efforts to gather required information, we must do much more than gather these forms to achieve our purpose of overcoming inequality. And that begins with building relationships with families.

Imagine how much we miss by being too information driven!

One of the key activities that we should engage in during enrollment is ensuring that students and their families are welcomed and supported to feel safe, a sense of belonging, value, and competence. In the opening of this segment of our book, we shared how much time Mrs. Pérez and Álvaro spent with the school's family coordinator to learn about her son's prior schooling and life experiences and Mrs. Pérez's involvement with her son's school. Taking time to meet with families at enrollment is not only important; it is an essential partnership-building effort with families, especially in terms of overcoming inequities.

Forging Partnerships at Enrollment

Every school and district has its own unique system for enrolling students. Before COVID-19, this might have encompassed a parent/guardian going to their local school or a centralized enrollment facility. Often, children would accompany their families and participate passively or actively in the process (e.g., watching their parents/guardians complete enrollment forms such as emergency contact and medical history, engaging in a series of screenings). Since the onset of the COVID-19 pandemic, the enrollment process has changed throughout the United States and other countries from an in-person to a remote event. It has also resulted in many educators rethinking the importance of supporting students and families to feel welcomed to whatever lies ahead in person, remotely, or via a hybrid of both in their new school and local community.

We suggest that whatever type of enrollment process is initiated, it should include a staff person who takes actions that immediately welcome a child and their family, show a sense of caring for and about them, and demonstrate an assets-based curiosity to get to know them with the intent of building positive, reciprocal partnerships. If we look back to the information that was gathered about Álvaro and Mrs. Pérez, it is impossible to imagine that any document would ever result in the depth of information, care, commitment, and human curiosity that meeting with a staff person does. However, it is also true that this can only happen when we show empathy, compassion, and a truly collaborative partnership spirit.

The following list of questions is intended for this purpose. As you read each topic and suggested question for discussion with parents/guardians, take time to imagine your own questions and write these in the space provided in Figure 3.3. In addition, add one or two topics that you think should be included.

Figure 3.3 • Suggested Topics and Questions for Building Parent/Guardian Partnerships

TOPIC	SUGGESTED QUESTIONS FOR DISCUSSION	MY OWN QUESTION
1. Find out about the qualities and values that make the student unique to their family.	1. What makes [name of child] special (things that set him/her apart from others, qualities he/she has, things he/she values)?	1.
2. Find out about the hopes, dreams, and interests of the student.	2. What are [name of child's] hopes, dreams, and activities/interests that he/she looks forward to doing in and outside of school?	2.
3. Seek information about what makes the relationship special between the parent/guardian and their child.	3. What are some things you enjoy about your child? What are some special activities that you do with him/her?	3.
4. Find out what qualities and values the parent appreciates from their child.	4. What particular talents and skills would you like me to know about [name of child]?	4.
5. Find out about the family's values and ways that they share their life together.	5. What are things you enjoy doing as a family, especially during COVID-19?	5.
6. Find out about how the family might like to be involved with their child's school experience, specifically to show that they are valued members of contributors to the school community.	6. We want our in-person, remote, and hybrid learning spaces to be a welcoming place for you and your child. What would make the experience of being involved with your child's school experiences more enjoyable?	6.
7. Set the stage for partnerships while leveraging the family's input and assets.	7. What special talents or interests would you consider sharing with the students in [name of child's] class or with students' families?	7.
8. Find out about the family's hopes and dreams for their child.	8. What are your hopes and dreams for [name of child's] education/future?	8.
9. Find out about any concerns the parent/guardian has about their child's health and well-being.	9. Do you have any concerns about your child's physical health, including medical or dental needs?	9.

TOPIC	SUGGESTED QUESTIONS FOR DISCUSSION	MY OWN QUESTION
10. Find out about any concerns the parent/guardian or child has about the child's classroom or school experience.	10. Do you have any concerns about your child's education or classroom or school experience?	10.
11. Set the stage for honesty, trust, partnership, and collaboration along with a clear message of inclusion and belonging.	11. What questions do you wish I had asked and would like to be sure are included?	11.
12. Find out when parents/ guardians are available to attend and participate in events.	12. When would you be available to attend and participate in school events? ☐ Before school (7–8 a.m.) ☐ At the beginning of school (8:30 a.m.–10 a.m.) ☐ During lunch (11:30 a.m.–1 p.m.) ☐ After school (4–5 p.m.) ☐ In the evening (5–7 p.m.) If remote, what is the best way for you to be involved? ☐ Phone ☐ WhatsApp ☐ Online ☐ Other:	12.
13.	13.	13.
14.	14.	14.

Securing information about a family's experiences is so important if we are ever to overcome inequality in our actions for many reasons. First, it helps us see from the first meeting we hold that parents/guardians and their children are partners with us. Second, and most importantly, it acts as a catalyst for using a systemic approach that will help us map out and leverage community partnerships that will enhance children's and families' assets and address challenges that all families experience.

Family and community partners can provide unlimited opportunities for multilingual learners to engage in meaningful interactions that support their health and well-being, social, and classroom experiences.

Mapping a Systemic Approach

The African proverb "It takes a village to raise a child" is an important concept for us to consider as we build a whole-community, whole-school, whole-classroom system. Children flourish because each of these three forms a whole to ensure that our students are safe, feel a sense of belonging and membership in these systems, feel wholly valued by these systems, and feel they are competent members of them.

A helpful way to see these working as a whole is to visit Maslow's hierarchy of needs to envision these three—community, school, and classroom—as parts interacting and interconnecting interdependently as one whole. Very briefly, Maslow's (1987) hierarchy builds from the foundation that people are motivated by achieving five successive degrees of needs: (1) the most important and basic of physiological needs, such as food and shelter: (2) safety, which includes freedom from fear and a feeling security; (3) love and belongingness to our family, social groups, and communities; (4) esteem for oneself, including dignity, mastery, and independence, as well as respect and value from others; (5) self-actualization, where a person can achieve their potential "to become everything one is capable of becoming" (Maslow, 1987, p. 64).

Figure 3.4 provides a list of needs and supports that the community can provide on behalf of our students and families. Maslow's hierarchy can help us map out a systemic plan for building community partners that will help students and families achieve their individual, self-realized potential. Let's look at this a little more deeply. Earlier in the book, we provided an example of a student who was in desperate need of dental care. We stated that his teacher secured assistance from her dentist. The action the teacher took addressed that student's most basic needs, his health and well-being. If that same student and his family needed help with housing or nutrition, those would also be in support of their most basic needs.

Figure 3.4 • Community Partnership Supports

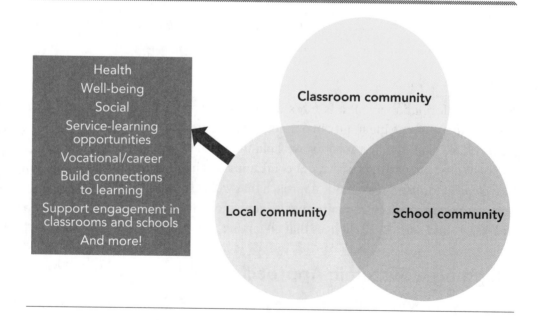

However, as humans, following the same train of thought as Maslow's hierarchy, the same family also has the need to feel and be safe, to be members of their community, to belong and be cared for and about by social groups and communities, to feel valued and respected by others, and, just as importantly, to be able to achieve their human potential. Those key conditions can be met only when we engage in partnerships with community members who will support students and families to be part of the social fabric of our classrooms, schools, and communities.

The systemic approach needed for this happens when we map out and leverage community partnerships that enhance the assets of students and families and address their challenges. We must intentionally build sustained partnerships that continuously collaborate to

✓ enhance the success of students and the active participation of their families;

✓ employ various sectors of the community to ensure students' well-being and physical, social-emotional, and intellectual growth; and

✓ address identified challenges that need to be strengthened to overcome barriers that do not allow children and families to demonstrate their assets and be connected to the various networks that are needed for a whole-child experience.

Further, we can forge partnerships among family, community, school, and classroom members to support an integrated focus on students' health and well-being and social-emotional and academic development. One way to visualize this is thinking of schools as the hubs to bring partners together.

Building Community Resources

In our effort to map out and leverage community partners, it is helpful to look closely at the various types of supports and after-school, out-of-school, and classroom-based activities that children engage in. As we can see from Figure 3.5, there is a lot that our community can provide when we tap into these resources to enhance students' assets and address challenges.

As important as it is to draw from community resources, it is equally important that staff have an awareness of them or, at the very least, know who to contact to support students and families to engage in these when they are needed or desired and to build staff awareness from there. Figure 3.1 provided us with a survey to take stock of staff awareness in our school or district. When we have provided this survey during our consulting and professional development work, two outcomes have generally occurred. First, we have seen that most participants are not aware of the services/ supports that are provided to students and families. Second, most are not sure how to help students from diverse experiences participate in them.

PART I • COMMUNITIES

Figure 3.5 • Health and Well-Being, After-School and Out-of-School, and Classroom-Based Supports

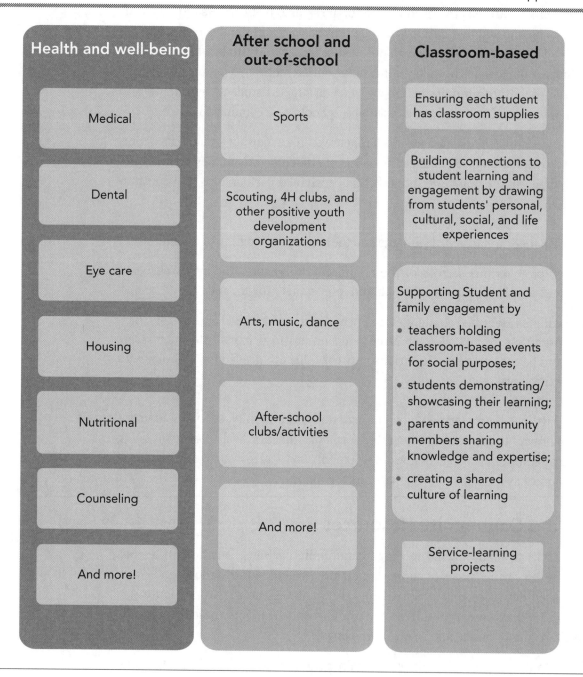

With so many potential community partners at our fingertips coupled with many multilingual-multicultural students and families whose experiences are distinct from our own, it is critical to plan and build community partnerships and our collective awareness of them. As we do this, we must keep in mind that these partnerships must be based on a reciprocal assets-based ideology that sees students and families as valuable strengths-based contributors to the community's success. Figure 3.6 presents some steps to follow for this purpose.

Figure 3.6 • Mapping School Community Partnerships

Create School Partnership Team: Principal or a designee should select a point person (e.g., liaison) to facilitate partnerships with the community and a team of administrators, nurses, counselors, teachers, parents/guardians, and students from the multilingual-multicultural community to form the School Partnership Team.

School principal and liaison should gather the School Partnership Team monthly, or more often depending on intensity of need, to identify health and well-being, social, and classroom activities/services that can potentially be fulfilled by community resources and make a list of potential partners.

Liaison (and School Partnership Team, where needed) meets with potential community partners to ensure that they possess an assets-based ideology and to identify ways that the community and school-based partnerships can be enacted positively.

IMAGINE

Think about your own map of school–community partnerships. Imagine who you would like involved on the School Partnership Team. Imagine the specific health and well-being, social, and classroom activities resources that you would like to be included by tapping into community resources.

_____

_____

_____

_____

_____

_____

Figure 3.7 • Mapping My School Community Partnerships

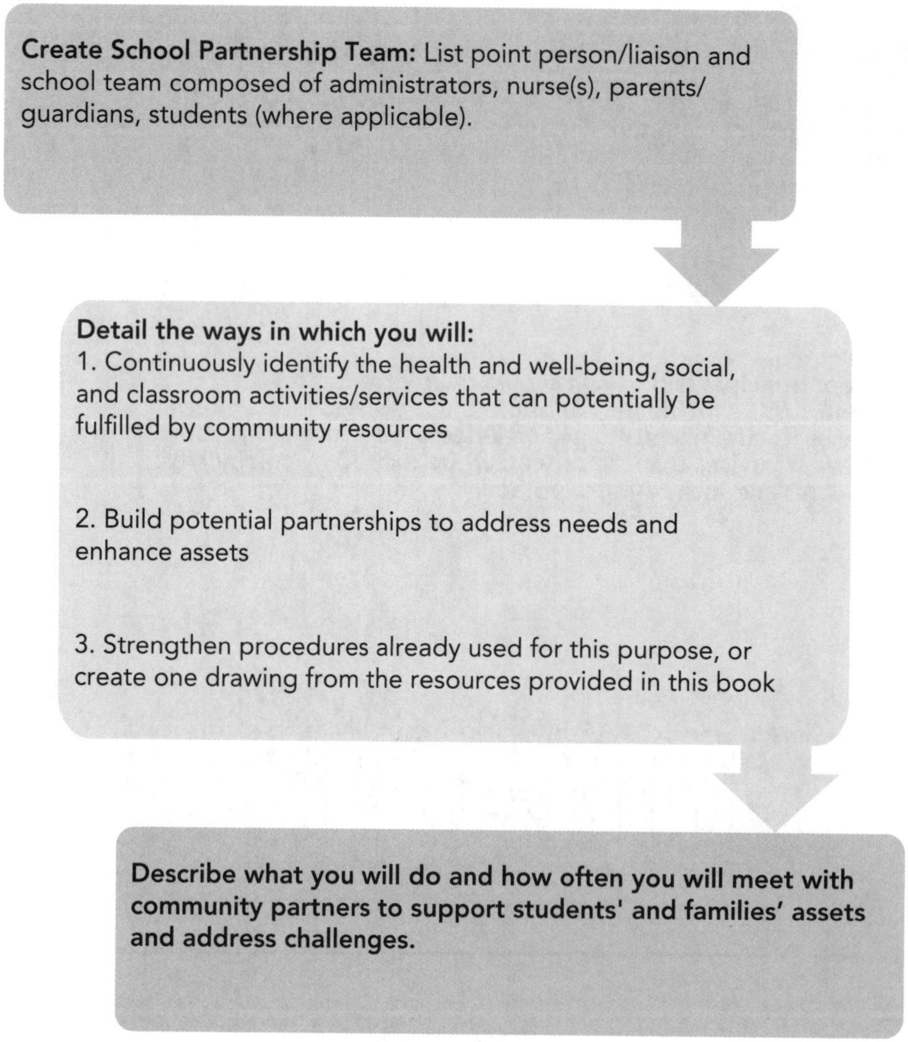

Create School Partnership Team: List point person/liaison and school team composed of administrators, nurse(s), parents/guardians, students (where applicable).

Detail the ways in which you will:
1. Continuously identify the health and well-being, social, and classroom activities/services that can potentially be fulfilled by community resources

2. Build potential partnerships to address needs and enhance assets

3. Strengthen procedures already used for this purpose, or create one drawing from the resources provided in this book

Describe what you will do and how often you will meet with community partners to support students' and families' assets and address challenges.

Figure 3.7 provides a format for mapping our community partnerships. It is helpful for district leaders, school principals, parent and community coordinators, and school- or district-based teams to engage in the mapping process together.

Identifying Interests, Desires, and Needs

An essential effort that a school- or district-based team should routinely engage in is identifying the needs, desires, and interests of students and families. The following two surveys, one for staff (Figure 3.8) and the second for parents/guardians (Figure 3.9), were created for this purpose. These can be adapted to the particular needs, desires, and interests of your students, families, and community. While some schools may disseminate and collect these annually, it's helpful to do this as student and family populations change (e.g., an increase in available housing or dramatic shifts in populations results in new groups of multilingual-multicultural students enrolling).

Figure 3.8 • Staff Survey

The purpose of this survey is to help us understand the health and well-being and social interests and desires of our students and build strong community partnerships on behalf of our students. Our collective responses will greatly help us in these efforts.

Please select your classification below:

☐ School administrator

☐ School teacher

☐ School support staff (counselor, social worker, custodian, lunch staff, etc.)

☐ Other:

Please check the resources that you believe are most needed by the students in your classes:

☐ Medical

☐ Dental

☐ Eye care

☐ Housing

☐ Nutritional

☐ Counseling

☐ Other (please list):

Please briefly describe why you believe these resources are needed.

Please check the three family–school partnership activities that you think would be most helpful to our students:

☐ Family gatherings for social purposes

☐ Family gatherings for students to showcase their learning

☐ Ways for families to share resources

☐ Creating a shared home-school culture of learning

☐ Other (please describe):

Please briefly describe why you believe these activities are needed.

(Continued)

PART I • COMMUNITIES

PART I • COMMUNITIES

(Continued)

Please check three activities that you believe would be most helpful to students:

☐ After-school clubs and recreational activities

☐ Before-/after-school programs

☐ Field trips

☐ Buddy programs

☐ Other (please list):

Please briefly describe the activities you believe are needed.

Figure 3.9 • Parent/Guardian Survey

The purpose of this survey is to help us understand the health and well-being and social interests and desires of your child and to build strong family–school partnerships. Your responses will greatly help us in these efforts. Thank you!

Please check the resources that you believe are most needed:

☐ Medical

☐ Dental

☐ Eye care

☐ Housing

☐ Nutritional

☐ Counseling

☐ Other

Please check the three family–school partnership activities that you think would be most helpful to your child:

☐ Family gatherings for social purposes

☐ Family gatherings for students to showcase their learning

☐ Ways for families to share resources

☐ Creating a shared home–school culture of learning

☐ Other (please describe):

Please describe how these activities might be helpful.

What is the best means to contact you to support our efforts?

Please check three activities that you believe would be most helpful to your child:

☐   After-school clubs and recreational activities

☐   Before-/after-school programs

☐   Field trips

☐   Buddy programs

☐   Other (please list):

Please briefly describe the type of clubs, programs, or trips that you think would be helpful to your child.

Once these surveys have been disseminated and collected, a school- or district-based team should

✓   engage in a systematic review of the findings to collate the type of community resources and supports that would be most helpful,

✓   determine the steps that a coordinator/liaison will take to recruit individual, institutional, and agency resources/supports.

Using Asset-Based Interactions

It is essential to recruit community partners that use the same assets-based ideology as we do. And a helpful first step in building partnerships is looking closely at the optimal types of interactions that we, as educators and community partners, should be having across all of our circles of interactions within our classrooms, schools, and community—namely, that they are positive and continuously show our students, their families, ourselves, and others the assets and strengths that we identify and infuse in our work to support our students' overall success, especially because we believe in their endless potential!

Let's look at different responses to the same sentence frame to show the difference between a deficits- and an assets-based response. Let's also say that the prompt is an example of an interaction between one staff person and another about our focal student, Álvaro, and his mother.

Sentence Frame

Álvaro, his mother, and his younger sister experienced a tragic volcano in Guatemala, where they lost their father and older sister. I feel . . .

Educator A: *so badly for them, and I don't speak Spanish so I can't tell them how awful I feel.*

Educator B: *that it must have taken a lot of courage for them to come to the United States! He told our liaison that his favorite subject is math, and I am excited to work with Álvaro and his mother.*

REFLECTION

As the caring educator that you are:

Create your own assets-based response to the prompt.

_____

_____

_____

_____

_____

_____

> Look back to the response from Educator A. As an assets-based educator, what might you say in response to support that educator to shift from a deficits- to an assets-based stance that demonstrates that you care about both Álvaro and Educator A?
>
> _____
>
> _____
>
> _____
>
> _____
>
> _____

online resources ➤ Available for download from **resources.corwin.com/BeyondCrises**.

Using assets-based interactions on a regular and consistent basis with multilingual-multicultural students and families and, as just importantly, with others including the community partners we recruit requires that we examine our feelings, assumptions, and biases about the students and families with whom we work, particularly those whose personal, social, cultural, racial, ethnic, academic, and life experiences are distinct from our own.

The deaths of George Floyd, Breonna Taylor, and Ahmaud Arbery and the life-changing injuries sustained by Jacob Blake raise the level of urgency for our undertaking of this critical work. Whether we are working in a community that is mostly white, multiracial/multiethnic, or mostly people of color, we must understand our personal experiences and feelings about sensitive issues such as discrimination and bias. Race relations writer Ijeoma Oluo helps us consider how, in our words and deeds, we must take actions that are intentionally uplifting and inspiring to others and not oppressing. This is particularly relevant considering that most principals and teachers in the United States are white (U.S. Department of Education, 2016). Taking actions to build community, school, and classrooms to truly overcome inequities involves our willingness to imagine the positively powerful and influential partnerships that can occur when we work with students and families by infusing their assets and strengths into our work together.

Here are some implementation steps for seeking and engaging in these types of community partnerships:

✓ Be open-minded, curious, nonjudgmental, and respectful.

✓ Actively listen to students and families.

✓ Ask questions that demonstrate your curiosity, respect, and neutrality.

✓ Show respect and value for families and students.

✓ Regard families as having invaluable assets and strengths.

✓ Focus on shared interactions that demonstrate that everyone has something very valuable to say and demonstrates your natural curiosity and caring for others through active listening as opposed to talking. (Remember that the most important partner is the one who listens the most!)

✓ Create a *mistake-safe* culture. Mistakes, as we all know, are a necessary part of what we do to grow and learn together. At the same time, one of the biggest challenges that we should expect in building and sustaining community partnerships is knowing when we should speak up and offer advice, correction, and guidance and when we should step back so that our partners have space to make adjustments and corrections on their own (Zacarian & Silverstone, 2020). We strongly suggest selecting partners who already possess an assets-based stance for addressing challenges and enhancing the strengths of our students and families so that we can build and grow most successfully together.

There are three conditions for engaging in this type of assets-based community partnership:

1. Foster a safe and nurturing environment where asking questions about the assumptions and perceptions that people have is wholly supported and welcomed.

2. Support discussing concerns and worries so that these can be consciously addressed.

3. Understand that building trusting relationships is a process during which we are all likely to make errors and create responses that fail. The adage "One step forward, two steps back" and the proverb "Even monkeys fall from trees" are both helpful and essential for encouraging ourselves and our partners to see our trials and errors as opportunities for individual and collective growth.

With this in mind, seek community partners that will

✓ use the same assets-based ideology that we are striving to use,

✓ address and enhance the health and well-being of students,

✓ build social ties and networks with families by engaging in events both online and in person that accentuate human connections,

✓ provide service-learning opportunities that enhance students' academic and social-emotional growth,

✓ provide vocational/career pathways,

✓ build connections to learning,

✓ continuously support community engagement in classrooms and schools, and

✓ do more!

Create a welcoming family-school-community partnership environment:

✓ Ensure that everyone is welcome in the classroom and school (remotely or in person) by assigning greeters at the door or as partners join meetings.

✓ Invite former families and community leaders to support family partners to feel and be welcomed.

✓ Ensure that there are bilingual-bicultural translators to meaningfully support family-school-community communication, and plan additional time for this critical activity to occur.

✓ Include a closing activity that affirms everyone's participation and contributions and seeks future involvement.

Engaging in Collaborative Assessment

It is also helpful to engage in a collaborative assessment of a team's activities as we create, implement, and assess our collective partnership efforts. Figure 3.10 provides a model for engaging in the steps needed.

It is also very helpful to gauge our partnership efforts. Figure 3.11 provides a tool for this purpose. It can be adapted to the particular efforts we make as we imagine the endless possibilities of the community, school, and classroom partnerships that can be built together.

Figure 3.10 • Planning Next Steps for Building and Sustaining Community, School, and Classroom Partnerships

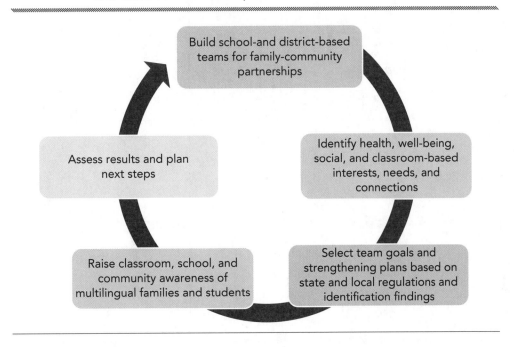

Figure 3.11 • Assessing Community, School, and Classroom Partnership Efforts

IMPLEMENTATION COMPONENT	QUESTIONS WE MIGHT ASK OURSELVES	WHAT WE HAVE STARTED (WHAT ELSE IS NEEDED TO STRENGTHEN OUR EFFORTS?)	WHAT IS SHOWING SUCCESS NOW (PROOF)?
Do we have school- and district-based teams for family and community partnerships?	What steps have we taken to create school- and district-based teams for family and community partnerships?		
	How are we including our multicultural, multilingual, multiethnic communities?		
	Do we regard families and communities as having valuable assets and strengths for creating partnerships that are mutual and reciprocal?		
	How do we collectively determine the needs, interests, and desires of students and families?		
	Do we meet regularly to systematically build and strengthen our partnerships with families and individuals, agencies, and organizations from the community?		
Do we meet with families at enrollment to secure information about students' health and well-being and social interests?	What efforts have we made to secure information about students' health and well-being and social interests (see Figures 3.3 and 3.9)		
	How do we demonstrate the linguistic and cultural skills needed to work closely with multicultural, multilingual, multiethnic, economically diverse families?		

IMPLEMENTATION COMPONENT	QUESTIONS WE MIGHT ASK OURSELVES	WHAT WE HAVE STARTED (WHAT ELSE IS NEEDED TO STRENGTHEN OUR EFFORTS?)	WHAT IS SHOWING SUCCESS NOW (PROOF)?
Do we value students' and families' personal, cultural, linguistic, and life experiences?	In what ways do we support students and families to feel safe, a sense of belonging, value, and competent?		
Do our school- and district-based teams include representatives from our multicultural, multilingual, multiethnic communities?	What efforts have we made to recruit and include members from our multicultural, multilingual, multiethnic communities on our staff? What roles do our multicultural, multilingual, multiethnic staff fulfill?		
Do we continuously raise our school's and district's awareness about our dynamically changing students and families?	In what ways is our staff informed about our multicultural, multilingual, multiethnic communities? How are these efforts included in our professional development efforts to raise awareness? Does each staff member have a list of current school, district, and community resources from which to draw?		

(Continued)

69

Figure 3.11 • (Continued)

IMPLEMENTATION COMPONENT	QUESTIONS WE MIGHT ASK OURSELVES	WHAT WE HAVE STARTED (WHAT ELSE IS NEEDED TO STRENGTHEN OUR EFFORTS?)	WHAT IS SHOWING SUCCESS NOW (PROOF)?
Are we systematically meeting to recruit, sustain, and assess the strengths of our community partnerships to support our students' academic and social-emotional, service learning, and career interests and needs?	Does the team meet regularly to recruit and sustain family and community partners that draw from the strengths, interests, and needs of our students and families? How do we determine the interests, needs, and desires of our multicultural, multilingual, multiethnic communities? What steps are we taking to support student engagement in service-learning projects? What steps are we taking to support students in their college/career interests? What systems do we have in place to assess our community partnership efforts?		

In this segment of our book, we imagined what a community might look like as we move beyond crises to overcome inequity. As you begin to use these ideas in your practice, revisit this segment often as it is intended to help us all imagine and reimagine ways that we can encourage the potential of community resources to enhance what we do to help our ever-changing student and family populations flourish. Our next segment looks more deeply at the second of our three interconnected domains: the school community.

Part II

IMAGINING SCHOOLS

Chapter 4: Designing and Enacting
Strengths-Based Schools

Chapter 5: Sustaining Growth and
Momentum in Schools

Chapter 6: Striving for Interdependence
and Interconnections in Schools

Designing and Enacting Strengths-Based Schools

4

"Today is day three of our whole-school professional development. Before it begins, let's review what we have implemented so far." After a brief pause, Principal James continues, "I'll go first. Let me share my screen."

Imagine the principal of a high school in your district setting the stage for all teachers, assistant principals, counselors, and specialists as they attend a two-week comprehensive professional development on addressing instructional, social-emotional, and physical needs of newly arrived multicultural students. After a daily two-hour session, everyone selects an aspect of the information and implements or joins a think tank where implementation plans, designs, and evaluation criteria are drafted. Teams of language arts and English as a second language (ESL) teachers get together to add the new methodologies to their co-teaching lessons. Math teachers practice teaching new strategies with their math peers to get feedback on their delivery. Science teachers script experiment and lab instructions to make them comprehensible for the beginning-level English learners. This is what we call a whole-school commitment to ELs.

IMAGINE

Imagine that you are a teacher assigned to this school, knowing you would have at least five newcomers at English proficiency level one. What advantages do you see here for you?

_____

_____

_____

_____

_____

_____

Imagine being on the opposite side of the spectrum and you are a new teacher who will have five newcomers, but your principal has informed everyone that due to budget cuts, there will be no professional development this year. The school has opted for remote instruction, and self-paced guides are emailed to all teachers with instructions on how to deliver instruction virtually. Imagine not getting to meet your colleagues and not knowing who to ask for help. Now you wish you had taken that optional ESL course in college. Imagine how new and experienced teachers feel when they are informed that these newcomers need to be ready to graduate in the next two years.

IMAGINE

How is this sink-or-swim situation similar to what newcomers experience in a new school without adequate supports?

_____

_____

_____

_____

_____

_____

_____

_____

_____

_____

_____

_____

---

online resources   Available for download from **resources.corwin.com/BeyondCrises**.

Imagine Principal James at Kennedy Middle School, where the first day of professional development is spent with staff in team-building activities for the purpose of getting acquainted and creating a feeling of family who will work together throughout the year to jointly accomplish goals. One of the goals at the top of the list is "take good care of you so you can take good care of your students." They use virtual breakout rooms to brainstorm ways to approach this goal. Ideas are shared with the large group, and everyone agrees to continue to work on the self-care goal each month. Before breaking up into disciplinary teams and thinktanks, consensus is reached on norms of interaction. Hence, the climate is set for whole-school collegial learning.

IMAGINE

What are some key features of collegial learning that are missing from your school? What shifts would you like to see?

_____

_____

_____

_____

_____

_____

_____

_____

_____

_____

online resources — Available for download from **resources.corwin.com/BeyondCrises**.

Imagine our focal student, Álvaro Pérez, being introduced to his seventh-grade teachers with the help of Camila Morales, the community liaison, and Rose Rozier, the ESL teacher. As a newcomer to English and to Kennedy Middle School, he was delighted that Mrs. Morales was there to interpret for him and that Ms. Rozier was there to introduce him to his pre-algebra, history, and science teachers. He immediately liked Ms. Rozier and felt very lucky that she would spend thirty minutes a day teaching him English and ten minutes at the end of the day answering any questions he might have. She would also be there in his science and history classes, teaching key words at the beginning of class to help him understand those lessons. His former teachers in Guatemala used to tell him he was very good in math, and that gave him a little more confidence going into math class. He wondered why his ESL teacher wasn't going to be in his math class. Soon he found out that the math teacher spoke Spanish! After being in those content classes for a week, he realized that all his teachers used similar instructional strategies and techniques that made the content easy to understand—for the most part. He still had to s truggle, but he saw that as a challenge. The support he was receiving from his teachers made him feel more confident.

In Part II of this book, we focus on middle and high schools. However, the same principles and processes apply to elementary schools as well as dual-language K–12 schools.

Designing and Enacting Schools

What do we mean by whole-school commitment to English learners?

✓ commitment to ELs' academic achievement

✓ commitment to their teachers' expedient support

✓ commitment to the school administrative leaders' efforts

Commitment to ELs' Academic Achievement

A whole-school commitment is where every teacher and administrator cares for and is committed to multilingual students' success, particularly English learners. In this section, we use EL as an inclusive term for newcomers, students with interrupted formal education (SIFE), and long-term ELs (LTEL). Additionally, the term *multilingual, multicultural, multiethnic, multiracial, and multicultural learners* includes ELs and former ELs who have exited the EL program, but schools are still required by law to monitor for the next four years. The term *multilingual-multicultural learners* also includes heritage language learners who might be doing very well in school or any multilingual learner who needs support to sustain academic achievement goals. The term *academic language learners* also is often used to include all students in a classroom or school. In essence, all students are academic language learners this year. *Because of the COVID-19 pandemic, all students in the schools are SIFE.*

ELs in middle and high school are a diverse group, and their distinct abilities and needs require linguistic, academic, and social-emotional support from well-prepared content and ESL/ELD teachers. In spite of a broad range of experiences, schools must support these students to be college and career ready along with all multilingual learners. In this section, we focus on ELs since they are the students who need the most support. However, all these recommendations address the social-emotional, cultural, and academic needs of all students when they are implemented schoolwide.

Schoolwide commitment to ELs is where every teacher is being supported and appreciated, because the task of providing quality instruction to ELs is not easy. Teacher commitment implies adapting the way they taught before, the way they were taught before, shifts in their former beliefs and mindsets. For this reason, all teachers must have the tools and continuous technical support to provide congruous instruction to diverse ELs. Teachers need to learn new ways to integrate language, literacy, and social-emotional learning into their content instruction. Since the learning slide from the effects of COVID-19 has affected most students, not just ELs, the integration of academic language and more literacy skills in each content area will benefit all students in the school.

Commitment to Their Teachers' Expedient Support

This shift will take time, courage, and self-determination. Therefore, in this school (as exemplified in these chapters), the administrators establish teacher support systems such as integrated comprehensive professional development, follow-up coaching for each teacher, and teachers learning communities where teams of teachers work together to integrate evidence-based instructional strategies to ensure success for ELs. Teachers are given built-in time to connect one-on-one with ELs and their families because this will be one of the keys to success this school year and hereafter. Teachers' voices are part of necessary changes. Teachers' social-emotional well-being and sense of safety and security are also a major part of student success, therefore teachers will require more support in this area.

Commitment to the School Administrative Leaders' Efforts

In Kennedy Middle School, Principal James and her leadership team recognize that success for ELs starts with building success for teachers and for themselves. A whole-school commitment warrants enacting the shift from isolated pockets of teacher excellence to a schoolwide commitment to excellence for all teachers and students. It starts with support from the district level for the school-site administrators in order to fully move from a focus on achieving federal compliance to concentrating on excellence. The shifts begin with top-down messages from the state and district acknowledging the reality of the student population and its needs in this current era.

When Álvaro arrived at Kennedy, a team of math, science, social studies, language arts, physical education, and ESL teachers and a counselor met to plan for the welcome of Álvaro and the other eight EL students who would be arriving in the next two weeks. They began by studying the guidelines from the state and the district. Other teacher teams are planning for the previous year's former sixth-grade ELs, and one team is specifically analyzing data they received about the long-term ELs they inherited from elementary schools.

In this segment of the book, we examine how all stakeholders—state, district, and school administration, coaches, teachers, co-teachers, liaisons—can revamp their roles now that they have new roles and are adjusting anyway! We can imagine how school improvement can become a reality when everyone is working together, learning together, while focusing on a fantastic implementation. We can imagine how these collective dispositions and actions will have an amazing impact on academic growth, equity, and social justice for all our students.

Figure 4.1 illustrates how everyone in the school focuses on ELs and how the school district and state support the school's focus on ELs.

PART II • SCHOOLS

Figure 4.1 • Professional Development on ELs: Influences That Impact Linguistic and Academic Development

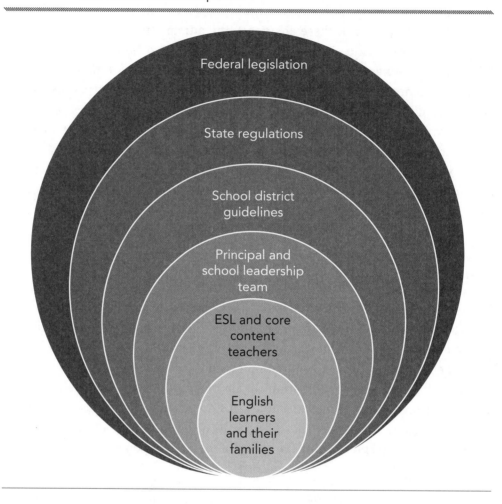

Envisioning Strengths-Based Roles for

- ✓ federal legislation and state personnel,
- ✓ school district,
- ✓ principal and on-site administrators/supervisors,
- ✓ deans and resource specialists,
- ✓ teachers,
- ✓ instructional coaches,
- ✓ students, and
- ✓ community liaison and families.

The Role of the Federal Legislation and the State

Every Student Succeeds Act (ESSA) requires attention to—and action on—equity. States and districts must ensure that low-income students and students of color are not taught at disproportionate rates by ineffective, out-of-field, or inexperienced teachers, and must measure and report on progress toward eliminating inequities.

The purpose of this title [ESSA] is to provide all children significant opportunity to receive a fair, equitable, and high-quality education, and to close educational achievement gaps.

An equity-focused school system—one that sets high expectations for all students, provides resources necessary for meeting those expectations, measures and reports progress toward them, and ensures action when any school—or any group of students—falls off track. https://www.congress.gov/114/plaws/publ95/PLAW-114publ95.pdf

The state's main role is to hold schools accountable for serving the needs of English learners according to guidelines by the Offices of Civil Rights in the U.S. Department of Education (USDOE) and U.S. Department of Justice (USDOJ; 2015). Concomitantly, it allocates the funding for addressing the guidelines. Some states are highly involved in the development of standards and curriculum guides for English development. They bring together experts in the field to stay informed of best practices. All this plus positive messaging is disseminated to all districts. It may be beneficial at times when school committees might want to become more acquainted with the services that state offices can provide. If there are questions or discrepancies, it is best to go to this source.

In determining whether state educational agencies or schools take appropriate action to comply with a student's civil rights through their language and academic programs, the U.S. Department of Justice applies the standards established by the *Castañeda v. Pickard* decision. The three-prong decision, according to USDOJ (Every Student Succeeds Act, 2015), looks for the following:

1. The educational theory underlying the language assistance program is recognized as sound by some experts in the field or is considered a legitimate experimental strategy.

2. The program and practices used by the school system are reasonably calculated to implement effectively the educational theory adopted by the school.

3. The program succeeds, after a legitimate trial, in producing results indicating that students' language barriers are actually being overcome with a reasonable period of time.

In essence, USDOJ emphasizes number three, saying that if the current programs are not creating success for multilanguage learners, they must do something different promptly. To the extent that states select EL instructional models that their schools must implement or guidelines for models, they must follow *Castañeda*'s requirements. This is a good time to revamp all those programs that are not producing excellent results.

The Role of the School District

In order to comply with the "qualified teacher" requirement, a district superintendent and department directors become the custodians of the comprehensive development model(s) that schools can adopt and that should adhere to the ESSA requirements. The model(s) sanctioned and disseminated by the district to address multilingual student instructional needs should show evidence that (1) both content (evidence-based EL instruction) and process (modeling, practice, feedback, embedded learning) are connected, (2) the approach is evidence-based by empirically tested components in experimental-control schools, (3) it addresses the need for rigorous instruction for all students in low- and high-diversity schools, (4) it proposes content-focused collaboration opportunities for all teachers and administrators, and (5) it contains effectiveness measures to evaluate designs, teacher efficacy through growth-oriented feedback from a valid and reliable observation tool, implementation and evaluation tools, and administrative and structural support systems.

In the district offices, the roles of all directors and specialists must shift to

- ✓ make ELs a priority for all departments that have not done so in the past,
- ✓ provide flexibility for schools to remove some existing barriers to EL success,
- ✓ send continuous messaging about the priority, and
- ✓ be present in the schools demonstrating support.

The Role of a Principal

The commitment is carried out by school administrators. Principals, assistant principals, and deans or coordinators attend the professional development on EL success along with the teachers to learn what teachers will be implementing. Moreover, they attend an additional two days on creating teacher support systems, observing and coaching teachers implementing new strategies, and sustaining the motivation and quality of the implementation.

The role of administrators in a school with small or large numbers of ELs/multilingual learners encompasses the following:

- ✓ implementing whole-school comprehensive professional development on EL services and academic success
- ✓ attending the professional development with the teachers
- ✓ attending an additional professional development on how to observe and coach teachers integrating language, literacy, and social-emotional learning into core content
- ✓ sustaining and monitoring quality implementation and impact on ELs
- ✓ working closely with other principals, district content directors, language specialists, and instructional coaches on designing and evaluating the infrastructure
- ✓ working with the community, parents, and students to keep everyone safe while also ensuring that students are learning

The Role of the Dean/EL Resource

There is a specific role in most schools with substantial number of ELs. Sometimes they are called deans, EL resource teachers, EL coordinators, or liaisons. Their role varies, but they are mainly in charge of ELs for the following and other purposes:

- ✓ meeting with students for course schedules, discipline issues, and home concerns
- ✓ administering language assessments

✓ keeping records of language development and state standards exams data

✓ communicating with parents/caregivers when necessary

✓ communicating with the community liaison

✓ providing information on ELs to the school and district

✓ providing information on ELs to teachers

✓ conducting workshops and/or coaching for teachers as necessary

An interview with a seventh-grade dean gives us a glimpse into the multiple roles that are called for in a school with large numbers of ELs, particularly newcomers. In addition to her work with seventh graders, she is also a professional learning facilitator and coach for the teachers.

In Her Own Words

Giuliana Jahnsen Lewis, Dean, Sterling Middle School,
Loudoun County, Virginia

Giuliana, what are some things you have done as a dean to support multilingual learners?

We fulfill various roles in the building as there are three of us in our school, one per grade level. Our duties rotate each year so we can get exposure to various areas. I supervised the EL department for my school as well as other areas pertaining to instruction and day-to-day operations. Each dean works along with an assistant principal.

At Sterling Middle School, we believe in the power of teamwork for the benefit of our students, in addition to students advocating for themselves. Therefore, we began a process in which each EL teacher works with a group of students to establish individual academic goals. At the beginning of the year, teachers meet with each individual EL to discuss their WIDA ACCESS levels, testing accommodations, classes, and goals for the year. Students are mentored on learning their starting point for the school year. Sometime midyear, students meet with their teacher mentors to discuss WIDA ACCESS testing, logistics, and individual goals for the assessment. By working with the assistant principal on WIDA ACCESS testing, along with our EL teachers, we noticed a great difference. Students were working diligently on each domain of the assessment. They knew exactly what to do in regard to their testing schedule, procedures, and their levels prior to the assessment. They were working arduously! The beauty of our school is that we work as teams, so students were receiving the necessary supports in all of their classes. A lot of cross-curricular sharing happens!

Afterward, we meet with all our grade-level teachers in small teams to inform them of their students' scores and discuss where they need help. We know every kid in our grade levels very well. In addition, we have provided professional development on language acquisition, understanding the WIDA Can Do Descriptors, and instructional strategies for ELs.

(Continued)

PART II • SCHOOLS

(Continued)

I have an extra role that I love. I am bilingual, so I get to call Spanish-speaking parents from my grade level quite often and establish connections with them to better support their children while they are in school. As a former EL teacher and newcomer student in the county, I understand the necessity of powerful connections between the families and the school, and of students advocating for themselves.

Having gone through all of the ExC-ELL professional development models that integrate language, literacy, and content and received the certification of an ExC-ELL coach, provides me with the opportunity to support teachers at my school. I work along with our internal coach to provide series of professional development opportunities for our teachers at various levels and depending on the current need. We have designed and delivered differentiated professional development sessions to better support our staff, in addition to classroom observations and coaching debriefs. I enjoy working with our teachers in providing supports for their ELs in the classroom. Working with ELs brings me back to when I first moved to the United States as a newcomer student in the ninth grade. I am able to speak to them and relate in many situations.

The teachers at Sterling work strenuously to provide the best instructional experience for our students. Being at Sterling takes a special heart, and our teachers truly have it!

The main heroes in every school's story are the ESL and core content teachers. Often, in elementary schools, there are dual-language teachers or other language teachers who work with classroom teachers. All teachers have emerged as heroes over the past several months, especially when schools began with so much uncertainty and unfamiliarity, unaccustomed to the new ways of teaching. Teachers continue to rise to the occasion daily with cognitive, social-emotional, and reinvigorated strength. They continue to study and learn from websites, books, and online workshops how to use technology to provide engaging instruction. They turn to peers through Zoom, Twitter, Facebook, and other resources to discuss how to set up their classroom and keep improving their lessons. They worry about grading. With fervent nonstop enthusiasm, they hold out their virtual hands to their students, class period by class period. They strive to build quality relationships with their students based on trust, empathy, and respect. They too have specific roles.

The Role of the ESL/Dual-Language/ English Language Development Teacher

The ESL/DL/ELD teacher is to explicitly teach the following on a daily basis:

✓ basic and academic language (vocabulary and discourse)

✓ beginning reading skills (e.g., phonemic and phonological awareness, vocabulary, fluency, comprehension), modeling with read-alouds, having students practice reading with a peer, and following up with instructional strategies that anchor language, discourse, and reading comprehension

✓ basic writing protocols (syntax, grammar, editing, and revising techniques)

✓ social-emotional competencies that enable students to participate in learning with confidence and tenacity

Plus, they have to work diligently with the core content teachers.

The Role of the Core Content Teacher

Core content teachers' role encompasses the following:

✓ teaching core content in a way that it is understood and processed by ELs

✓ integrating Tier 2 (connectors, transition, polysemous words) and Tier 3 (subject-specific) vocabulary into every lesson

✓ integrating reading comprehension strategies specific to a selected text, video, directions, and online learning tools

✓ modeling writing skills relevant to each writing assignment and providing scaffolding tools

✓ teaching the social-emotional competencies that will enable ELs to approach learning with confidence and tenacity, as well as those that general education students need to collaborate with, accept, and respect diverse students

✓ working diligently with ESL/DL/ELD teachers

The Linked Role of Co-teachers

Virtual, in-person, or hybrid co-teaching takes on a new concept and procedures. Co-teachers have a specific commitment to make to each other and to co-plan, which involves the following:

✓ division of equitable tasks

✓ instructional turn-taking

✓ communication with parents/guardians

✓ assessments and grades

✓ continuous collaborative learning

Co-teachers will experience doubts about what they are doing, the impact on their students, and the relationship they are building with their peer. They can use Figure 4.2 to remind them that it is OK to pause and take stock of their situation. They can also use Figure 4.3 to delve a little deeper into the stress, fears, or barriers that students might be experiencing. That figure can be modified to learn about the experiences and fears of newcomers as they arrive. It can also help to connect to students of color and students in general who have gone through traumatic experiences.

Figure 4.2 • Taking Good Care of Me

SOME SUCCESSES I HAD THIS SPRING	HOW I PLAN TO BUILD ON THEM	SOME FEARS I HAVE FOR THIS SCHOOL YEAR	HOW I PLAN TO OVERCOME THEM

Figure 4.3 • Taking Good Care of Our Students

SOME SUCCESSES WE AND OUR STUDENTS HAD THIS SPRING	HOW WE PLAN TO BUILD ON THEM	SOME FEARS WE AND OUR STUDENTS HAVE FOR THIS SCHOOL YEAR	HOW WE PLAN TO OVERCOME THOSE FEARS

The following interview with a high school reading teacher portrays how her work scope has been adapting to the changing population in recent years. As part of the leadership team, but working closely with newcomers, she is instrumental in creating necessary changes.

In Her Own Words

Lisa Tartaglia, Reading Teacher, Loudoun County High School, Loudoun County, Virginia

Lisa, how did you get your SIFE to graduate in four years?

Creative scheduling! Interventions, mediations, and being a cheerleader. We have block scheduling at our high school. Therefore, the principal, assistant principals, counselors, EL teachers, and I reconfigured the schedules so that our newcomers/SIFE would have English and math and English/reading every day instead of just once or twice a week on alternate days. They needed this continuity. We also added online tutorial programs that integrated phonemic awareness, phonics, vocabulary, reading, and writing. We designed special summer school programs for them.

We became mediators for all that is "high school life" when we noticed none were taking music, theater, or other extracurricular activities and clubs. A couple of the boys dabbled with guitar, but they were not in guitar class. None were on the student council. I had a meeting with the specials teachers and explained how to reach out and invite this group of students. Otherwise, they will not sign up on their own.

Academically, we developed a plan where each content teacher mentored a small group. Counselors and athletic coaches helped to promote equity. I worked with the EL teachers to help them fill out graduation papers, college enrollment, senior picture registration, and all those things that are such a part of schooling but not for newcomers.

Perhaps my biggest challenge was being mindful of the social-emotional ups and downs. They wanted to finish school but had so many barriers that they often gave up or were on the verge of dropping out. I became a cheerleader for them. I literally called a senior girl every morning: "Get up! Hurry up, don't miss the bus." Probably the coach called senior boys now and then. Since most of them lived far from the school, they had to take the bus. If they missed it, they had to walk and be late. When they arrived, we would gently say, "Glad to see you." The newcomers soon learned how to hold each other account-able. They called and texted each other all the time. Theirs is a culture of community, a big family, and we all learned to honor that. They celebrated each birthday with songs, balloons, and food. Food was shared daily. They took turns bringing pupusas and any-thing they could bring from home to share during second period for those who did not have breakfast. They were very quiet, subtle, and cleaned up meticulously. You can imag-ine how they celebrated their graduation!

The Role of the Instructional Coach

Instructional coaches can be extremely helpful for various reasons, including that they

✓ focus directly on instructional change/improvement;

✓ give technical feedback, not evaluation, on what the teacher wants to improve;

✓ provide feedback on student performance;

✓ focus on only a few items at a time;

✓ help with problem solving;

✓ help determine next steps for growth;

✓ provide moral support and companionship;

✓ help with methodology and curriculum adaptation and development;

✓ help with analysis of application; and

✓ provide a compassionate relationship.

The Role of All Students

All students are responsible for the following (which can be posted on a whiteboard and placed in their online folders):

✓ staying focused

✓ giving 100 percent

✓ practicing interaction

✓ making friends

✓ being kind and empathetic

✓ asking for help and giving help

✓ learning new vocabulary and reading and writing in every subject every day

✓ learning and practicing social-emotional competencies every day

✓ acting in accordance with school goals and values

✓ contributing to the school and the community

✓ talking to their teachers when they have a problem

The Role of the Community Liaison and Families

✓ Be the link between school staff, parents, and the community.

✓ Welcome parents to the school, and address their questions and concerns.

✓ Be a translator for parents.

✓ Send important messages to students' homes.

✓ Help newcomers connect with appropriate school staff.

✓ Sustain partnerships with community organization and service providers.

The Partnership With Families and Caretakers

Families and caretakers are invited to actively participate in their children's learning. A school compiles ways of reaching out to families, knowing that one approach does not work all the time. Notwithstanding, critical information on how to help their children at home is offered to parents/guardians by continuously reaching out. While we present this topic comprehensively in Part 1, it is important to underscore the essential role that parents and caregivers provide. Teachers and administrators meet frequently to discuss ongoing connections with families and ways to enhance engagement while respecting families' circumstances.

Principal James records her messages in English and Spanish so she can send them to newcomer families, inviting them and the students to contact her and the teachers. She gives them a menu of options to stay connected.

She also asks teachers to reflect on what worked and didn't work last time in distance learning and attempts to reach students and their families. Her message is that we all learn from our mistakes or half-attempts. She uses Figure 4.4 for teachers to reflect on their connections with family.

Figure 4.4 • Reaching Out to Students' Families

SOME RECENT SUCCESSES I HAVE EXPERIENCED	HOW I PLAN TO BUILD ON THEM	SOME OUTREACH I WANT TO ENACT THIS SCHOOL YEAR	HOW I PLAN TO EVALUATE THESE EFFORTS

PART II • SCHOOLS

REFLECTION

As you and your colleagues discuss these roles, you might want to invite someone from the state or district office to join your discussions. Ask: How do you see your role shifting now?

_____

_____

_____

_____

What other questions would you like to ask?

_____

_____

_____

_____

online resources ↗   Available for download from **resources.corwin.com/BeyondCrises**.

Projecting Barriers and Challenges

Even in the best situations, well-intentioned educators still have to contend with some barriers and hurdles:

- ✓ state and federal policies
- ✓ the school district's policies and processes
- ✓ lack of well-prepared teachers
- ✓ curricula and published materials
- ✓ the pandemic

The State and Federal Policies

One of the biggest challenge for schools is to determine, first of all, if they are compliant with the U.S. Department of Education, Office of Civil Rights (2020) requirements for addressing the rights of ELs/multilingual learners. The USDOE elaborates on what compliance means and provides guidelines, which we recommend you revisit at the beginning of each school year or as you meet while reading this book to gauge the status of your commitment and set your focus for improvement or celebrations.

However, compliance shouldn't be seen as its own end goal. For those who want to go beyond compliance and move to excellence, we recommend a recent publication,

Breaking Down the Wall: Essential Shifts for English Learners' Success (Calderón et al., 2020), which lays out in nine chapters how schools can go from compliance to excellence.

Figure 4.5 lists the ten requirements from USDOE and USDOJ (2015) and parallel efforts for going beyond compliance. You and your staff can use it to add ideas, thoughts, or areas you want to research further to move from compliance to excellence. Whereas the chart uses the language from USDOE and USDOJ specifically in reference to ELs, it could also apply to academic language learners, which includes all students in the school.

Figure 4.5 • Here's to a Better Normal: From Compliance to Excellence

USDOE AND USDOJ GUIDELINE	FOR COMPLIANCE, WE ALREADY . . .	FOR EXCELLENCE, WE NEED TO . . .
1. Quick and accurate identification of ELs' instructional plans		
2. Effective individualized language acquisition programs		
3. Highly qualified instructional and support staff for EL programs		
4. Equitable access to all curricular and extracurricular programs for all		
5. Inclusive whole-school nurturing learning environment indistinguishable of program or level of service		
6. Indistinguishable programs and services that provide a nurturing learning environment inclusive of dually identified ELs		
7. Language acquisition assistance within the general classroom setting for all learners regardless of EL status		
8. Data documenting success and/or support of exited ELs		
9. Yearly evaluations and refinement at the multi-year level analysis of programs and changing needs of EL population		
10. Documentation of successful communication with limited English proficient parents		

PART II • SCHOOLS

An Example: The Virginia State Department of Education

State agencies such as the Virginia State Department of Education's Office of English Learners have shifted typical twenty-year professional development offerings by reorienting funding to professional development on the integration of language, literacy, and content for all teachers, as described in this book. Because of the COVID-19 pandemic, of course, the institutes will integrate virtual delivery of those components. As we have conducted some of these institutes throughout the state, we have heard from participants that the integration of language, literacy, and content works for all students—even gifted students in high school who are preparing to apply to Ivy League schools (Calderón et al., 2015; Calderón & Montenegro, 2021).

Beyond Crises: The School District Can Begin to Move Beyond the Status Quo

While the district's role is to ensure compliance at the school level, archaic district regulations prevail, and these create the artificial separation of content, language, and literacy for ELs and non-ELs who are struggling/striving readers and writers. The departmentalization of core subjects and ESL at the district level has led to EL isolation and discrimination. It also demolishes teacher collaboration around the integration of quality language, literacy, and core content instruction. Moreover, research continues to emphasize integration of these for all students (August et al., 2008; Carnegie Council on Advancing Adolescent Literacy, 2010; Graham & Perrin, 2007; Moats, 2020; Takanishi & Le Menestrel, 2017). District administrators can take advantage of this hiatus and critical juncture to rethink their own structures and offer timely support to schools for shifting to more effective ways of addressing obsolete policies along with past discriminatory injustices and watered-down instruction for ELs, particularly LTEL. Notwithstanding these limitations, schools such as the middle school where Álvaro is arriving and the feeder high school are able to go from compliance to excellence.

Beyond Crises: The Need to Retool Everyone at the School

Throughout the country, English learners, whether in levels 1–2 or 3–4 of English language proficiency, should spend a portion of the day with a credentialed ESL teacher. But the reality is that the majority of the day is spent with general education teachers who rarely hold credentials or certification to teach ELs. Before COVID-19, some ELs received barely five minutes of instruction when the ESL teacher went into a classroom to "teach ELs" scattered throughout a math classroom. The ESL teacher typically sat close to an EL and whispered either a translation or an explanation. In the meantime, the other ELs in the classroom had to fend for themselves until the ESL teacher came around. In a science classroom, the ESL teacher could cluster several EL students in the back of the room and try to address their divergent needs, attempting to keep pace with the science teacher's explanations and instructions. Before the COVID-19 crises, this was called co-teaching in the majority of the secondary schools.

In a typical elementary classroom, the ESL teacher sat close to the ELs on the floor while the language arts teacher conducted shared reading with a big book. In this case, the ESL teacher was silent, reluctant to interrupt the flow of the classroom teacher's read-aloud. Instead, he sat close to the silent ELs clustered in the back of the group, motioning to look at the teacher and stop fidgeting. The instructional coach came into the classroom with a checklist to observe the teacher's shared reading. The coach tabulated each time a student answered a question, usually a student sitting up front close to the teacher. After perhaps eight minutes, the coach gave the teacher a thumbs up and left. Later we asked the teacher when she and her co-teacher would get feedback from the coach. She answered, "I already did! She gave me a thumbs up!"

There is more to co-teaching than having ESL teachers sit close to ELs. What has typically been called push-in and pull-out has created these reductionist approaches to meeting the instructional needs of ELs. Depending on the English proficiency of the EL, they should receive thirty to sixty minutes a day from an ESL teacher and language assistance in every core content classroom.

Effective professional development prepares ESL and core content teachers to co-teach when they attend the same extensive PD on instructional strategies and shows them how to orchestrate equal responsibility and care for the students and themselves. When there is a lack of credentialed or certified teachers of ELs, and inadequate preparation of all teachers, instructional coaches, and school leaders, the crisis for ELs and other underserved students persists.

REFLECTION

Describe an instance that you have observed where the language teacher underserved ELs and did not meet U.S. Department of Education requirements for appropriate instruction. Why is that? If there is co-teaching in your school, what does it look like?

_____

_____

_____

_____

_____

_____

_____

(Continued)

PART II • SCHOOLS

(Continued)

What would you like co-teaching to look like at your school?

_____

_____

_____

_____

_____

_____

_____

_____

_____

_____

online resources ▷ Available for download from **resources.corwin.com/BeyondCrises**.

Beyond Crises: Co-teaching Reconfigured

Some great benefits of the "new normal" might be that this forced change is a great opportunity to learn together and work together toward the same goals. The often-ignored role of the ESL teacher can now be at the forefront. This focal point can engender greater collaboration between general education and ESL teachers and better practices for the benefit of all students. This will lead to opportunities for joint professional development and job-embedded collaboration.

Co-teaching models can be explored as a whole faculty, and everyone can be trained together. The typical co-teaching will no longer be applicable to online or hybrid instruction. More intense teaming and sharing delivery of synchronous or asynchronous instruction will have to be reinvented. Although ELs still need quality time with ESL teachers per the USDOE Office of Civil Rights, the grouping of the ELs will need thoughtful designs so that ELs are not isolated for long periods of time and do not miss out on general instruction or interaction with non-EL peers.

As schools shift to more remote teaching, everyone becomes a learner once again.

Álvaro's co-teachers, as well as his sister Inés's teachers, have attended professional development together and now share a virtual screen, classroom management, and breakout rooms. When planning a lesson, they also plan the turn-taking and time allocations for each with a planning guide such as the one in Figure 4.6.

Figure 4.6 • Co-teachers Turn-Taking

Who introduces objectives and expected outcomes?

1. Let's analyze our EL profiles.

2. What technology should we use (Flipgrid videos, Padlet, text boxes, self-paced units)?

3. How much time for full class? Pairs? Teams? How do we group ELs in each segment?

4. Who preteaches vocabulary?

5. Who teaches the first content segment?

6. Who monitors the chat box?

7. Who manages the breakout rooms?

8. What is to be taught/learned in the breakout rooms?

9. Who teaches the second segment?

10. Who monitors reading and writing?

11. Who manages what type of performance assessments?

12. How many minutes for each of these events?

13. Who checks which assignments?

14. How are one-on-one student conferences scheduled ?

15. Who communicates with parents?

Beyond Crises: Curriculum and Materials

Whether going back to school means returning in person, online, or with a hybrid model differs across the nation. Nevertheless, regardless of how students are going back to school this year, they should engage in a rich and meaningful curriculum that exposes them to a variety of texts as they learn concepts in science, literature, social studies, history, the arts, and culture—texts that provide the context for developing reading and writing skills (Moats, 2020). Louisa Moats (2020) reminds us that teachers need better training to carry out deliberate instruction in reading, spelling, and writing because they are rarely if ever taught the relationships between subject matter knowledge, domain-specific vocabulary, and reading comprehension. Hence, most teachers rely on publishers' texts with similar omissions to guide their instruction. Whereas Dr. Moats refers to students in general, it is important to emphasize that ELs are the ones who have been damaged the most from these omissions because their core content teachers have not been adequately prepared to integrate language, literacy, and content.

> *Fundamentally, these gaps are the result of differences in students' opportunities to learn—not their learning abilities (Moats, 2020).*

Reading failure can be prevented in K–12 second language readers. It is possible to teach most students how to be proficient readers if we start in the early grades and early in the year for newcomers, SIFE, LTEL, and striving readers. A significant body of research shows which practices are most effective for the EL variability, including biliteracy development. This segment highlights some instructional strategies that have been proven to be effective for the diversity of ELs (Calderón, 2007; Calderón & Minaya-Rowe, 2011; Calderón & Montenegro, 2021; Takanishi & Le Menestrel, 2017). Additionally, students living in poverty, students of color, and students who are eligible for remedial services can become competent readers. Persistent "gaps" between more advantaged and less advantaged students can be narrowed and even closed.

As publishers scramble to reposition their texts for hybrid teaching, we hope they rely more on scientific knowledge of linguistics, reading, and writing in the core content areas beyond language arts. As colleges of education pivot toward online courses, we hope their selection of textbooks and development of new courses also reflect current scientific knowledge.

Beyond Crises: Erase the Pandemic Divide

We imagine that schools will continue to open and perhaps close again thereafter, due to pandemic fluctuations. If we look back to the spring 2020 semester, we see the educational gap or learning slide start to widen. The tailored education that students with disabilities received before COVID-19 was rarely there. It was difficult for schools to deliver services such as speech, occupational, and physical therapy that were in their individualized education plans and guaranteed under the Individuals with Disabilities Education Act. Specialized services for English learners were scant due to limited access to technology. Yet we know that all these students were developing life skills since some had to work and some had to become the family translators or mediators. They now have enhanced communication skills in their home language and most likely in English.

There was an area where the divide grew exponentially. Privileged families turned to learning pods, academic pods, or microschools, hiring instructors to carry out virtual instruction for a handful of children. In contrast, let's think about people who live paycheck to paycheck (many in "front line" professions) who hold two or three jobs just to try to pay rent and put food on the table, and who feel guilty because they cannot afford to give their children more opportunities. Those who lost their jobs, no longer have a place to live, and/or experienced the loss of a loved one due to COVID-19 experienced horrific suffering and stress. The gap has widened more. Yet we saw and heard of many teachers and administrators giving a 150 percent effort to help these children, which means that those teachers and administrators were also under tremendous stress and morally suffering while trying to be compassionate. Hope and empathy persist!

Now, everyone is pondering how to deal with their own and students' anxiety, stress, trauma, and distress again. All that intensified in July and August when everyone was discussing whether to open in person, virtually, or hybrid. Teachers and families were and still are forced to choose between imperfect options based on factors including health, socioeconomic status, and tolerance for the unknown and whether to return to school in person. Making the ultimate decision exerted more pressure and emotional strain. All this tension coming from homes and schools has to be dealt with now. Social-emotional well-being is as important as academic learning. We must prepare our students with the social-emotional competencies that will help their psyches survive this pandemic and give them fortitude for the future. In spite of turmoil, it is great comfort to see teachers welcoming their students with caring positive messages and administrators working hard to keep their schools safe. Keep those welcoming videos going!

Now that you are thinking about some challenges, concerns, and things you know are working, fill in the blanks in Figure 4.7. Then compare with your colleagues. What is the consensus?

Once your school has reached consensus on what is in place and where there is room to grow, the next step is to plan the goals and the trajectory to reach those goals. The next chapter offers some suggestions based on empirical and ongoing case studies.

Figure 4.7 • Reflection on Challenges

Which of the four challenges is the one you and your colleagues are most concerned with? Why? Write your thoughts in the blank spaces.

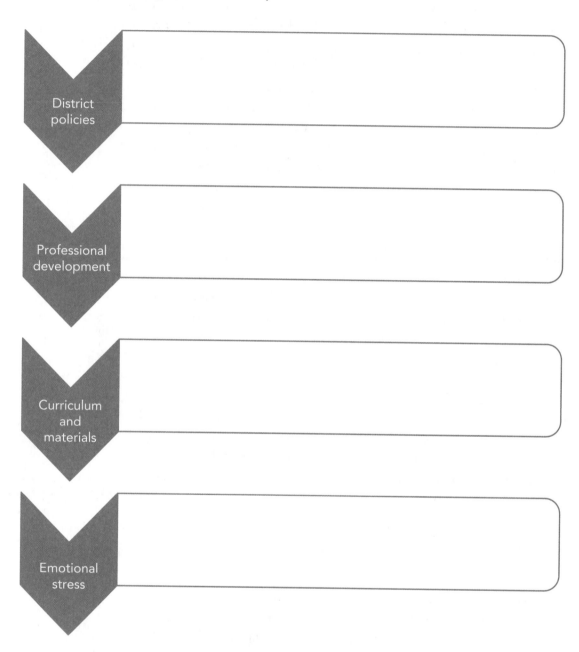

Sustaining Growth and Momentum in Schools

5

The secret of change is to focus all of your energy not on fighting the old but on building on the new.

—Socrates

Envisioning a Perfect Opportunity for a New Beginning

We Have to Change Anyway!

What a great opportunity to invent and innovate! Since we can no longer operate the same way we did in previous years, we might as well see this interlude as a great opportunity to create the school structures and protocols we have dreamed about. We have already seen that through technology ELs talk more, are more focused, and benefit from home assignments they can do at their pace or without interfering with their jobs. Using these observations as a point of departure, how can we ensure excellent participation for all ELs? This beginning will, of course, be supplemented and honed over time, but its goal is to bring continuity, consistency, quality, and comprehensiveness to the many aspects of student success.

This is a great time to collaboratively make changes to the barriers that keep ELs and other students from achieving their potential. In addition to considering the four macro challenges listed in the previous chapter, here are some micro shifts for school committees to add:

- ✓ more collegiality and coaching
- ✓ more student interaction
- ✓ more social-emotional learning for everyone
- ✓ sustaining quality implementation

More Collegiality: Better Co-teaching

Here's to a Better Normal: Co-teachers Keeping the Flow

The flow charts that follow are examples of how co-teachers map out and deliver instruction in thirty-, sixty-, or ninety-minute blocks. It is important to stay on task within projected time limits for each. As partners, they also model how student partnerships can work effectively without wasting time. The co-teaching modeling is critical for Álvaro in his middle school, his sister Inés in her elementary school, and their partners. The teachers are aware that the partners' relationship takes precedence, and they allow time and assistance for it to develop. The co-teachers are just as mindful that it is important to be flexible. There will be times when a student experiences an unexpected or unfortunate occurrence that will warrant a pause and special attention.

Below are three examples that illustrate all-school professional development for all core content and ESL/ELD teachers. The co-teachers keep the flow while preteaching vocabulary, modeling reading comprehension before students read, and explaining the drafting-editing-revising processes before students write. Teachers' turn-taking and timing are included in the flow of activities. A graphic organizer is given to students so that they can anticipate time slots and transitions. It helps students internalize what ten minutes (or whatever time frame you use) is like.

Co-teaching Vocabulary

The ten minutes of preteaching five Tier 2 words (e.g., transition, connectors, polysemous words) from the text students are about to read help Álvaro and all students. It provides specificity even for native English speakers. It facilitates word recognition and meaning in context once the ELs start to read the assigned text. There is still a lot of misconception and wrong information about preteaching those five words. Some educators think that the words should come from a long list of words in isolation that someone says they should teach this year. Others think that if they are doing inquiry-type lessons, ELs should not be given the meaning and they should discover it during inquiry. Regrettably, we have seen ELs discover a word by copying its meaning from someone else without comprehending its meaning and relevance to the lesson. They waste time on task and don't understand why or what they are supposed to be doing. Hence, even with those methods, it is important to preteach ELs five or so Tier 2 words, but not preteach Tier 3 words (content-specific ones like *photosynthesis* or *germination*). Later, the inquiry teacher or ESL teacher can make sure ELs know them or teach them at the end.

A frequently asked question is "Do I reteach these words the next day?" Not really. There is no need to worry about having to reteach those words. By the end of the instructional cycle (see Figures 5.1, 5.2, and 5.4), the ELs will have used those five words in their reading, verbal summaries, discussions, and writing, at least thirty-five to forty times. Students master vocabulary by applying it in all the domains (listening, speaking, reading, and writing).

Preteaching five words takes only ten minutes. For each word, Ms. Rozier has a PowerPoint slide or Google Doc that explains the meaning, gives examples, and demonstrates how to pronounce the word, which only takes one minute. Pairs of students practice using the word with their own examples guided by a sentence frame or sentence starter. Each partner gives five or six examples during the course of one minute. Thus, it takes two minutes total for each word. Preteaching helps students remember the meaning when they read it in the text. They use the new words again as they read aloud with their partner and stop to verbally summarize after each paragraph, using the pretaught words as well as other new words they picked up as they read each paragraph.

Álvaro's peer practice of vocabulary and partner reading with summarization after each paragraph is usually done remotely in breakout rooms. The content teacher monitors the practice, and when the whole class comes together again, the teacher calls on one or two pairs to share their examples with the class. Figure 5.1 conveys the flow of the delivery of vocabulary instruction before reading.

Figure 5.1 • Co-teaching Tier 2 Words From the Text Students Are About to Read

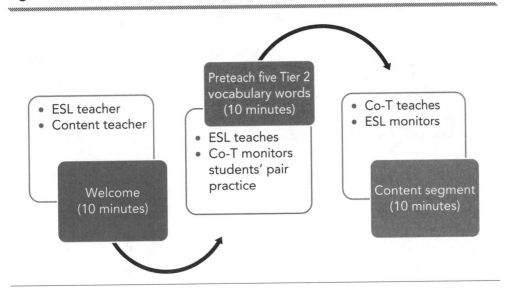

Co-teaching Reading

Science, social studies, language arts, health, and math problems have distinct jargon/discourse conventions, grammatical features, and structures. Syntax and semantics are different across the disciplines. Students have to read in all the disciplines, more so now due to asynchronous learning. For this reason, it is a must that all subject teachers teach how to read the assigned texts.

There are also some theories out there, without evidence, that say ELs learn to read by reading. This is true only if they have been shown through modeling, lots of practice, and feedback on how to read each genre. Think of newcomers or other students who have not had the luxury of being read to or taught fundamental reading conventions. Besides giving them some comprehension strategies, give them a nice buddy to do partner reading with, preferably a partner who is a native English reader to serve as a model. Students learn more from each other when given the opportunity. Partner reading or pair reading is also beneficial for striving readers and special education students from any cultural background. When all teachers show the text features and text structures that pertain to the assigned text, all students are able to delve deeper into comprehension. Moreover, they actually begin to like reading. Figures 5.2 and 5.3 show how the ESL and core content teacher plan and deliver their instruction, taking turns instructing, monitoring, and collecting student performance data during partner reading.

Figure 5.2 • Teaching Reading Comprehension and Student Pair Reading

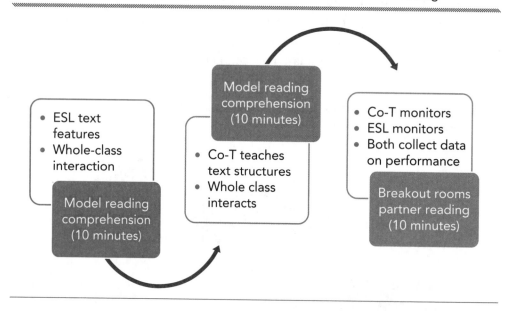

Co-teaching Writing

Academic writing in the content areas is one area that receives the most complaints from teachers, colleges, and the business sector. All students need explicit instruction on drafting, editing, revising, editing again, and writing powerful and accurate conclusions that vary across the disciplines. Students use the words the

Figure 5.3 • Teaching Writing and Editing to High School Newcomers

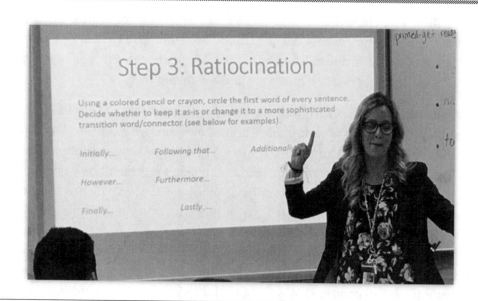

teacher pretaught at the beginning and additional words they learned when they read and summarize aloud with a partner. Teachers explicitly teach the words they want to see in students' writing, assign readings about the content they want students to explore, and provide discourse protocols and sentence frames on Padlets or Google Docs to enable deep discussions. Teachers or students formulate questions that take them back into the text or additional texts on the subject to immerse themselves into the subject and the language before they start drafting. Because of practices such as these, students in Advanced Placement classes report that their test scores have risen, particularly their SAT scores (Calderón & Montenegro, 2021). In Figure 5.3 we see Lisa Tartaglia, high school reading teacher, teaching Newcomers/SIFE to edit their own writing.

Figure 5.4 illustrates the beginning of the writing process, which is drafting. Similar processes would be used by co-teachers for the subsequent stages of writing: editing, revising, final editing, and composing a powerful conclusion and title.

Figure 5.4 • Teaching the Writing Process for Content-Based Academic Writing

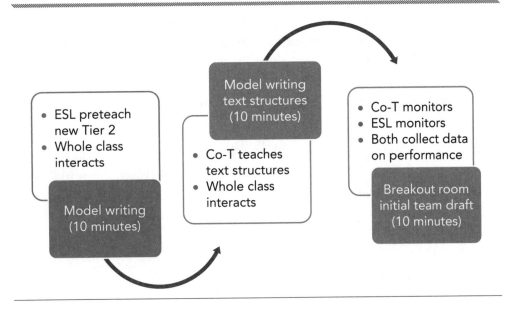

REFLECTION

How do you see your remote job-embedded collaboration between ESL and general education teachers in this new reality for teaching vocabulary, reading comprehension skills, and writing?

_____

_____

_____

(Continued)

(Continued)

_____

_____

_____

_____

_____

_____

online resources ► Available for download from **resources.corwin.com/BeyondCrises**.

We know from empirical research in the 1980s and application of that research since then that teachers' collective efforts yield the highest student effect sizes, particularly for schools with a great deal of diversity (Calderón, 1984; Hattie, 2017; Joyce & Showers, 1982). Collegiality will be most advantageous now that teachers have to transition to unfamiliar instruction modes because of the pandemic and have so much to learn and unlearn. Teachers need companionship to do problem solving, get targeted feedback, share lessons, share successes, motivate one other to keep trying, and occasionally cry on each other's shoulders, albeit virtually (Calderón, 1999).

Teachers have shared tips with us about what helps them get through difficult times or times when they have to adapt to fit in a new curriculum or textbook adoption. These seem quite relevant to the changes they now have to make. We asked some teachers to submit one or two tips under the label "change is difficult," and Figure 5.5 is a selection of what they shared.

Figure 5.5 • Change Is Difficult: Voices From the Field

- It takes a lot of courage to change. It is easier when there is support from peers, coaches, and supervisors.
- Moving away from generic instruction is quite difficult—it takes time and collegial support.
- Teacher observation protocols focusing on quality instruction for ELs that are specific to academic discourse, reading comprehension, and writing help teachers create that positive change and climate in the schools.
- Teacher observation protocols specific to teaching vocabulary, reading comprehension, and writing guide our lesson designs and the delivery of that lesson.
- Practice one new strategy at a time, video record your lessons, and use the observation protocol to reflect as you view the video. Take notes.
- Once you feel comfortable with recording and self-reflection, use a video to seek feedback from trusted peers and experts.

- Know that coaches and supervisors need a lot of support and professional development to give accurate feedback—particularly for observing quality instruction for ELs in secondary schools.
- Coaching is a powerful tool, but a comprehensive staff development program that focuses on student outcomes must precede it.
- Coaching is caring. It takes a lot of love and skill to be a good coach.

Beyond Crises: More Peer and Expert Coaching

There are two old sayings we want to highlight here: "Feedback is the breakfast of champions" and "You get worse before you get better." Two good reasons for wanting to build a wonderful coaching relationship. We want someone to coach us through those worse moments. The coach can be another teacher whom you trust and respect, the school-based instructional coach, or an expert coach who delivered the training that you and your colleagues are about to implement.

Consider the following roles for coaches of ESL and core content teachers with ELs in their classrooms.

The Role of Instructional Coaches

✓ Provide support for co-teachers who need more help integrating their content areas with reading and writing through second language instruction.

✓ Provide support for experienced teachers who may not have had training on new research-based integrated approaches and virtual instruction.

✓ Provide support for new teachers in the areas in which they need help.

✓ Provide motivation and support for all teachers for shifting from a mindset that "ELs are the ESL teacher's responsibility" to "ELs are my responsibility."

✓ Help create a cross-cultural climate to promote equity and enrichment.

✓ Facilitate group and individual teacher development, by content areas or topics that cut across all disciplines.

✓ Observe, demonstrate, and confer with teachers on EL strategies.

✓ Schedule and create collaboration and reflective dialogue in teachers' learning communities centered on EL issues.

✓ Promote a shared vision for policy and practice for quality EL instruction.

✓ Help identify opportunities in the community that can give students authentic opportunities to learn about nature, community development, community services, the media, and politics. Part 1 provides resources and tools for engaging communities.

Expert coaches and school-based coaches are more effective when they attend or provide the professional development along with the teachers. Otherwise, they will never be on the same page. A certain level of distrust or apprehension will persist. Now that everyone is learning and experimenting with virtual instruction, it is easier to bring coaches and teachers together to co-construct and co-plan a lesson and then observe that lesson in order to have specific feedback on what the teacher wanted observed and analyzed.

Teachers Invite the Coaches and Specify Their Need

The ESL and content teachers choose from observation protocol categories for vocabulary, reading, and writing one specific strategy they are currently working on and could use some coaching on. When teachers request the focus of the observation, they are more open to feedback and continuous coaching. For example, a science teacher might request, "Observe me introducing question formulation so you can give me feedback on the clarity of my instructions before I send students to their breakout rooms." This observation would probably take no more than ten minutes. However, the information would be most valuable and feedback most welcome by the teacher.

Whole-School Teachers Learning Communities

Effecting fundamental change is the mission of staff collegial efforts in multilingual settings such as Principal James's school. We call the collegial efforts *teachers learning communities* (TLCs). The apostrophe is dropped from the word *teachers* to reflect the active voice of teachers who are learning (Calderón, 1999). TLCs are structures that remain constant after an initial comprehensive in-service on an evidence-based instructional model that addresses the needs of diverse students. TLCs occur during the working day when teachers get together to analyze school improvement efforts, share accomplishments for the week, do problem solving, exchange instructional strategies, brag about their students' accomplishments, learn to analyze student progress, set up peer coaching relationships and schedules, and learn what they need to learn. This is where diverse teams of teachers co-construct knowledge and meaning related to their craft as they are faced with new challenges. In our experimental control study, in the schools where TLCs persisted, co-teaching and coaching became exemplary and resulted in higher student scores than those in the control school (Calderón, 1999).

We also found in that study that TLC activities need to be brief since teacher time is precious. Here is a typical thirty-five-minute agenda of a weekly TLC:

- ✓ five minutes for sharing successes
- ✓ five minutes for problem solving
- ✓ fifteen to twenty minutes for instructional demos or for analyzing student work
- ✓ five minutes for celebration

A Space for Courageous Conversations

TLCs are safe places for teachers to have courageous conversations around equity. However, these conversations will require more than thirty minutes. At times, teachers show newspaper clippings, headlines, podcast or video snippets, or samples of uncomfortable language to embark on a conversation. Some teachers may not be comfortable sharing their views aloud at first. It is all right to pass once or to submit thoughts in writing.

Topics dealing with immigration and racial justice are difficult but necessary if we want to build a civic future where students' identities and worldviews are different from traditional views. After exploring the topics with colleagues, discussions on immigration or reimagining immigration perspectives shared with students will help prepare all students to develop informed perspectives and the ability to communicate across cultures (see Figure 5.6).

Figure 5.6 • Discussing Bias, Prejudice, and Equity

- Begin with a fun, trust-building activity.
- Co-create community norms of interaction.
  - Discuss how you will be an active participant in courageous conversations.
  - List: What topics do I find challenging to discuss?
  - Discuss: Why do I find ____ difficult to discuss?
  - Discuss: Are bias and prejudice evident in our school?
  - Read a book or article from a Black or Latinx perspective and discuss in your TLC.
  - How do we face that?
  - Add to equity plan.

Sustaining Productive TLCs

Principal James helps teachers and coaches support and sustain exemplary TLCs through the following decisions and actions:

✓ Secure additional training as requested by teachers when necessary to refine teamwork, trust building, team building, and productivity.

✓ Share leadership with coaches and teachers for this endeavor.

✓ Enact structures that support collaboration to ensure that TLCs are functional, productive, inclusive, and sustainable.

✓ Make TLC meetings part of the workday, once a week for collaboration between content teachers, specialists, and ESL teachers.

✓ Work closely with other principals, district content directors, language specialists, and instructional coaches on designing the infrastructure.

Administrators Learning Communities (ALCs)

Administrators from the Loudoun County Schools also have ALCs, where they have opportunities to collaborate for the following purposes:

- ✓ reflecting for deeper understanding of the new leadership practices for equity

- ✓ connecting the district's initiatives with each school's practice and vision

- ✓ improving the vision and culture of continuous learning at each school

- ✓ revisiting inequities and promoting social justice

- ✓ mentoring new principals

- ✓ revisiting structures for expanding the scope of ALCs and TLCs

With the new virtual structures for instruction, ESL teachers, reading specialists, and content teachers will need extra time to develop new designs to collaborate. Thus, the follow-up to comprehensive professional development must include support systems that give teachers time to jointly plan, invent, experiment, and keep working on new practices. Peer coaching, expert coaching, and TLCs should be part of every school budget. In fact, we always propose that 25 percent of the budget be set aside for workshops and conferences attendance, and 75 percent for coaching and collegial learning in TLCs.

In the following excerpts, principals share how they are now working toward a better normal that goes beyond crises. They have found ways to inspire their staff and create hope and positivity within these W-shaped turbulent times.

In His Own Words

Herman Mizell, Principal, Sterling Middle School, Loudoun County, Virginia

Mr. Mizell, How do you and your leadership team, teachers, and parent liaison sustain equity during this new normal?

Our new normal is the opportunity to bring about change and heightened awareness for many of the inequities in education. It sheds light on ways our education system caters to a majority population while leaving the rest in the margins with processes, decisions, and available resources.

We choose to reframe our thinking and processes to meet the needs of our families. What might work for the rest of the county does not necessarily work for our community. Virtual parent meetings, hearing the voices and questions of our families and students, and creating "brave spaces" led to growth in our awareness of what our responsibility is and looks like with readying and setting up families, students, and staff for success, growth, and community.

Sustaining this work requires moment-to-moment intentional thinking and decision making from our leadership team with the support of our parent liaison. We are closing the opportunity gap; we are teaching our families how their engagement supports their children. We are hearing parent, student, and staff voices, ideas, and questions. We are bringing all to the water and teaching them how to fish. We are creating opportunities for our students in the systems we create, such as scheduling, student groupings, and decision making with teaching and learning at the forefront through a culturally responsive lens.

Our students and parents matter, and how they perform *really* matters! They need to know and see this—not just lip service, but in our actions.

> *Why* we do what we do is because our belief is "every child, every day, whatever it takes."
>
> *How* we do what we do, although different, is by making decisions from the margins.
>
> *What* we do is nothing short of true heart work, passion, and, yes, teamwork.

NOTE: Mr. Mizell mentioned that in the past four years he learned to lead a school where he looks very different from the teacher and student populations. From our perspective, this difference has made staff and administration more sensitive and empathetic toward everyone and created the strong sense of equity that makes this school so special.

In His Own Words

Carlos Ramírez, Principal, Randolph Elementary School, Arlington, Virginia

Mr. Ramírez, what did it take to reengage your multilingual students who were not appearing or engaging at the beginning of the school year?

From connectivity issues to lack of technology savviness to language barriers, each family's story and needs were vastly different for this school year, 2020–2021. As the leader of a PreK–5 International Baccalaureate for Primary Years Programme, which also happens to have the designation of a Title I school, multiple challenges have become the order of the day, and the steep learning curve to problem solve and plan strategically has been, at times, insurmountable. Not only is there no historical knowledge of what to do in these circumstances in terms of running a virtual school and being a virtual instructional leader during a worldwide pandemic, but also the time needed to assess, plan, and execute has almost been nonexistent. School leaders are supposed to be ahead of the game! We still are, but by the skin of our teeth, as these rapidly changing times keep throwing a curveball at us and call for flexible thinking and a great deal of adaptability.

Since the beginning, the issue at large has been connectivity, or lack thereof, and the fact that societal inequities were exposed to the naked eye. It was as simple as having internet access at home and a device to be able to access instruction, or not having one or the other and being unable to access virtual learning. Considering the circumstances in my school community, where more than 50 percent of our students did not have reliable

(Continued)

(Continued)

internet service at home, the work was cut out for us as school leaders. Through advocacy and with the support of our school system leadership, a massive plan was devised alongside the county government. This plan included, at the high level, partnerships with internet providers to ensure that all families whose students were registered in school could apply for subsidized internet service. Additionally, families whose current living situation would not allow for receiving said internet service were provided with hot spots or a wireless access point was installed in their neighborhood. We have only one chance to educate our children, and the time is now! Therefore, no effort was spared to ensure the connectivity issue was tackled.

The first day of school was looming on the horizon. We knew we had to be more than ready to provide our students with the high-quality instruction they deserve. When the first day of school came, we went from 60 percent connectivity rates in the morning to 95 percent by the end of the first week. As we closed the second week of online learning, we were able to reach 98 percent connectivity, attendance, and participation rates. And the success stories started to pour in.

How was that possible? By looking at individual needs and providing targeted supports. We taught parents how to log in, how to connect, how to help their children navigate through the multiple learning platforms. This was safely done either in person or via teleconference. The support team we put together grew by the day in numbers. We started weeks before school opened its virtual doors and were able to recruit ten staff members (instructional technology coordinator, test coordinator, bilingual family liaison, administrative and instructional assistants, and teachers) who spoke different languages and were tech savvy and willing to "return" to work early. These individuals called the families of every single student enrolled at our school, equipped with a series of scripted questions, to find out whether they had internet access at home, Wi-Fi, a school-issued device, log-in information, and so on. Additionally, these callers inquired about any possible needs each family might have had in terms of applying for internet access, obtaining a new school-issued device, food insecurity, imminent eviction, and so on. As the reported issues began piling up on a common spreadsheet, more staff were added to this connectivity team to ensure proper communication, follow-up, and support in a timely manner. Our connectivity team grew to more than twenty staff members during preservice to all staff once school started. That was the key to success and the many stories that each team member relayed in the process of getting every student connected, attending, and participating in online learning. As the adage goes, "It takes a village."

We learned from these experiences that every challenge comes with learning opportunities and a chance to reinvent ourselves. Thinking flexibly and creatively has been at the heart of everything we have done and continue to do.

In spite of the current circumstances, I still would not change what I do for anything else! Being able to join a morning meeting and visit with students as they get ready to start the day on a positive note is priceless. Seeing how teachers and instructional assistants work so hard to ensure every student feels welcome, counted, and appreciated says a lot about their true professionalism. Not only do they teach the curriculum, but they also offer emotional support, donate their time and resources to help students and families when they are in need, and, above all, always find ways to bring fun, peace, and harmony to our students' lives. The work they do matters a lot!

Our school vision and mission states, "Developing balanced learners and global citizens." That means that every single effort we are making to educate our students will pay off in the near future, as we will graduate cohorts of risk-takers, caring and principled individuals who will be able to make their own decisions and influence the course of history. My hat's off to all educators and school leaders out there who may be taking a moment to read what this principal has humbly shared. Stay strong! This too shall pass, and we will be so much wiser and more knowledgeable afterward that we will be ready for the next challenge.

NOTE: This is Mr. Ramírez's second year as a principal. He immigrated from Venezuela and quickly became an exemplary EL teacher, resource teacher, professional development coordinator, then principal.

In Figure 5.7, we see the Sterling Middle School principal, assistant principals, and deans finishing a product in their administrators learning community at the end of a two-day session on coaching and teacher support systems (Calderón, 2017). They previously attended a three-day professional development session on instructional practices to reach ELs/multilingual learners in every classroom along with their teachers. Now, they are mapping out the goals for effectively implementing what they have learned, potential hurdles and barriers, and paths to accomplish those goals and improve outcomes for all student cohorts. These maps include the teacher support systems they will implement along the way.

Figure 5.7 • Administrators and Coaches Planning Teacher Support Systems

More Student Interaction

Strong relationships generate ample interaction. Relationships are essential to academic success and well-being. Whether in virtual or in-person settings, at the beginning of the year, semester, and every day, personal connections between teacher and student and between students need to be nurtured. Positive relationships help sustain motivation and enhance language development.

Álvaro's teachers begin each day by asking students how they feel, how their families are doing, how it went over the weekend or the previous evening. Initially, some students are reluctant and embarrassed to answer, and their silence is respected. Eventually, they begin to share what feels safe to share. A buddy system in breakout rooms is a safe context for sharing the answers to these personal questions. For newcomers, a few sentence starters or sentence frames such as "I didn't sleep because," "I feel good because," and "My mother/father helped me" will help. There are times when teachers pair Álvaro with the peers who have the same language background. Other times, they pair Álvaro with a proficient English speaker or a student with the same partner language.

There's an old saying that the person who is talking is the person who is learning. Therefore, we want all students talking more, especially the ELs. Unfortunately, Soto and Ward Singer (2020) found that talking for ELs has been very limited:

- ✓ typically, 2 percent per day

- ✓ in secondary classrooms, an average of fourteen to fifty-two seconds per class period

The researchers also state that structured talk with intentional practices increases academic language and content learning (Soto & Ward Singer, 2020).

Because of the pandemic, every student in a school will be a student with interrupted formal education this school year!

Every teacher in every school needs to be a vocabulary/language teacher these days because of the large number of ELs arriving in the school. Add to this the large number of other disenfranchised students who are thought to be part of the learning slide. After the COVID-19 hiatus, every teacher in the school *is* a vocabulary/language teacher since the majority of the students will be students with interrupted formal education (SIFE), lagging behind due to the lack of academic language practice.

Enhancing Oracy and Discourse

- ✓ Create a context that encourages voicing of understandings and misunderstandings, thereby enriching students' cognitive and linguistic repertoires (Fisher et al., 2012).

- ✓ Provide students with multiple opportunities to interact with peers about a text or what they are writing (Slavin & Calderón, 2001).

✓ Carefully plan, model, provide a psychological safety net, and scaffold in a way that makes ELs feel comfortable expressing their "English in progress" and native speakers of English feel they are refining their English.

✓ Honor students' home languages, including Black English, and help everyone understand that these languages are valuable and can be used as a path to academic English development.

✓ Select opportune moments for student discussions in their home language or, if preferred, in English.

Speaking, however, is not the only part of the interaction equation. Students need to practice academic discourse as well as academic listening. Listening is a discreet skill since it involves filling many omitted items. Oral grammar and syntax are different; they involve a good amount of probabilistic reasoning—predicting what comes next. Listeners need to be able to predict what word someone is going to say. Listening also involves a fair amount of reading body language and more pragmatic reasoning. Deciphering body language in Google Meet or Zoom is somewhat complicated.

Academic listening takes more cognitive energy than speaking. Information needs to be held in the short-term memory long enough to retain all the facts in order to make an informed reply. This is a process that is hard enough in a language in which you are fluent, let alone a language you are learning and now having to use in a virtual context.

Virtually Speaking

One of our tasks as soon as we go online is to model and teach speaking and listening skills (Calderón, Espino, & Slakk, 2019). Álvaro's teachers use strategies such as these:

✓ Go teach—similar to think-pair-share, but partners teach each other what the teacher has just explained. Randomly call on students to share.

✓ Turn-to-your-partner or think-pair-share—mostly used to answer a question.

✓ Chat stations in breakout rooms.

✓ Home language chat time—students with the same native language discuss/clarify a topic or chat at the end of the day to decompress.

✓ Round table summaries—four students use (sentence-starters initially, subsequently, moreover, finally).

✓ Discourse (using creative communication)—free talk about topics students want to discuss before writing.

Students can build up ideas through extensive talking with peers. Just as listening involves making predictions or interpretations, so do reading and writing. Interaction becomes the bridge between vocabulary, reading, and writing. Like-partner language opportunities for writing can be built in to ease some of the language stress some students might experience. Other times, it is important to have ELs interact with non-EL students for exposure to grade-level English.

Figure 5.8 • Developing More EL Interaction

- Program peer interaction every ten to fifteen minutes.
- Model adept diction in speech and writing.
- Recognize interesting or sophisticated word choices in their speech or writing.
- Promote word play, rhymes, use of idioms, clichés, and puns.
- Promote the use of linguistic similarities and differences across languages.
- Permit students to use their primary language to discuss complex topics.
- Organize community-based projects where ELs interact with community services, businesses, agencies, and organizations.

Students will greatly benefit from similar guidelines to those shown in Figure 5.8 in the form of a bulleted list that can be shared via Padlets or Google folders.

Developing Vocabulary and Verbal Summarization With Peers

During reading, even during your explanations or an experiment, let students stop every few minutes to summarize orally with a buddy what they are hearing, observing, or reading. Summarization is one of the most powerful tools for developing academic vocabulary, comprehension, clarification, and anchoring of knowledge. Summarization helps EL

✓ identify main ideas and supporting details,

✓ understand the essence and importance of the topic, and

✓ perceive the relationship among ideas to support or refute an argument.

Through summarization students also learn to use their own discourse with terms and phrases that the teacher has pretaught and many more that they learned while reading, writing, and summarizing verbally with a peer. Verbal summaries help students have clarity and discourse for their written summaries.

Summarization also enhances self-management by challenging students to be self-motivated and disciplined. They learn to regulate and manage emotions by being patient with their partner. They learn to build positive relationships with others and communicate positively and clearly.

Summarization has one of the largest effect sizes for all students (Hattie, 2017), which means that through verbal summarization with a peer or in a team, ELs will increase their verbal and information-processing skills. They will also begin to feel more confident when reading. Verbal summarization before writing also helps produce more cohesive and content-laden writing. Figure 5.9 emphasizes the need to discuss, ask questions, argue and defend one's point of view if necessary, and clarify thinking, facts, and opinions.

Figure 5.9 • Talking Before Writing

Take five to ten minutes to talk to your partner to

- clarify or support ideas, a concept, or a term;
- edit or elaborate a sentence;
- fill information gaps;
- discuss and interpret character traits;
- look up more information;
- find and discuss statistics; and
- look for or draft claims or counterclaims, basic principles, opinions, beliefs, relationships, and themes.

Some students are self-conscious about turning on their video in whole-class settings. ELs feel more comfortable in smaller groups. Discussions can take place in a synchronous or asynchronous environment, with message boards that allow students to respond to each other. Students can work in pairs in breakout rooms to solve the same problem in different ways or complete a written assignment. As students discuss, teachers moderate the conversation, prompting students to expand on their thinking or clarifying misunderstandings. Even with no internet access, teachers can still use the phone—calling students to talk through problems or convening two or three students on a group call to have academic discussions. Regardless of how teachers structure conversations, provide guiding questions and rubrics. Figure 5.10 shows how a teacher can convey information and build extra interaction support for newcomers (English levels 1 and 2) while also addressing long-term ELs' (English levels 3 to 5) needs for depth of learning.

Figure 5.11 is a way for you and your colleagues to summarize the interaction/discourse strategies mentioned so far and plan for more communication for students before reading, during reading, and during the writing process. Even newcomers/SIFE can participate in discussions when they are provided with discourse protocols and key vocabulary. You might want to fill in the first time for in-person learning, a second for virtual learning, and a third for blended learning.

Figure 5.10 • Virtual Interaction Example

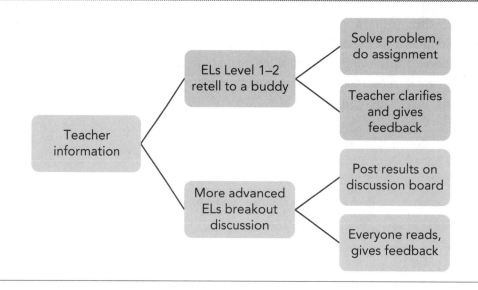

Figure 5.11 • Plans for More Interaction

What are some strategies and dispositions you plan to integrate into your instruction, whether blended, in-person, or virtual, to promote oracy/discourse development, peer interaction, and more communication for newcomers?

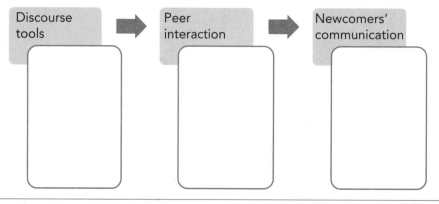

More Family Interaction

Communicating with students like Álvaro and Inés means also communicating with their families. We read earlier in the chapter how communication and good relationships with students' families is critical to engaging students. More than ever, constant communication with parents has become a vital part of each day. Principal James's school leaves one day out of the week for three crucial events: professional development, lesson planning and TLCs, and calling parents or having parents call in.

Mrs. Pérez, Álvaro and Inéz's mother, calls often because she is learning to use the computer and to understand her children's assignments. She wants to make sure they keep up with schedules and self-paced assignments. She gets concerned when she sees her children worry about something they do not understand. She has been reassured by Mrs. Morales that it is all right to call her or Ms. Rosier with questions or concerns.

Think of families/caretakers as an extension of the anxiety or stress an EL might be expressing. We recommend beginning with a friendly get-to-know-each-other conversation. In Chapters 1 and 2, we discussed the importance of listening, really listening, to parents/caregivers and the critical importance of creating a collaborative culture in which parents/caregivers are mutual partners with us. In Chapter 3, we presented a resource (Figure 3.3) for building partnerships. Something else to keep in mind: Latinx families don't like "get to the point quickly" conversations. Instead, we recommend the following:

- ✓ Start with a nice greeting and how nice it is to know the student.

- ✓ Listen to the family's experiences with earlier remote learning.

- ✓ Identify the family's preferred methods of communication.

- ✓ Provide information on how to communicate with and receive updates from school.

- ✓ Build on strong family networks that communicate regularly with each other via text, social media channels such as Facebook Messenger, or phone trees.

- ✓ Partner with EL and bilingual educators, interpreters, family liaisons, community partners, and the PTA to discuss opportunities and challenges.

- ✓ Share tips, questions, resources, and tutorials.

Social-Emotional Learning for Everyone

SEL for Students

Once considered secondary to academic learning and receiving marginal attention in the past, social-emotional learning (SEL) is now considered essential to the overall quest to prevent and resolve the challenge of failed efforts of large-scale and localized educational improvement initiatives. We know that adolescents in general struggle with the surge of hormones, self-identity crisis, and social pressures to belong and to be accepted. Left emotionally unregulated, teens run the risk of making unwise decisions and engaging in dangerous and socially unacceptable behavior in addition to experiencing higher rates of stress and depression. According to a recent Pew survey, 70 percent of teens say anxiety and depression are "major problems" among their peers, making anxiety the mental health tsunami of their generation (Flannery,

Social and emotional learning (SEL) is the process through which children and adults acquire and effectively apply the knowledge, attitudes, and skills necessary to understand and manage emotions, set and achieve positive goals, feel and show empathy for others, establish and maintain positive relationships, and make responsible decisions (CASEL, 2020).

2019). Imagine the personal and academic challenges that ELs and Black students are also grappling with as teens these days, knowing that due to language and cultural differences or barriers, they may lack access to adults who could help guide them through difficult times.

There are differing frameworks for SEL. The Collaborative for Academic and Social Emotional Learning (CASEL) encompasses the competencies mentioned in most other frameworks. The competencies can be adopted for K–12 students, teachers, administrators, and parents. Everyone will find something to appropriate: self-management, self-awareness, social awareness, relationship skills, and responsible decision making. These would be great topics to take up, one at a time, in learning communities.

A major caveat is to make sure we integrate SEL with equity. Rob Jagers from CASEL (Jagers et al., 2018) elevates the importance of calling out and attending to racial identity in the field of SEL. He states that developing self-awareness with an equity lens can help students and adults "examine what it means to belong to a group or community, including how ethnicity and race impacts one's sense of self and beliefs," and "recognize biases and understand how thoughts, feelings, and actions are interconnected." In addition, "SEL competencies can be leveraged to develop justice-oriented, global citizens, and nurture inclusive school and district communities" (Drummond-Forester, 2020).

The Center for Reaching and Teaching the Whole Child integrates SEL and equity, focusing on bringing SEL skills together with culturally responsive teaching practices. It points out that cultural competency is as important as social and emotional competency when it comes to providing a foundation for academic achievement and lifelong success. This means that understanding context is key—whether it is one's family, community, or the broader cultural and sociopolitical environment. The focus is on developing children's skills for recognizing and managing emotions, empathy, positive relationships, and problem solving. These competencies promote intrapersonal, interpersonal, and cognitive knowledge, skills, and attitudes that support lifelong success.

Being aware of our racial identity allows us to better understand the privileges that may accompany our identity and to see how those privileges shape students' lives and relationships. If we teach to students' strengths as they live through trauma, violence, and chronic stress, we can integrate the following into all content areas:

- ✓ listening skills
- ✓ empathy
- ✓ social-emotional language that is needed to express feelings to peers and others
- ✓ attention to their own and their peers' values, assets, and strengths
- ✓ mediating their own emotions
- ✓ resolution of conflict in a productive way (Zacarian, Alvarez-Ortiz, & Haynes, 2017, p. 92)

Cooperative/Collaborative Learning, SEL, and Interaction

Cooperative learning strategies or peer collaboration on tasks that have always reinforced SEL competencies embedded in the curriculum are an effective way to enhance the academic achievement of all students. This is especially true for ELs at all levels of language proficiency. They greatly benefit from the opportunity to learn and practice social-emotional competencies along with English when they work in small groups, have multiple opportunities to use language in an academic context, make mistakes and take risks, and learn from peers who are at various academic and language levels. Studies have found that incorporating cooperative learning strategies in the content areas allows teachers to assess ELs' understanding, determine what needs to be retaught, and get a clearer picture of the degree of their participation (Calderón, Hertz-Lazarowitz, & Slavin, 1998; Takanishi & Le Menestrel, 2017).

Cooperative and Collaborative Learning

- ✓ Create student-centered learning environments, opportunities for differentiated instruction, integrated lesson development and experiences, and interactive grouping practices, and promote inclusiveness and acceptance of all students.
- ✓ Provide maximum opportunities for ELs to practice social and academic language in safe and supportive environments with peers.
- ✓ Use heterogenous groupings for some activities, same-native-language groups for others, and same pairs for comfort.
- ✓ Instruct all students on the collegial norms and social-emotional competencies that they are to practice during each activity.
- ✓ Remind them that the purpose of cooperative/collaborative learning is to learn the content.

SEL for Teachers' Resilience and Well-Being

Principal James believes that building resilience is an important part of growth, change, and efficacy. Building resilience for teachers means enhancing the ability to adapt well to stress, adversity, trauma, and personal loss for themselves and for their students. Connecting with family, peers, and students strengthens resilience and well-being. However, that can also be stressful at times. Think of all that has been weighing on teachers! These are just some of the predicaments:

- ✓ being exposed to the coronavirus if attending school in person
- ✓ living though an uncertain school calendar
- ✓ having to learn new ways of teaching virtually or hybrid
- ✓ keeping student interest online
- ✓ maintaining daily routines

PART II • SCHOOLS

✓ taking care of their own children's education at home as well as their students'

✓ connecting with multilingual-multicultural families more often

✓ dealing with constant change

Principals' Resilience and Well-Being

Every facet of the school day has changed. Think of all the decisions principals and their administrative teams have had to make these past several months! So many responsibilities:

✓ protecting students and teachers from the coronavirus if in-person learning is taking place: masks, social distancing, washing hands, cleaning rooms, monitoring health, well-prepared nurse or designated COVID-19 contact person

✓ securing enough technology for remote instruction: iPads/Chromebooks for all students, network, alternative devices, equipment for teachers

✓ teaching and learning for ELs: professional development for teachers on incorporating technology and SEL into language, literacy, and content instruction

✓ scheduling the whole year: instructional blocks for all subjects, bus and lunch schedules, shifts to in-person or blended learning, unexpected events

✓ establishing communication lines with families: new ways of communicating with parents who might not have access to the required technology

✓ estimating costs: trying to stay within a set budget when so many variables are intangible and there are so many competing needs

✓ dispelling ambiguity: everyone looks to the boss, the principal, for answers

✓ considering new attendance issues: finding students who had to move but are still in the area, students constantly absent, students who are present online but not during in-person sessions

✓ consistently offering support to school personnel, students, and families

A District's and Principal's Dilemma: Teacher Evaluation

Principals are now questioning teacher evaluation. If going easy on student evaluation is highly recommended, should we go easy on teacher evaluation as well? Principals feel uncomfortable observing live instruction remotely. They feel that watching a Zoom recording will not capture enough for meaningful feedback. Much worse, it will be more impersonal not being face-to-face. The quality of the relationship with each teacher might be on the line. How to connect and sustain a positive relationship with each teacher is principals' paramount dilemma.

Although teacher evaluation will be quite different from before, the expectations for quality instruction for ELs are the same. The approach will be different. The conversations between teacher and principal/supervisors will be more important than ever. It will be similar to the way coaches approach the coaching process by having a preconference, where teacher input is essential. That will guide the observation and feedback. For example, in the vignette below, the teachers and supervisors attend professional development on coaching and evaluating, and teachers lay out a growth plan based on an observation protocol that encompasses the language, literacy, and content instructional attributes. After the observation, teachers and principal debrief, reflect, and set next steps using that observation protocol.

In times of uncertainty, leaders are looked to for strength, guidance, and direction. Even if they do not have the answers, and may be scared of doing the wrong thing, they have to project confidence and calm, and they have to make smart decisions. With all the issues that principals have to deal with during the pandemic, they truly deserve a lot of TLC! In this case, when principals work together, we call those spaces *principals learning communities* (PLCs), and these are more important now than ever. School districts should reconsider more support, remove the overload of job duties, and give principals more decision-making power.

REFLECTION

What are your plans for SEL for everyone at the school? Begin with key words here, then develop a whole-school plan.

Our diverse students

_____

_____

_____

_____

_____

Teachers

_____

_____

_____

_____

_____

(Continued)

(Continued)

Instructional coaches

_____

_____

_____

_____

_____

_____

Other school staff

_____

_____

_____

_____

_____

_____

Principal and leadership team

_____

_____

_____

_____

_____

_____

online resources   Available for download from **resources.corwin.com/BeyondCrises**.

Sustaining Quality Implementation: Professional Development and Follow-Up Support

Research-Based Professional Development and Follow-Up Support Systems

It is during difficult times that the best in us emerges. A collective best in every school can have a great impact on all students, including ELs. We have the knowledge and research to help everyone on this journey toward positive change. For decades, we have known what works to develop educator efficacy. There are always special funds to support quality professional development. The issue is that schools and districts do not pay enough attention to this powerful tool that, when planned diligently, renders the outcomes a school desires.

There are documented examples of changes in practice resulting from well-designed professional development programs. Many of these cases followed the well-known model of theory-demonstration-practice, feedback, and follow-through advocated by Joyce and Showers since 1982. Their model emphasizes the importance of comprehensive designs followed by coaching and technical assistance in the classroom. Unfortunately, as USDOE (1995) states, "the intensive training and frequent follow-up advocated by Joyce and others are rarely used and should not be confused with the one-shot workshops that are more characteristic of staff development in local districts" (para. 16).

On the whole, most researchers agree that professional development programs typically have weak effects on practice because they lack focus, intensity, follow-up, and continuity. Even where there are substantive efforts in integrating language, literacy, SEL, and content, inconsistency and lack of follow-up weaken potential effects on practice and student achievement.

Designing an Effective Professional Development Program

The Features of Effective Professional Development

✓ The foundational feature of any professional learning in schools is that it must be a whole-school endeavor.

✓ All core content, ESL, teachers, specialists, administrators, instructional coaches, and counselors should attend together.

✓ The content for everyone encompasses and integrates language, literacy, equity, SEL, and subject matter pedagogy for in-person or virtual instruction.

✓ The process consists of presentation of theory and research, modeling and demonstrations, and participant practice with feedback at each workshop.

✓ The duration of the process should be eighteen hours minimum for the initial session, with additional eighteen hours throughout the year for at least three years.

Follow-Up Support System

✓ Teachers continue to refine their practice in TLCs.

✓ Administrators and instructional coaches attend additional days on how to build teacher support systems; how to observe using specific protocols for vocabulary, reading, and writing in all content areas; and how to coach the integrated model.

✓ Every teacher receives three or more coaching episodes from the experts who conducted the training, in addition to frequent peer coaching and coaching from school-based coaches.

Why Professional Development Does NOT Work

✗ The integration of all key features cannot occur in one or two workshops.

✗ Without coaching and TLCs, the implementation will have disappeared by the end of the year.

✗ Without sustained implementation, student outcomes remain stagnant.

✗ When schools change professional development and instructional models every year, student outcomes remain stagnant.

✗ When there are two or more competing models that teachers "have to implement," student outcomes remain stagnant.

The case study below illustrates some of the ways Loudoun County Public Schools has already approached going beyond the multiple crises. They have carefully selected a professional development on instructional strategies that cut across all subject areas. They have sustained it over four years. That makes it easier for teachers to work collaboratively and for the administrative teams to observe, coach, and support as necessary.

Under the leadership of Superintendent Eric Williams and his specialists in the Office of English Learners, Loudoun County Public Schools has become an example for many schools and districts in different states. The following is a synopsis of some of their professional development designs and ongoing implementation.

Exemplary Professional Development: A Follow-Up Coaching and Learning Communities Model

Loudoun County Public Schools, in Virginia, has been implementing a comprehensive professional learning program for the past four years. They began with four middle and high schools and added six elementary schools in year three.

They committed to a whole-school model that prepares math, science, social studies, language arts, and ESL teachers to teach academic language that encompasses vocabulary, discourse, listening and speaking skills; reading comprehension in the subject areas, including close reading; and writing skills for each core content genre. Social-emotional competencies taught through cooperative learning undergird all activities as students learn to communicate and collaborate in pairs and teams throughout each lesson.

All teachers, instructional coaches, and administrators from each school attend an initial three-day professional development institute together. Administrative teams and instructional coaches, along with school district specialists and administrators, attend two additional days on implementing teacher support systems (teachers learning communities) and observing and coaching the integration of language, literacy, and core content.

The multiyear commitment includes trainers going into the school to systematically coach teachers several times a year. School and district administrator teams participate in classroom visits to practice how to observe, collect data to share with the teacher, give feedback on student performance, and jointly plan the next steps. Thereafter, site-based coaches and administrators coach the teachers in between trainers/coaches' visits.

The observation protocol used during coaching focuses on lesson delivery and participation of ELs during instruction. They use the ExC-ELL observation protocol because it dovetails with the features for teaching vocabulary, discourse, reading comprehension, and academic writing they learned in the professional development institute. Feedback helps teachers and administrators see where students are succeeding and where they need extra help. Their participation in the observations and feedback sessions creates momentum and sustains the yearlong implementation. Yearly summer institutes for new teachers or as refreshers help to give everyone the message that this mode of instruction is here to stay and it's not one of those here today, gone tomorrow initiatives.

During the repeated visits, local teams and trainers have been able to select six exemplary teachers and four school and district specialists who would be trained as the District Support Cadre to offer refresher workshops in their schools, coach teachers, and assist with the teachers learning communities in order to sustain the innovation.

ELs continue to achieve and graduate due to the preparation of all core content teachers in a school with targeted interventions for newcomers, SIFE, and LTEL. Ample collaboration among district and school administrators and specialists is the key.

In fall 2020, all the instruction was remote. There was a solid foundation and now it is a matter of making that shift to virtual instruction.

The professional development and follow-up support system for Loudoun is now virtual until it can become hybrid. The theory, modeling, practice, and feedback are delivered through Zoom, Google Docs, Padlets, breakout rooms, and all the new things everyone has discovered. The classroom observations and coaching are live or videotaped, using the same observation protocol with the same instructional and coaching processes.

There is great hope for ELs and all students in these schools.

The professional development design for workshops at these Loudon County schools as illustrated in Figure 5.12, is a recurring cycle of presenting research, modeling strategies, practicing and getting feedback from trainers/facilitators, and integration into the lessons they bring to the workshops. These workshops are offered in person or remote. The content and features are the same, the delivery is of course different. Albeit even with virtual technology, the valuable peer interaction is possible throughout. Conducting the workshops in virtual modes helps teachers experience how they can build interaction with their students.

Figure 5.12 • Successful Features of Professional Learning

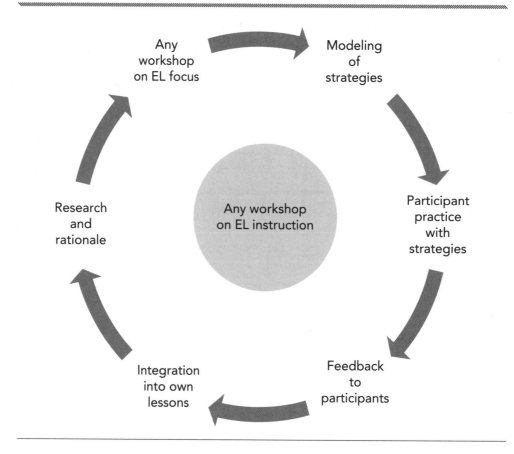

In addition to Loudon County Public Schools, others have begun the whole-school approach to professional development and instructional practices for developing academic language, literacy, and SEL skills/competencies integrated into all subject areas. A new study funded by the U.S. Department of Education Office of English Language Acquisition is capturing all the benefits of this type of implementation. The next chapter adds further detail to this integration and the interdependence among district, schools, and classrooms as well as the connections with equity and excellence.

Figure 5.13 • Design Your Own Professional Development

Which of these essential components need more attention in your school's evidence-based comprehensive professional development design and its implementation?

Check the boxes here and then develop a year's plan for effective professional development systems.

ESSENTIAL COMPONENTS	IF IN PLACE, DESCRIBE WHAT IT LOOKS LIKE	IF NOT IN PLACE, WHAT MIGHT YOU PLAN TO DO?
1. Theory and research foundations		
2. Modeling/demos in every workshop		
3. Practice and feedback from presenters at every workshop		
4. Follow-up coaching by experts and peers for each participant		
5. All principals and instructional coaches participate in all professional development with teachers		
6. Teachers meet in teachers learning communities on EL success once a week		
7. Principals and leadership team participate in coaching		
8. Principals and leadership team participate in quarterly implementation monitoring		
9. Professional development providers participate in implementation quarterly monitoring		

PART II • SCHOOLS

Striving for Interdependence and Interconnections in Schools

Interdependent people combine their efforts with the efforts of others to achieve their greatest success.

—Stephen Covey

Interdependence and Interconnections

The roles of state, district, and school personnel as described in previous chapters have helped many schools in their student-driven efforts and school improvement all around. Their efforts center on

- ✓ integrating language, literacy, and social-emotional learning into all core content instruction;
- ✓ overcoming inequities in schools; and
- ✓ forecasting transfer from professional development.

Now, because of the COVID-19 pandemic, is a great opportunity to adjust the context of the school and classroom levels. As we continue to experiment with remote and hybrid instruction, we might as well change all the old norms that we know haven't worked. Figure 2.8 illustrates the integration of all the features that ought to be included in content lessons.

The schools described in Chapter 5 and the one described in this chapter are examples of schools that have made great efforts toward interdependence and interconnection. Their districts have played a major role in giving them support and autonomy with a purpose. *These schools pay special attention to Black, Indigenous, and people of color, and all marginalized bilinguals as well as monolinguals from disadvantaged urban and rural communities.* The teachers are constantly looking for better ways to reach their students, particularly those they did not see often or at all in the spring of 2020 when the pandemic hit. Figure 6.1 illustrates the classroom and school connections with community.

Figure 6.1 • Interdependence and Interconnections

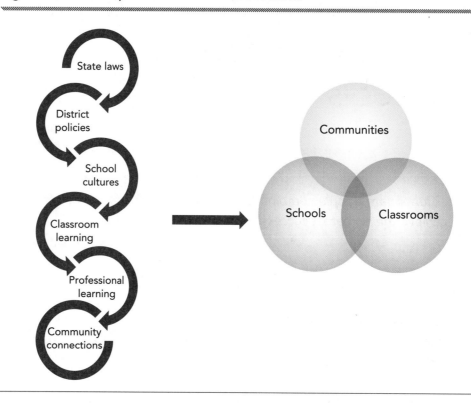

Interdependence of state law, district policies, school culture, classroom learning opportunities, professional learning systems, and community connections yield student results. If English learners, students of color, and striving readers manifest the same academic results year after year, it is time to change the systems and interconnections even though we are in the midst of so many crises.

In the section that follows we hear from a principal from a middle school in New York City, who approached the crises by building interdependence into everything he and his staff could think of before the 2020–2021 school year began.

In His Own Words

Ysidro Abreu, Principal, Middle School #319, New York City

Mr. Abreu, how is your school reconstructing the meaning of school in the new normal?

In a matter of hours, the meaning of what school is was transformed for me and many other principals. The idea of paper, bulletin board decoration, books, social interactions, working in groups, providing immediate feedback to student papers was gone. The lunchroom that many students complained about now seemed like a pleasant dream!

There was not much time to think about, just to do, pack up the school, and make it virtual. Up until this point, the word *virtual* for me was used in futuristic films. What should

I take home? How can I support teachers and students from home? How do I ensure students continue with a new normal? What are my tools? What is my role in the school community now? What is the role of the principal in this pandemic?

Students, parents, and teachers were going through so much: sick family members, jobs lost, illness, lack of resources, need for food, emotional anxiety, need for computers and other equipment. It was clear to me that this was a new normal, and it required a new type of leader.

There have been many studies defining transformational leadership. Now, it sounds great in books, but it has not been written for this W-shaped experience. Every staff development plan, curricula guideline, and benchmark was out of commission when we went virtual.

Last spring was the moment that redefined my twenty-eight years as an educator and sixteen years as founding principal of the school. Now, I needed all these tools I learned along the way to start this new journey: teamwork, positive and caring staff building, honesty, and becoming the best listener possible.

I began by highlighting everyone's talents, one by one, and how we would need each of them in this journey. We divided into teams: organizational team, attendance team, and instructional team. We created a virtual center composed of three cells, one per grade level. The main function of each cell was to create a tight community to support each other, to learn about each student, and to ensure that everyone was afforded emotional, physical, and academic support. Each consisted of a lead administrator, teachers who teach the same students, a team advocate (student support), lead coaches for vertical and horizontal instructional support, and tech support leads and teams. It helped to quantify collected information and bring the necessary support from outside expertise to support the school community. Some of the artifacts produced by this virtual center were an instructional weekly flow with resources for multilingual learners; student scaffolds; professional development plans; attendance reports; emotional and academic support for students, teachers, and parents; and weekly meetings to analyze the impact of strategies as we monitored student engagement.

As the teams began working independently, I focused on creating a culture of patience and empathy. I spoke less, listened more, and asked questions about their thinking and ideas.

Developing patience began with me. I sent emails to advocate for self-care, organized sessions for relaxation techniques, and called by phone to know how everyone was doing. At first conversations were a bit difficult because they wanted to talk about work. I had to say, "I called to talk about you taking care of yourself. Tell me how you are doing." Soon, our weekly conversations became easier and we got to know each other better. We shared ways we were trying to take care of ourselves and our families.

We shared ways to help other members of the school community. Empathy developed naturally, and my role changed from supervision and managing to one of support and inspiration. I visited classes to cheer, celebrate, hear what was needed, support, and help students, parents, and teachers. It was clear that I needed to develop a set of skills I had not developed. I registered for multiple sessions that were offered in our school system

(Continued)

(Continued)

for social-emotional intelligence, how to deal with crisis, taking care of self, and so on. My "Dear colleagues" greetings became "Dear brothers and sisters."

Daily questioning and ongoing change strategies to improve student engagement resulted in change of programs, software, and food deliveries and a closer look at equity. Which students were not fully engaged? Who needed programs that were more visual, needed closer guiding, needed more user-friendly strategies or an entire change of resources and curricula? Addressing these questions immediately boosted engagement in the classroom.

The racial inequalities that were occurring in our country became part of the equation. The instructional teams had to address this. Not only with readings and writing, but with opportunities to allow students to express their anxiety in art or multimedia formats.

The new norm asked for a closer and more real-life community of learners, including parents. In addition to learning how to use technology, parents had to learn how to complete surveys to provide feedback to our school as to how to we could maintain open communication. Teachers also had to learn ways to bring in students to a classroom atmosphere that was supportive and celebrated those little sisters and brothers, mothers and fathers, and other family members of our students who invited themselves at times to appear on camera.

Our professional development began with working with technology: how to use Zoom, Peardeck, Google Jam, and other software. Afterward, staff attended an institute on remote instruction: integrating vocabulary, reading comprehension, writing, and social-emotional learning (SEL) into core content lessons. One of the presenters was responsible for the SEL integration and how to get 100 percent participation, another for how to pair and team students during these activities, and another for how to teach vocabulary/discourse, close reading, and writing strategies virtually. Teachers learned to bring all the components together into their lessons.

Leadership is often situational, and a leader needs to adapt to ensure that the school community soars. It is only now with the provided staff development and new district guidelines that the school community is ready to center and define its vision of excellence for a better new normal.

This transformational process calls for principals to adapt leadership to utilize the existing human resources in their schools by creating teams to identify needed change and develop a community vision to guide the needed change through inspiration, empathy, and patience.

In our weekly parent and student virtual town halls, I hear parents thanking the school. I walk around the school and see teachers training each other. My office sees people coming to bring ideas, new teachers leading with expertise, and a strong team of teachers helping me as a leader in this transformational process with a path to a better new normal. I have to say, it is satisfying and motivating to live by our basic principles: persevere, achieve, and excel.

Disclaimer: I am writing from my personal capacity, and my views expressed are my own.

One of Mr. Abreu's early decisions was to provide professional development for his English language development (ELD) and content teachers on integrating technology, instructional content, and strategies with social-emotional learning, as seen in Figure 6.2.

Every teacher is a first-year teacher again!

Figure 6.2 • Integrating Language, Literacy, and SEL in Core Content Instruction

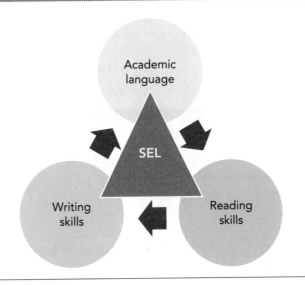

A New Beginning: Overcoming Inequities in Our Schools

Imagine the school of your dreams (but realistically), with optimism and forward thinking. It can start with small teams of teachers working on specific elements of quality implementation. We share the following checklist (Figure 6.3) as a tool for self-reflection and group discussions.

Figure 6.3 • Reflections and Actions

Every teacher and instructional coach in the building reflects before planning and delivering instruction:

☐ In my vocabulary instruction, I need to . . .

☐ In my reading instruction, I need to . . .

☐ In my writing instruction, I need to . . .

☐ In my complete lesson involving vocabulary, reading, writing, curriculum, and assessment, I need to . . .

☐ I can incorporate social-emotional strategies into language with these cooperative learning activities . . .

(Continued)

PART II • SCHOOLS

(Continued)

☐ I can incorporate social-emotional strategies into reading with these cooperative learning activities . . .

☐ I can incorporate social-emotional strategies into writing with these cooperative learning activities . . .

☐ I can incorporate social-emotional strategies into anchoring content with these cooperative learning activities . . .

☐ To collaborate with my colleagues and to make these changes, I need to . . .

☐ I can attend and actively share, help, and continuously learn to . . .

☐ I can ask for feedback and coaching from . . .

☐ I can invite colleagues and school and district leaders to observe how my students are learning . . .

As ESL and content co-teachers, reflect on how and when they will:

☐ Go through the same training sessions to learn and use evidence-based instructional strategies remotely and in person

☐ Plan and develop lessons together

☐ Use these strategies with the whole class

☐ Pair ELs with non-ELs for more practice

☐ Meet with newcomers or other students to help them practice structured talk for contributing to discussions, verbal summaries, and peer interaction

As a principal/assistant principal/instructional coach, I will:

☐ Attend all the professional development sessions with our teachers to establish these support systems for the teachers

☐ Ask teachers what they need in order to implement with frequency and fidelity to quality and creativity

☐ Participate in classrooms walkthroughs and coach/provide feedback to teachers

☐ Continuously collect evidence on what we have accomplished

As school district leaders, we will support our schools with ELs and multilingual students by:

☐ Giving principals the resources and flexibility necessary to focus on multilingual students' needs

☐ Helping principals use data to inform necessary adaptations to implementation efforts

☐ Funding principals' professional development and follow-up support

☐ Providing appropriate funding for new activities

☐ Conducting frequent meetings to share implementation progress, do problem solving, and celebrate with the school administration

☐ Participating in classroom walkthroughs and coaching/feedback to teachers

As the state education agency, we will support our local education agencies by:

☐ Providing ongoing evidence-based professional development

☐ Providing additional funding to schools that are ready to implement follow-up coaching from our professional development academies

Educational equity means that all students have the same access to educational success. It means using research-based/evidence-based instructional strategies and interventions that support student learning and mitigate student poverty and language issues, and create stronger bridges between community health and social services and the schools. It also means developing a network of schools and districts that go beyond the status quo or the new normal to become models for others.

Imagine these schools, where there are polite, profound conversations about what is happening to our students. After analyzing inequalities, school teams begin to build competent staff in all subjects to offer rigorous but thoughtful instruction that leads to graduation and college attendance or lucrative work skills. Instead of watering down the curriculum and adding remedial courses, these schools develop accelerated courses that teach students the way they learn instead of the way we have always ineffectively taught them. If we want to see changes in student outcomes, we need to change ourselves. We need to change the barriers that keep teachers from being their best.

One of the most difficult tasks in schools now is how to serve students from vastly different backgrounds. Teachers encounter a diversity of social, emotional, and academic challenges. Even privileged students who had the luxury of learning in a pod with a handful of equal peers during the pandemic will have lost the social-emotional skills learned from heterogeneous interaction. All students need to recover something they lost. The frameworks we share in this book are comprehensive enough to apportion auspicious learning opportunities.

The approaches taken by the educators described in the case studies in Chapter 4 were constructed out of love and by being there with the students as much as possible to learn all they could about them. Moreover, each set out to inform teachers and request that they each take small groups of the neediest students under their wings. They also met regularly in their TLCs to gauge their own and their students' progress. Figure 6.4 manifests the implementation of these various components. A similar figure can be used for your implementation plan and its evaluation.

The schools that we present throughout the book also see family connections as a priority. The principals have allocated paid time for teachers to connect with families. They also have staff dedicated to reaching out to and staying in touch with families. They have invested in families as co-educators by providing professional learning opportunities and openness to continuous conversations or call-ins for answers or emotional support. Parents were also brought in as co-constructors of a better system to benefit all students.

The Every Student Succeeds Act's Title II program provides grants to states and districts that can be used on activities that improve access to strong teachers and leaders for low-income students and students of color. These funds can be used to, among other things, address inequities in access to effective teachers, provide professional development, improve teacher recruitment and retention, and develop and implement evaluation systems.

Instead of worrying about overcoming the COVID-19 learning loss, think about overcoming academic inequities.

PART II • SCHOOLS

Figure 6.4 • Analyzing Specifics of Equity

IMPLEMENTATION COMPONENT	WHAT WE NEED TO WORK ON	WHAT WE HAVE STARTED (WHAT ELSE IS NEEDED)	WHAT IS SHOWING SUCCESS NOW (PROOF)
Do we have quality instruction in every core content and ESL/ELD class for ELs/dual-language students?	Do all core content, ESL/ELD, and special education teachers who instruct one or more ELs demonstrate the skills necessary to effectively teach academic vocabulary, discourse, reading comprehension, and formal text-based writing to their ELs? Is their teaching reaching all ELs?		
Do we value students' home cultures and languages?	Do we show respect and value the range of home cultures and languages as well as translanguaging, including Black English/African American Vernacular? Do we provide spaces for students to use their language and culture? Do we inform parents how we value and foment the home culture and languages and translanguaging?		
Do we have a whole-school culture of acceptance and implementation of social-emotional teaching and learning?	First and foremost, is the whole school conscientiously teaching and practicing social and emotional skills, norms, and the language students need to express their social-emotional needs.		

IMPLEMENTATION COMPONENT	WHAT WE NEED TO WORK ON	WHAT WE HAVE STARTED (WHAT ELSE IS NEEDED)	WHAT IS SHOWING SUCCESS NOW (PROOF)
Do we address the diversity of ELs?	Do we know what each of our long-term ELs needs to excel in each subject area? Do we have an evidence-based ELD intervention for our newcomers? Have their core content teachers received specific professional development for teaching newcomers? What about the quality of dually identified instruction?		
Are we systematically using different types of assessments to inform instruction?	Are teachers using student performance assessments for each component? Do teachers meet with peers to compare assessments, learning progressions, and implications for adjusting instruction? For requesting additional professional development?		

(Continued)

Figure 6.4 • (Continued)

IMPLEMENTATION COMPONENT	WHAT WE NEED TO WORK ON	WHAT WE HAVE STARTED (WHAT ELSE IS NEEDED)	WHAT IS SHOWING SUCCESS NOW (PROOF)
Are we providing comprehensive professional development on the language and literacy components for all teachers and administrators for at least three years?	Is there a plan to train every teacher, administrator, and support person in the school by the end of three years? Which cohort of teachers and administrators will be the pioneers for Year 1? Year 2? Year 3?		
Are principals and other administrative staff tasked with evaluating teachers sufficiently trained in the academic language, reading comprehension, and writing in the content areas instructional components to meaningfully evaluate teachers who deliver instruction to ELs?	Has the required teacher evaluation instrument been adapted to include the language, literacy, SEL, and content components? Are administrators, instructional coaches, and peers trained to use an aligned observation/coaching protocol?		
Are we using an appropriate observation protocol to capture transfer from training into each classroom?	Are we setting aside time, funds, and expertise to coach every teacher who goes through the training each year at least three times by experts and at least six times by in-house experts and administrators using a valid observation protocol?		

IMPLEMENTATION COMPONENT	WHAT WE NEED TO WORK ON	WHAT WE HAVE STARTED (WHAT ELSE IS NEEDED)	WHAT IS SHOWING SUCCESS NOW (PROOF)
Do the school district and state education agency provide supplemental professional learning opportunities, when necessary, to ensure that the EL program is implemented effectively?	Do district EL specialists and core content coordinators or directors attend the professional development and come to the school to coach teachers and support the administration? Does the state department of education sponsor additional institutes? Do they provide grants for additional on-site coaching?		
Are collegial learning/sharing opportunities well established?	Do teachers meet systematically once a week by grade levels or disciplines to further their instructional success with ELs? Do co-teachers (ESL and content) meet at least twice a week to plan co-teaching?		

Forecasting Positive Change

With full state and district support, schools need to reinvent themselves. Rapid, constant, and disruptive change is now the norm, and how we did school in the past is no longer applicable for the most part. Everyone needs to learn how to adapt to constantly changing environments in ways that will unleash fresh energy, innovation, and commitment. This means that school leaders' new job is to draw energy, creativity, and learning out of the people with whom they work (Ibarra & Scoular, 2019).

As mentioned in the previous chapter, one-day or even three-day workshops will not yield positive outcomes for students if there are no follow-up systems to support teachers' constant implementation and adaptation. Figure 6.5 illustrates the outcomes that can be expected. If our efforts reflect the trajectory of the boxes along the top horizontal line, we can see that the teachers' skill and disposition will not have enough support to develop fully. This is when most new learnings from professional learning erode since teachers feel no one cares if they implement it or not. Worse yet, the growth for ELs will be nil (Calderón, 2007, 2017).

However, when there is systematic coaching and collegial exchanges in the teachers learning communities (TLCs), the trajectory takes a few twists, but teachers develop the expertise and the sense of efficacy that helps them reach ELs and all students in an effective way. This more profound study and feedback from experts develops higher levels of skill and disposition. This stage may need to last two or three years. Typically, by the end of year two or three, teachers attain stage three, become

Figure 6.5 • Forecasting the Impact of Transfer

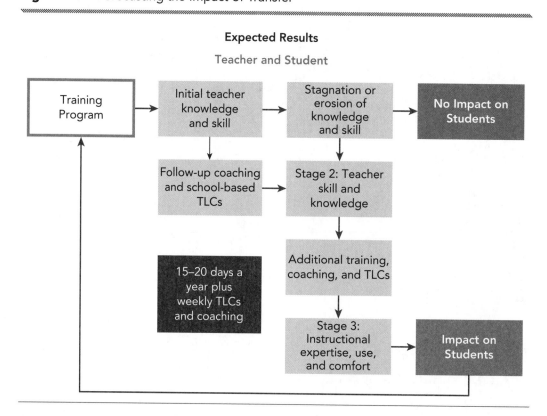

instructional experts, and can become trainers of other teachers in the school. Even better, there will be significant growth for students.

These are great times to shift to more effective instruction for multilingual learners. These are hopeful times!

Teachers are actually excited to be learning powerful ways to offer distance learning. They are encountering more collaborative learning and sharing. *Education Week* reports that they are learning more from peers than from six days of professional development on how to use technology (August 30, 2020). The fact that educational infrastructures and instructional approaches are being reshaped means there is a great opportunity to rethink and reform professional development for educators who are seeking better ways to reach ELs, multilingual learners, and students of color.

We have the research- and evidence-based knowledge and practices. What needs to happen now is for decision makers to think "comprehensive and inclusive for all students" professional development for all teachers in the school on teaching language, literacy, and SEL integrated within each content area. All students need language development now!

Teachers are experiencing a heavy workload doing both remote and hybrid teaching to a diverse student population at different levels of language proficiency. That is extraordinary in itself, but some of their students might not even be showing up, and some might not be engaged while they seem to be online. Yet teachers do not have to go through this alone. Principals and teachers are using their peer coaching virtual sessions to help teachers find ways to improve student engagement, since it is the responsibility of the whole school for all multilingual learners to succeed.

Moreover, as the new educational structures emerge, we know that the home schooling, whether full- or part-time, is going to play a vital role. Therefore, parent professional development will need to be aligned with ESL/core content professional development, with similar practices and a lot of SEL adapted to the home situation.

Uncertain times call for great leadership from principals and teachers. Collectively, they create a nurturing supportive context for everyone so that learning can take place for everyone. In light of this, the New York City schools' chancellor, Richard Carranza, is planning more support with direct resources for training and asks schools to prioritize the following:

✓ Allow time for teachers and students to readjust/adapt to changes.

✓ Dedicate the first few weeks of school to providing social-emotional support as part of the school reopening plans.

✓ Integrate social-emotional learning and trauma-informed care into core academic instruction.

✓ Prioritize mental health supports throughout the 2020–2021 school year. (New York City Department of Education, 2020).

Equity means equity for all—Black students, Indigenous students, and other students of color, regardless of race, religion, gender, language, or socioeconomic status. It will be a challenging and controversial balance. Now, with steady news coverage and social media posts about bewildering events, we face a moment that highlights the ongoing struggle for racial and social equality in the United States. We can begin as a whole school to work on educational equity through quality instruction for all. The good news is that schools such as the ones we have invited to share in this book are serving students and teachers well.

IMAGINING CLASSROOMS

Designing and Enacting Strengths-Based Classrooms

7

In school I feel safe. My teacher takes care of me. She says, "Hijita, no llores, vas a estar bien." I stop crying and try to smile. I pray that nobody comes to take me and my family away.

—Second-grade student

Imagine, like this second grader, being in a classroom where you truly belong, where your languages and cultures are on full display every day. Imagine your family members are invited to participate with you in classroom discussions in their preferred languages, using technology such as a computer or a phone when you are not physically in school. Imagine that as part of your time at home, you have opportunities to experiment with family members in your kitchen to make discoveries about chemistry while cooking and engaging in mathematics by following recipes.

Meet Inés, the second grader. Imagine she works in a small virtual group to make up questions to ask Álvaro, her brother, and Mrs. Pérez, her mother, about life in Guatemala. The group then plans to compare feelings during times of crises. Imagine that Inés gets to be an explorer in her community, where she can investigate and draw a variety of plants and trees for science, reproduce models of different kinds of buildings with everyday objects for social studies, and research the languages that she sees and hears around her for language arts.

IMAGINE

How can home be a stimulus for student learning?

_____

_____

_____

_____

_____

_____

(Continued)

(Continued)

What in your community might pique a student's curiosity as stimulus for a grade-level theme or unit of learning?

_____

_____

_____

_____

_____

What are some connections you can make among students' lived experiences, their home life, and school, whether classes are held virtually or in person?

_____

_____

_____

_____

_____

_____

_____

online resources   Available for download from **resources.corwin.com/BeyondCrises**.

Now imagine you are Alma Ortega-Miller, Inés's second-grade teacher, whose parents immigrated from Guatemala just a generation ago. Because of your personal experiences, you are especially sensitive to the lives of multilingual learners in your school, their families, and their connections to community. Being the eldest of four children, you were a translator for your parents at the local clinic and a babysitter for your siblings. Very early on you knew you wanted to be a teacher, and when you received a scholarship to attend the state university, you were able to pursue your dream.

At the beginning of every year, Ms. Ortega-Miller makes a pact with her students to co-create classroom norms. As her class represents many different languages, she wants to make sure students have ample opportunities to interact in their partner language. She imagines how students might forge friendships through paired activities in their multiple languages. In particular, she thinks about how the historically marginalized students in her room can be drawn into conversations to share their stories and histories to better understand their upbringings and to gain her trust.

Imagine as a language specialist and part-time coach how you might share time to co-plan, co-teach, and co-assess with Ms. Ortega-Miller. As co-assessors you decide what information serves as evidence for learning and how it is to be collected, analyzed, interpreted, and reported. Sometimes, you simply agree on specific language to use in giving concrete actionable feedback to students. Together you brainstorm a draft protocol for observing second graders in multiple contexts that you plan to share with the grade-level team.

Now imagine, as chair of the school's curriculum committee, how you are charged with inspiring teachers to embed linguistic and cultural relevance into units of learning. In addition, you and other teacher leaders are to ensure that there are multimodal (e.g., graphic, visual, digital, oral, textual) ways for students to show evidence of learning for each unit's final projects. Imagine that your principal supports your team in designing common assessment across grades with accompanying criteria for success that teachers and their students can then convert into "I can" statements.

Imagine you are Inés's principal at Sally Ride Elementary, a K–5 school, who invites the leadership team of teachers, community members, and students to join in optimizing equity and social justice. Imagine how you might set up a network of families of like languages and cultures to work with teachers to build curriculum projects that resonate with students' personal, cultural, linguistic, and life experiences. Imagine how you might highlight multilingualism and multiculturalism in your school's mission, vision, and values. Imagine how you might create a communal website for families in multiple languages where individual classrooms contribute on a rotating basis. Imagine how you would make the school an inviting and welcome sanctuary for all students and families, such as by having individual classrooms design an exhibit to display in the main entrance to showcase students' learning and their connection to family and community.

IMAGINE

How might school leadership facilitate the coalescence of family, school, and community in times of crisis and beyond?

_____

_____

_____

_____

_____

_____

(Continued)

(Continued)

How might you bring in the linguistic and cultural capital of the community and begin the process?

_____

_____

_____

_____

_____

online resources Available for download from **resources.corwin.com/BeyondCrises**.

Change has been occurring in Sally Ride Elementary. Over the past three years, dual-language education has finally become a reality under new school leadership, coupled with avid support from the community and families. In preparing to inaugurate dual language throughout the school over the next five years, much time has been devoted to planning and oversight wherein partnerships, community organizations, family members, and Ride's leadership team have revisited the school's mission, vision, and values as well as formulated a language policy. Grade-level instructional teams have begun to design culturally responsive curriculum prototypes for project-based learning in multiple languages with input from students and an array of standards.

Last year, Ride launched its inaugural dual-language kindergarten. This year, as another dual-language kindergarten class enters, the first cohort has moved to first grade. Each subsequent year, the dual-language strand will extend to the next grade until it has spread throughout the entire building.

You are about to enter Ms. Ortega-Miller's classroom, a microcosm of the multilingual-multicultural community and school that feeds into Ms. James's middle school. It is filled with twenty-seven enthusiastic second graders, an eclectic mix of seven-year-olds, the majority of whom are Latinx from a variety of Spanish-speaking countries, including Puerto Rico, Mexico, Guatemala, and the Dominican Republic, but also children whose families are from Vietnam, India, and Egypt. Some, like Inés, are refugees, and others were born and raised in the United States. It is amazing to watch the interactions among the children in their many languages, whether in person or at a distance, and how their teacher supports each and every one of them.

In Part III, we take a closer look at vibrant classrooms and the relationships they form within schools and communities—the three circles of influence or ecosystems that ground our book. We think about the transformation of classrooms that have been thrust into a COVID-driven world amid other crises and imagine the range of possibilities in overcoming linguistic and cultural inequities. In the classroom context, we explore the important roles of teachers, students, and family members as partners who are unified in initiating and sustaining change in teaching and learning as they become empowered stakeholders in the pursuit of educational excellence.

Education is not the filling of a pail, but the lighting of a fire.

—W. B. Yeats

Designing and Enacting Classroom Change

Life as we have known it has changed drastically since March 2020. Everyone has faced unforeseen challenges, increased levels of stress, and confusion over what to do. We have witnessed communities in turmoil, and yet we have come together for common causes. We have seen how schools have been dismantled and how we have become more connected to students in their homes or other places in the community. And we have watched how classrooms have been reconfigured as we have strived to maintain connections to students and families. As educators, we are entering a new phase, hopefully beyond crises, as we work to overcome inequities that have ravaged our communities, schools, and classrooms.

Characterizing Ideal Classrooms

Classrooms are reflections of the schools and communities in which they reside. Whether classrooms are in brick-and-mortar buildings or are at a distance as virtual realities, the relationships formed among their members reflect the social nature of learning in the sociocultural reality of a place known as school. We witness the strengthening of the bond among teachers, students, and families by unforeseen events and circumstances—whether a remote volcano, a recent hurricane, wildfires, racial unrest, or a global pandemic—and how these personal experiences and struggles have helped reshape our thinking. All the while, we center our attention on children, our students, as valuable sources of knowledge and resources to tap as we co-construct the educational experience.

In this first section of the chapter we look beyond crises and imagine that all classrooms have been transformed into

- ✓ warm caring corners of refuge,
- ✓ student-centered hubs of learning,
- ✓ vibrant ecosystems,
- ✓ extensions of community,
- ✓ protected places for student interaction,
- ✓ linguistically and culturally sustainable spaces,
- ✓ data-responsive centers of equity,
- ✓ areas for discussing standards and learning targets, and
- ✓ focal points for student-driven activities.

PART III • CLASSROOMS

Classrooms as warm corners of refuge

During times of crises, it is critical that students feel safe, secure, and wanted. Many students' lives are filled with uncertainty from day to day as they continue to live with significant adversities; school also can be a place where students feel more isolated than ever. But we hope that school can become a haven for students, filled with interesting routines, growing friendships, and rigorous expectations.

As in Ms. James's middle school and at Ride Elementary, so many schools today, especially in urban and metropolitan suburban areas, are composed of a heterogeneous mix of students, including newcomers or recent arrivals to the United States who are trying to become acclimated to a new set of customs and languages on top of the angst of living in crisis mode. In fact, as we learned in Part I of this book, multilingual learners and their families have permeated every region of the country, every state and territory. Despite all its challenges, however, somehow COVID-19 and its unforeseen upheaval of schooling as we had known it has provided a common, relatable experience for students, families, and teachers.

In the second-grade classroom, Ms. Ortega-Miller supports Inés and other Latinx students in Spanish; she is able to amplify their language practices and cultural understandings. At the middle school, Álvaro and other newly arrived immigrants from Central America, Africa, and the Middle East, speaking twenty-eight languages from just as many countries, are becoming acclimated to school and learning content in large part through English. These older students, many of whom were terrorized by gangs and endured long passages to the United States with little to eat for weeks on end, finally feel safeguarded. Said one student, "Here, I feel more protected. I don't feel scared when I go out of my house. I can come to the school. I can have certainty that nothing bad will happen to me" (quoted in Taketa, 2017, para. 5). Indeed, school has traditionally been a place of solace for many students, and now is not the time to abandon their hopes and dreams.

Student-centered classrooms provide spaces for multilingual learners to safely interact in the languages of their choice.

Classrooms as student-centered hubs of learning

The pandemic has marked a huge change in every facet of our lives. Even if not in virtual spaces, classrooms of today don't have the same physical appearances, and rightfully so, as one of the responsibilities of education is to guard the health and safety of its youth. These rearranged spaces, often with desks partitioned or many feet apart from each other, may appear as barriers to interaction; however, adept teachers can take on this challenge as an opportunity to encourage students to be active participants in their own learning.

Imagine yourself walking into a student-centered classroom. What are the students and the teacher doing? What does the room look like? If we believe that learning is an active process, then language should be reflected in action. Teachers with classrooms that are considered student-centered hubs for learning

- value students' social-emotional development, mental health, and learning from play as much as from content, literacy, and language learning;

- create areas and time devoted to student performance and communication in multiple languages;

- extend learning outside the classroom and school walls to the community, including students' homes, the neighborhood, local markets, and beyond;

- offer spaces for co-working to give students a sense of ownership;

- incorporate multimodalities, including kinesthetic, graphic, and visual scaffolds, into academic tasks; and

- leverage multilingual learners' languages and cultures as springboards to further learning.

IMAGINE

Besides the features mentioned above, signs of student-centered learning include, but are not limited to, active learning, collaboration, student voice and choice, and technology integration as powerful supports for learning.

Which of these attributes are apparent in your classroom?

_____

_____

_____

_____

_____

_____

What else might you add for your multilingual learners? Share examples with your colleagues.

_____

_____

_____

_____

_____

_____

online resources — Available for download from **resources.corwin.com/BeyondCrises**.

Classrooms as vibrant ecosystems

Classrooms, as schools and communities, are ecosystems in their own right. If classrooms are indeed healthy ecosystems, students serve as the primary producers of their own education. If classrooms are vibrant, they tend to have purposes that reflect the vision and values of the school.

By taking a more student-empowering approach, teachers are able to build students' self-awareness and motivate them. In that way, students become the drivers and energy source of the ecosystem (France, 2018). In learning environments that are considered ecosystems, there is a cultivation of strong relationships and an interdependence between teachers and students.

Classroom ecosystems accentuate the assets of every student and are places where linguistic and cultural sustainability reigns. These classrooms are regarded as

- more multimodal than only relying on print,

- more responsive to students' interests and needs than reactive or preprogrammed,

- more inclusive and accessible to all than exclusive for some,

- more connected to students' lives than divorced from them,

- more collaborative and cooperative than competitive,

- more active and stimulating than passive, and

- more responsive to multilingual learners' linguistic and cultural strengths than seeing students through a monolingual lens.

IMAGINE

Think of your classroom as an ecosystem. What are its components, and how do they work together?

_____

_____

_____

_____

_____

How might this ecosystem change during difficult times and strange circumstances?

_____

_____

_____

_____

_____

_____

online resources — Available for download from **resources.corwin.com/BeyondCrises**.

Classrooms as extensions of community

Classrooms have often been described as communities—communities of learners, learning communities (Watkins, 2005), and communities of practice (Lave & Wenger, 1991). In all instances, community entails coming together around shared interests and goals. What is distinctive in students' and teachers' formation of a community, however, is that there is still an inherent power structure in place. Notwithstanding, if a true community spirit prevails in classrooms, there are overriding advantages to this positive learning climate.

Classrooms that build a sense of community demonstrate the following:

- a sense of belonging
- a common set of norms
- shared responsibility for each other's learning
- display and respect for diverse languages and cultures
- acceptance of difference in perspectives
- acknowledgment of contributions of all members of the classroom community

In classrooms that build a sense of community, students do the following:

- share information
- help each other learn
- regard each another as equals
- co-construct knowledge
- feel comfortable engaging in inquiry
- collaborate in their pursuit of learning
- discuss and resolve issues with each other

PART III • CLASSROOMS

> *In classrooms with a sense of community, students feel safe, care for and respect each other, and are engaged in learning.*

In classrooms that build a sense of community, students tend to have increased curiosity, participation, motivation, confidence, engagement, and agency.

Classrooms should be considered communities unto themselves, where knowledge is co-constructed and shared. In that process, there is much negotiation and dialogue to create and maintain a culture of learning. Classrooms should also be interconnected with school, families, and local communities. Extending the identified attributes of community listed above, Figure 7.1 offers an opportunity for teachers to come together to identify and discuss which traits best represent their classrooms as communities or how their school acts as an extension of community. Teachers may then wish to personalize the columns that describe what constitutes community for their setting.

Figure 7.1 • Attributes of Classrooms That Build a Sense of Community

In classrooms where a sense of community is built, there is . . .	In classrooms where a sense of community is built, students . . .	In classrooms where a sense of community is built, students tend to have increased . . .	In classrooms where there is a sense of interconnection of school, family, and local community, there is . . .
• comradery • caring	• feel protected • trust their teachers and each other	• empathy • enthusiasm for learning	• security • unity

As a classroom community, whether meeting remotely or in person, the same strategies for instilling student motivation apply, including establishing high expectations and setting clear goals with students along with student-led assessment (Gottlieb, 2016; Saphier, 2017; Wilcox, 2018). When Ms. Ortega-Miller is teaching remotely, she likes to start the day with virtual nonjudgmental energizers for her class. She might throw out a question that students can quickly answer in popcorn style, one right after another, such as "What is your favorite day of the week?" Sometimes she has students extend their content learning, as in asking them to show an object and describe different shapes (e.g., "Look, my drinking glass is a cylinder"; "My crayon is a cylinder with a point at the end"). She often has her students imagine and think critically, such when she asked, "What magical power would you like to have and why?" In that way, students are able to bond over a common experience where everyone contributes.

After coming together and feeling more at ease, students can then generate questions and engage in inquiry to design and work on collaborative projects. It is an opportune time to seek answers to community-related issues, such as "How efficient are our neighborhood recycling efforts?" or "What do we need to know and do to participate in a food drive?" Ms. Ortega-Miller ends the day by having students take ownership of their learning and generate agency in some small way. For example, she often volunteers an answer to a question such as "What little thing can I do to make a difference today?" before giving her students time to reflect and respond as they sign off.

Classrooms as protected places for student interaction

During the pandemic many multilingual learners, while confined at home, have spent much time navigating and communicating in more than one language. Classrooms should be an extension of home, where multilingual learners are encouraged to interact in multiple languages with peers (or their teacher). When students are given the freedom to express themselves in the languages or dialects of their choice, they generally act with determination to reach their goals and thus become empowered. Languaging is the way we make personal sense of the world and become conscious of ourselves as communicators as we form our identities. In essence, languaging conveys an action through a dynamic process of using language to make meaning and to shape knowledge and experience within sociocultural contexts (Swain, 2006; van Lier, 2007).

Classrooms are sacred places for interchange where content and language learning co-occur. In classrooms where multilingual learners share a language, translanguaging (the natural interaction between languages in oral and written communication) is bound to happen. As a powerful resource for learning, in the translanguaging classroom, the practices of multilingual students are on display as they access and deploy their full linguistic repertoires (García, Ibarra Johnson, & Seltzer, 2017). To legitimize translanguaging as a classroom practice, students should be given a voice in formulating a language policy that sets the norms and circumstances for language use (Gottlieb, 2021).

Interactive classrooms with multilingual learners, where languaging and translanguaging are accepted routines, are indeed noisy busy places as students exchange information and build on each other's ideas. Student interaction is powerful when it promotes collaboration and team building. To maximize the strength of collaborative partnerships, teachers must do the following:

- design complex activities that invite and stimulate students to contribute to conversation and problem-solving
- provide opportunities for students to develop metacognitive awareness (understanding one's thought processes) and metalinguistic awareness (understanding how languages function) by comparing texts, multimodal sources, or experiences

PART III • CLASSROOMS

- motivate students by giving them genuine reasons to work together

- practice teaming among students so that they understand the rationale behind collaboration and become intrinsically aware of its benefits

- build in individual and group accountability with meaningful team roles that directly relate to the content of the task

- make discussion and consensus building integral to decision making

- strengthen and stretch the expertise of each student (Burns, 2016)

What we have imagined as a typical classroom that encourages student interaction has been totally reshaped by the pandemic. Unlike Ms. Ortega-Miller, who has a multilingual-multicultural classroom in a metropolitan suburb, Caroline Carter Curtice is an ESOL teacher at five schools in a rural area of South Carolina where the number of English learners is relatively small. When COVID-19 hit, a couple of schools became completely virtual, others converted into hybrids, still others maintained in-person learning as long as possible. Ms. Carter Curtice had to adjust to all the different modes of teaching in an instant. The one advantage of this configuration is that in the virtual environment she has been able to combine students from different schools. Thus the idea of promoting collaborative partnerships between students and between students and teachers, although desired, just does not always depict reality.

Classrooms as linguistically and culturally sustainable spaces

When classrooms exhibit linguistic and cultural sustainability (Paris, 2012), we know that there has been a shift in the mindset of educators. This shift takes us beyond an awareness of linguistically and culturally responsive instruction (Ladson-Billings, 1994) to committing to creating classrooms that are firmly rooted in multilingualism and multiculturalism. The presence of linguistic and cultural resources that reflect students' and families' lived experiences and traditions is evident throughout curriculum, instruction, and assessment, ideally across classrooms and throughout school.

As exemplified in Figure 7.2, linguistic and cultural sustainability is as much a philosophy or a way of being as it is an action to preserve the collective multilingual-multicultural identities of a community. La Guelaguetza (a Zapotec word) epitomizes linguistic and cultural sustainability as evidenced in this annual festival celebrating the eights region of Oaxaca, México. Traditional trajes of local historical and cultural significance are on display in a lavish parade followed by indigenous dances and song that are testimony to the rich heritage and the bond between families and community.

Linguistic and cultural sustainability as well as linguistic and cultural responsiveness are rooted in the strengths that multilingual-multicultural students bring to the classroom to make learning more interesting, real, and effective. As such, one

Figure 7.2 • Annual Celebration of Indigenous Dances of Oaxaca, México

intent of being inclusive of languages and cultures is to reverse patterns of inequity of access and opportunity to marginalized students. In classrooms, linguistic and cultural sustainability starts with utilizing the cultural capital of the students as a springboard for learning. It extends to teachers' and other school leaders' consciousness of the whole child as a valued member of a classroom, family, and community. You may wish to gauge the extent of the linguistic and cultural sustainability of your classroom by completing the rating scale in Figure 7.3.

Classrooms as data-responsive centers of equity

Classrooms are data-rich spaces as every minute that students are present is an opportunity for assessment. Teachers often have to make instantaneous or contingent decisions about the next instructional move, and students are invited to give feedback. Data are drawn from multiple sources, such as observation, everyday activities, or long-term projects, and in multimodal ways, including visual, graphic, digital, written, and oral means. Students, along with teachers, are involved in decision making and bring equity to the process. Integral to instruction and assessment, students are given options in pursuing learning and in showing how they have grown.

In Ms. Ortega-Miller's classroom, students gradually take responsibility for their own learning as they keep tabs on where they are in relation to their learning targets and where they need to go next. In their study of domestic and wild animals, for example, multilingual learners select an animal and the language of their choice in which to conduct their research, understanding that in this unit, their end product can be in one or more languages along with drawings or photos. For each unit of

Figure 7.3 • Self-Assessment Rating Scale of Linguistic and Cultural Sustainability in a Classroom

To what extent are the following traits present in your classroom?

LINGUISTICALLY AND CULTURALLY SUSTAINABLE TRAITS	ENORMOUSLY SO	QUITE A BIT	A TAD
1. Bias in curricular materials has been identified, discussed, and addressed in direct ways.			
2. An anti-bias curriculum is in place that is sensitive to linguistic, cultural, gender, sexual orientation, and religious issues.			
3. Learning is viewed through a multicultural lens.			
4. Others' perspectives are acknowledged as viable points of view.			
5. Students' languages and cultures are leveraged throughout the day.			
6. Controversial real-world issues are subjects of critical conversations and study.			
7. Family and community members are invited to school, whether in person or remote, as experts and cultural envoys.			
8. Families receive communiques in multimodal ways, including in multiple languages.			
9. Classrooms welcome family members and the local community.			
10. There is insistence on respecting and sharing linguistic and cultural differences.			

learning throughout the year, students have a digital folder where they place all their work that they have scanned as evidence of learning. Ms. Ortega-Miller guides and scaffolds learning by providing technology tips and reviewing the e-portfolios with each student; she wants to ensure that students are able to see their own growth over time.

Classrooms as areas for discussing standards and learning targets

For the past thirty years, standards have been integral to school life. Standards are guideposts that offer parameters for infusing rigor into teaching and learning.

In K–12 settings there can be academic content standards minimally in language arts, mathematics, science, and social studies; Common Core en Español (Spanish language arts standards); English language development/proficiency standards; and Spanish language development standards. While Spanish-English dual-language classrooms use all these standards in crafting learning targets, Ms. Ortega-Miller carefully selects the state's academic content standards in conjunction with English language development standards for her students.

When standards are converted into attainable learning targets and are coupled with culturally responsive teaching, we see increases in student motivation and engagement that, in turn, prompt higher achievement (Saifer, Edwards, Ellis, Ko, & Stuczynski, 2011). Student standards for learning offer a uniform set of expectations to ground curriculum, instruction, and classroom assessment. In turn, learning targets offer realistic goal posts for students—in essence, expectations for learning.

Together, teachers and students should devote time to creating "I can" statements from standards to present as learning targets to attach to units of learning. Reconfiguring standards in the words of students represents a "can do" spirit and strengths-based philosophy. In this way, teachers, students, and even family members are encouraged to approach teaching and learning through an assets-based lens. The Common European Framework of Reference for Languages with its Can Do Statements, NCSSF-ACTFL with its Can-Do Statements, and WIDA with its Can Do Descriptors have long seen the value in having a strengths-based vision for language education.

A strategy that Ms. Ortega-Miller uses to enhance student comprehension of standards and learning targets is to analyze standards statements as examples of "juicy sentences" (coined by Wong Fillmore and shown in https://www.youtube.com/watch?v=uN8A-nimkqI). Here, phrases within complex text are deconstructed with students to become understandable and meaningful. Having an agreement up front as to what constitutes academic success, along with exemplars, provides a guide for students to reach their learning target.

The following is an example of a second-grade standard for reading literature. Ms. Ortega-Miller points out the italicized phrases of the juicy standard statement, which the class then discusses as a whole group before the crafting the corresponding "I can" statement.

Describe *the overall structure* of (multicultural) stories, including describing how *the beginning introduces the story* and *the ending concludes the action.*	**I can** describe the parts of stories (from around the world) from beginning to end.

Classrooms as focal points for student-driven activities

Lastly, ideal classrooms are typified by student-driven activities focused on learners as members of a close-knit community. As such, classroom tasks are authentic, are meaningful, and invite multiple pathways to solutions, where students co-construct knowledge and match it to criteria of success. Self- and peer assessment offer opportunities for students to think deeply about the evidence they provide for their learning.

Hands-on, performance-based activities in student-centered classrooms are stimuli for students to

- exchange information and ideas with each other;

- share their life experiences and perspectives related to the activity;

- pursue their own interests;

- be challenged, but within their academic reach;

- teach each other;

- select options, such language choice, to reach their learning goals;

- access multimodal resources (written or spoken language in combination with visual, audio, gestural, tactile, and spatial means of communication); and

- offer and give timely, concrete, actionable feedback to their peers.

Hands-on activities are not confined to the classroom; they happen all the time at home. Inés and Álvaro's mother, for example, enjoys cooking with her children; sometimes she reads recipes aloud in Spanish while her kids gather, measure, and mix the ingredients. Other times the three prepare special Guatemalan dishes such as pepian, a thick stew, or they experiment with food that they have in their refrigerator to make a meal.

Inés's family's escape from the ravaging effects of a volcano left her, although traumatized, questioning the enormity of what she had experienced by its eruption. Ms. Ortega-Miller, in consultation with the family liaison, school counselor, and bilingual family therapist, thought it might be therapeutic for Inés to share with her classmates the account of what she had seen and heard. Ms. Ortega-Miller first presents the idea to Inés's mother, who agrees and volunteers to participate in the reenactment. As a result of the presentation, the class decides to investigate volcanoes in their families' homelands and around the world.

Ms. Ortega-Miller divides students into small groups to research the location of volcanoes and their causes. Facilitated by the teacher, each group plans to show what they learn in a different way—one group is going to conduct an experiment that will recreate the volcano experience, one group is going to gather photos and descriptions of volcanos to make an album, and a third group is going to create a story based on their families' knowledge of volcanos and books that they find. While the groups actively pursue their learning goals, Ms. Ortega-Miller converses with each group to take the pulse of their understanding and gives personalized feedback to move each student's learning forward.

IMAGINE

Review with your colleagues the traits of classrooms described in this section.

Which features might you prioritize in your teaching?

_____

_____

_____

_____

_____

_____

Which are most important to your grade-level or department team?

_____

_____

_____

_____

_____

_____

Decide on a course of action to incorporate the ones you choose into your teaching practice.

_____

_____

_____

_____

_____

_____

 Available for download from **resources.corwin.com/BeyondCrises**.

PART III • CLASSROOMS

Envisioning Teachers as Caretakers

Next to parents, guardians, and close family members, teachers are the most influential people in students' lives. In particular, research shows that having a teacher of color can be helpful and make a difference for students of color by

- serving as a resource and role model,

- forging social-emotional ties,

- boosting the students' academic performance, and

- increasing students' aspirations to attend postsecondary institutions (Carver-Thomas, 2018).

Despite these benefits, there remains a cultural divide in the teacher workforce, with every state reporting a higher percentage of students of color than teachers of color. The U.S. Department of Education (2016) reinforces the need for having a more heterogeneous mix of teachers: "Diversity is inherently valuable. We are stronger as a nation when people of varied backgrounds, experiences, and perspectives work and learn together; diversity and inclusion breed innovation" (p. 1).

In this section, we look beyond crises and think about envisioning the work of teachers, especially those of minoritized students. Let's imagine that classrooms have teachers who are

- ✓ advocates for students, families, and communities;

- ✓ change agents;

- ✓ linguistically and culturally responsive envoys;

- ✓ thought leaders; and

- ✓ co–assessment designers.

Teachers as advocates for students, families, and communities

Today it is more important than ever for teachers to establish and maintain ties with students, their families, and the communities in which they live. Classroom teachers are in the best position to support, encourage, and advocate on behalf of students and families. However, we also need to recognize that family members and students are teachers in their own right, with linguistic, cultural, and experiential strengths that are recognized as *funds of knowledge* (González, Moll, & Amanti, 2005). Indeed, students, family members, and school personnel can all become empowered because they

- possess assets that contribute to classrooms, schools, and communities;

- have accrued knowledge and expertise;

- lend encouragement and social-emotional support; and

- provide constructive feedback during learning.

There are many ways teachers can create two-way communication in their advocacy efforts to connect home to school and school to home. Inés's teacher, Ms. Ortega-Miller, goes to the public library to secure cards for her class and makes sure that her students and their family members are invited to community events there. In Inés and Álvaro's local branch of the library, there is a multilingual storytelling hour every week, and once a month it is in Spanish. The Pérez family enjoys attending and sharing their country's folktales, both orally and in print. In that way, they remain connected to Guatemala while strengthening ties to other Latinx cultures.

Ms. Ortega-Miller also conducts virtual home visits in Spanish and, when she can, in person. She believes that it is important to gain insight into the interaction between mother and daughter and to record Inés's mother's impressions of school and her daughter's milestones and lived experiences that could impact her education. Maestra, as Ms. Ortega-Miller likes parents to call her, feels personally connected to the Pérez family as her own heritage can be traced back to Guatemala.

During the fifteen-minute call, Ms. Ortega-Miller, who is a member of the school–community support team, shares the names of several agencies that may help the family through these difficult times and to overcome the residual trauma from losing such close family members. (Being deeply familiar with and committed to her Guatemalan and school community, Ms. Ortega-Miller has worked with the family liaison to build these strengths-based partnerships.) Together la maestra, Inés, and Mrs. Pérez set the goals for learning for the year. Inés proudly shows her teacher one of her favorite artifacts from her cultural collection, Guatemalan worry dolls (Figure 7.4).

Figure 7.4 • Guatemalan Worry Dolls in Inés's Cultural Collection

Teachers as change agents

Taking on the role of facilitators, rather than transmitters or technicians of learning, teachers guide their students in self-discovery and individual sense-making. By being eager to learn and be reflective themselves, today's teachers focus on instilling lifelong learning as well as being accessible, positive, committed, trustful, self-assured, and collaborative (van der Heijden, Geldens, Beijaard, & Popeijus, 2014). By being catalysts of change, teachers are able to

- envision interrelationships among classrooms, schools, communities, and society;

- challenge social inequities related to schooling (e.g., access to technology) and seek local solutions;

- assist students in developing the knowledge and skills necessary for becoming empowered in their own right;

- take genuine interest in students to learn more about them, their families, and their living situations;

- approach any conflict or potential discrepancy as an opportunity to negotiate a solution;

- have a voice in planning, collecting, analyzing, and reporting student-level data; and

- have decision-making power in their own right.

As school leaders and members of equity councils, learning networks, curriculum design committees, or school–community support teams, teachers have input in school and district decision-making processes and become part of policy-making bodies involved in collective leader efficacy. As part of distributive leadership teams, teachers are given responsibilities for co-facilitating or co-developing whole-school staff meetings. In co-planning yearlong professional learning, teachers are able to build on their own passions or perceived needs. In that way, teachers are able to own their learning.

IMAGINE

Based on these characteristics, might teachers in your school be considered change agents?

_____

_____

_____

_____

_____

_____

_____

_____

Imagine what you and your colleagues might do to initiate change and how you would go about pursuing that goal.

_____

_____

_____

_____

_____

_____

_____

online resources ↖ Available for download from **resources.corwin.com/BeyondCrises**.

Teachers as linguistically and culturally responsive envoys

Culturally responsive teaching can serve as a vehicle for stimulating (and sustaining) teacher change that is rooted in knowing, understanding, and acting on behalf of students. Teachers embark on instructional and assessment practices to ensure that all students are affirmed and supported so that they can reach their full potential. Culturally responsive classroom practices apply to the following:

- **What**—curriculum with its focus on content and language integration; themes, topics, and issues of interest to students, relevant to their lives and lived experiences, that invite multiple perspectives and combat stereotypes and biases

- **How**—methodologies for teaching and learning that involve students in the co-construction of knowledge using the language(s) of their choice, build on students' linguistic and cultural repertoires, and engage students in solving problems through inquiry

- **Who**—relationships that form among teachers, students, and families that show caring, concern, curiosity, and empathy

Wherever there are multilingual learners and other minoritized students, teachers have the responsibility to accentuate what these students can do. This practice is essential when welcoming students back to physical classrooms after a long hiatus. For example, Ms. Ortega-Miller asks her students to describe something special to them (e.g., anything personal and meaningful, such as a drawing or an experience) to ease the transition and connect home to school. In addition, she has set up a buddy system so that, upon her arrival at school, Inés is assigned another Spanish speaker, Jorge, to be her linguistic and cultural ambassador.

There should always be a presence of students' identities in school, and teachers should seamlessly incorporate multilingual learners' linguistic and cultural assets into classroom life. Space should be filled with personal memorabilia and student-generated displays. Figure 7.5 is a checklist that offers some ideas for how classrooms and schools can highlight the languages and cultures of their students. As part of professional learning, the checklist serves as a needs assessment for teachers to evaluate the linguistic and cultural sustainability of their school. Each grade-level team can then meet to discuss the results and plan how to improve the visibility of multilingualism and multiculturalism.

Figure 7.5 • A Linguistically and Culturally Sustainable Environment on Display

Which of these artifacts of linguistically and culturally sustainable environments are in your school or classroom, or simply resonate with you?

- ☐ Students, if given the option, post photos of themselves and their families with a brief description on classroom walls.
- ☐ There is a running video as you enter the school of students introducing themselves in multiple languages.
- ☐ There are inviting posters of students' homelands, flags, or personal heroes in rooms and throughout the hallways.
- ☐ Colorful murals depicting indigenous cultures have been painted by community members and students.
- ☐ Meaningful cultural artifacts are on display in prominent cases.
- ☐ Hallways are peppered with multicultural projects or students' writing in multiple languages.
- ☐ Signs (e.g., Entry/Exit) are posted in multiple languages.
- ☐ Offices are decorated with student quotes in multiple languages.
- ☐ There are multilingual banners of upcoming school or grade-level events.
- ☐ Broadcasts over the intercom by students and adults are in multiple languages.
- ☐ Classroom and school newsletters include students' drawings and are in multiple languages.
- ☐ The school's website is a welcoming place where information is available in multiple languages.

IMAGINE

Imagine having a school where every classroom reflects its students and their linguistic and cultural assets.

What would it look like?

_____

_____

_____

_____

_____

Which artifacts would you have your multilingual learners include?

_____

_____

_____

_____

_____

What can you and other teachers do to increase the linguistic and cultural relevance of your classroom and school?

_____

_____

_____

_____

_____

PART III • CLASSROOMS

Figure 7.6 • Fifth-Grade Project of Spanish and Latinx Artists Displayed in a School's Corridor

Internal to classrooms, teachers can also instill linguistic and cultural sustainability with materials, resources, and instructional approaches. Here are several reminders to help maximize student accessibility to multiple languages and cultures, to the extent feasible:

- Secure authentic literature and stories as curricular exemplars and resources.
- Provide websites in multiple languages to complement those in English.
- Ensure that textbooks, if used, are culturally sensitive and have accurate information.
- Choose materials that present alternative perspectives or worldviews.
- Incorporate students' home and community life, such as traditions, community history, art, music, and dance, into the curriculum.
- Facilitate courageous conversations on sensitive issues that directly impact students' lives.
- Reinforce curricular topics with outreach to family and community members.
- Bring family oral storytelling to life.
- Stock your classroom library and school resource center with multilingual books and materials.

IMAGINE

Imagine having a linguistically and culturally sustainable classroom with many of the traits described in this section.

What kinds of materials would you like to secure?

_____

_____

_____

_____

_____

_____

_____

_____

How might you and other teachers create an ongoing list (or spreadsheet) of books, websites, videos, and other resources for yourselves and your students?

_____

_____

_____

_____

_____

_____

_____

_____

_____

 Available for download from **resources.corwin.com/BeyondCrises**.

Teachers as thought leaders

Teachers may think that they have to attend webinars or conferences to connect to thought leaders, but actually all they have to do is to look around for colleagues in their school! The Center for Collaborative Education (2016–2020, para. 1) defines thought leadership as "an extension and continuation of valued collaborations and partnerships" In essence, a thought leader is someone who offers guidance and insight to others. In schools that means that many teachers and paraprofessionals qualify as effective leaders for each and every student. In addition, we look to mentors, coaches, and co-teachers in assuming that role; in some small way, they help chip away at the hierarchical power structure often present in schools and help to bring greater equity to the workforce.

Mentors are generally experienced practitioners who guide, challenge, advise, support, and advocate for colleagues who are generally, but not necessarily, newly minted teachers. Mentors listen, offer alternate perspectives, appreciate differences in teaching methodologies and strategies, share educational theory, and provide relevant research and resources. Mentor teachers also give constructive feedback to their mentees to gently move their practice forward. Teachers may volunteer to assist mentee colleagues, at times, in unofficial informal capacities while coaches, department chairs, and lead teachers are expected to be mentors. Multilingual-multicultural paraprofessionals, often hired directly from the community, can also serve as mentors as they are close to students and families.

This year Ms. Ortega-Miller is serving as a mentor to the dual-language kindergarten and first-grade teachers. She is very excited as she is enrolled in a master's program in multilingual education and she enjoys sharing the most current research articles and children's literature with the teams. In becoming immersed in some of the issues that arise, Ms. Ortega-Miller is becoming thoroughly immersed in the curriculum and hopes to bring continuity next year by taking the position of the second-grade dual-language teacher.

Instructional coaches are usually teachers with deep knowledge and experience who have release or contracted time to work with other teachers, during which they offer advice, give direction, or customize solutions. For example, Ms. Ortega-Miller and other second-grade teachers have requested that their instructional coach help them develop an observation protocol for their classrooms. The coach, who also doubles as Ms. Ortega-Miller's co-teacher, has brought literature to the team on assessment *for* learning (aka formative assessment) and has discussed how the tool, if implemented uniformly, might eventually be used schoolwide. After brainstorming ideas, the coach volunteers to videotape the teachers in action so, as a group, they can develop a code for interpreting the information.

At times, coaches are unofficial point persons who are curious about planning and enacting novel strategies (Wolpert-Gawron, 2016). At other times, the responsibilities of coaches evolve or are molded by requests from teachers who wish to have a partner with whom to exchange ideas for activities or lessons, evaluate or secure resources to share with departments, or adapt curriculum for individual students, such as those with disabilities. Lastly, coaches are often asked to model lessons using techniques for specific student populations or for educational technology.

Co-teachers are two teachers who work together in a classroom for part or all of a school day and take collective responsibility for co-planning, co-teaching, and co-assessing shared groups of students. As the value of mentors and instructional coaches is a function of positive relationship building, so too are co-teachers helpful resources for each other. The careful pairing of teachers in a co-teaching setting allows for the ongoing exchange of thought partners where both teachers flourish and grow professionally.

Generally co-teaching brings two educators with differing areas of expertise together to serve students; for example, a language specialist partners with a content area teacher or a general education teacher works in tandem with a special education teacher. Looking into Inés's second-grade classroom, although Ms. Ortega-Miller is a bilingual Spanish speaker, it is her co-teacher who brings expertise in language development; together, the duo offers a tremendously rich learning environment to the students. At the beginning of the school year, Ms. Ortega-Miller makes the initial contact with Inés's mother and the other families, gathering information about the students' interests, fears, and favorite things, and then she shares the information with her co-teacher. Together they co-plan next steps.

IMAGINE

In what capacity might you describe yourself as a thought leader?

_____

_____

_____

_____

_____

How might you lend a hand to colleagues or families in some small way? What expertise do you have, and how might you share it with others?

_____

_____

_____

_____

_____

_____

 Available for download from **resources.corwin.com/BeyondCrises**.

PART III • CLASSROOMS

Teachers as co–assessment designers

Let's agree that one of the goals of education is to shape a student's personal and group identities and, in doing so, lead students to challenge dominant perspectives and develop a critical consciousness (Lebeaux, 2020). If that is the case, then assessment, as a critical component of any educational system, would be remiss if it did not reflect students' views and was not inclusive of students themselves. Thus, assessment *as* learning, where students play a central role in decision making, comes to be a critical approach in the everyday functioning of classrooms and in taking an equity stance (Gottlieb, 2016).

When teachers are co-designers of assessment with students, they enter into a partnership, most notably in crafting assessment *for* learning. Figure 7.7 lists ways in which teachers can directly involve students in the assessment process and provides examples of what that engagement might look like. It is presented as a checklist for teachers and their teams to contemplate how to expand the participation of students, particularly multilingual learners, in classroom assessment.

When we say that teachers are assessment co-designers, the *co* can refer to a partnership with students, other teachers, or leadership teams. Teachers and students who engage in assessment *for* learning work together to co-construct or refine learning targets and instructional activities, agree on which multimodal ways to show evidence for learning, and give and act on feedback. Teachers, conversing with grade-level or content team members, may create and share different ways of interpreting information, such as a standards-referenced rating scale. If proved effective, protocols developed by teacher teams can then be brought to the school's leadership team to adopt for common assessment.

Designing and enacting change is a long process; when it occurs spontaneously as in the many crises we have had to endure that still persist, it is confounded by additional stressors. Over the last year we have seen how classrooms and teachers along with students and families have risen to the occasion to overcome challenges they have faced. As we move beyond crises, we begin to reconceptualize schooling so that our students, families, and their collective assets are front and center.

Imagine how teachers like Ms. Ortega-Miller have helped to reshape education. She teaches to her students' strengths, invites family participation, and places them both as first and foremost in her teaching priorities. In these transformative times we have to marvel at the remarkability of our students' resilience and applaud their fortitude in facing and hopefully overcoming the hardships we all have had to endure. Yet, while we wish to remain optimistic throughout these crises, we also must face the challenges and reality at hand, which we reveal in the next chapter.

Figure 7.7 • Bringing Students Into the Assessment Process: A Checklist for Increasing Classroom Equity

I HAVE . . .	YES/NO	DESCRIPTION OF WHAT TO DO
1. Involved my students in formulating learning targets for lessons and units of learning.		Students and teachers craft integrated learning goals (combining content and language) for units of learning and integrated learning targets (again, combining content and language) for individual lessons.
2. Deconstructed applicable standards for language and content with students so that they have a shared understanding of the expectations for learning.		Students and teachers analyze what is stated in standards and convert it into student-friendly language.
3. Generated ideas for multimodal representation with students to demonstrate evidence for learning.		Students have opportunities to express their learning through visual, graphic, digital, oral, or written means (e.g., multimedia presentations, voiceover videos).
4. Surveyed or interviewed students to ascertain their interests, passions, and experiences to connect to themes or projects.		Students help generate and select an essential question they wish to pursue for a unit of learning based on their interests and goals.
5. Designed and modeled criteria for success with students.		Teachers analyze student work with students in relation to criteria or descriptors to determine what makes an exemplar.
6. Allowed multilingual learners to use the language(s) of their choice to make inquiries, investigate issues, and seek solutions.		Multilingual learners who are knowledgeable of multiple languages are given opportunities to explore, research, draft, exchange ideas, or discuss issues in English, their other language, or both.
7. Guided students in assessment *as, for,* and *of* learning.		Students evaluate the extent to which they meet learning targets or goals (assessment *as* learning), then discuss it with their teacher (assessment *for* learning), and compare their performance to that on a unit test or final project (assessment *of* learning).
8. Had students apply the criteria of success in peer assessment and give concrete feedback to each other.		Students check off the criteria they have met along with their evidence before peers confirm the students' responses with actionable feedback.
9. Had students self-reflect on their learning and plan how to use their new knowledge.		Students reveal their successes and challenges in journals or learning logs, or respond to questions, checklists, or rating scales.
10. Empowered students by facilitating the preparation and presentation of student-led conferences that personalize their accomplishments.		Students show their work to their teacher (and parent/guardian); together they discuss the evidence for meeting current goals and set goals for the future.

Sustaining Momentum and Growth in Classrooms

8

Real change, enduring change, happens one step at a time.

—Ruth Bader Ginsburg

In no time in our history have educators been pushed to the limit more than when COVID-19 hit. One day school was in session, the next day everyone was sent scurrying to set up technology and initiate remote learning. With the severing of emotional and physical ties with students, the frustration of teachers and administrators was palpable; the uncertainty of the situation was unbelievably stressful. Teachers of multilingual, multicultural, and multiracial learners immediately saw resources stretched and everyday inequities become exacerbated—the digital divide, unemployment, housing, hunger, and vulnerability to catching the virus, to name a few. The question then becomes: How can we sustain our students' momentum and growth when we are confronted with so many competing priorities?

In this chapter we identify the challenges facing our classrooms that have been imposed upon us by external forces and factors. In offering recommendations for how we might confront these issues, we center our attention on the opportunities that have opened up during these difficult times to be carried forward in productive ways. With newly formulated goals, we look beyond crises with hope for expanded collaboration among communities, schools, and classrooms.

Challenging Issues

So far this part of the book has painted a scenario of ideal classrooms along with courageous, innovative teachers. With the abruptness of global change in March 2020, however, many teachers had to assume new roles to help students and their families. Jennifer Iamele Savage, a literacy coach in South Carolina, is a prime example of an educator who jumped into action to assist families in meeting their basic needs:

> During the school closure, our district provided free lunch pick-up sites as well as other food distribution opportunities. Additionally, personally I was able to obtain a grant through DonorsChoose to provide care packages to many of our families in need. The care packages included things like laundry detergent, toilet paper, and hygiene supplies in addition to learning materials. (personal communication, October 10, 2020)

Furthermore, Ms. Savage's district took extra steps to confront and respond to the pandemic. Along with reimagining schooling, the district's family and community outreach included the following:

- partnering with the local library, setting up individual student accounts, and providing ebooks

- sending home book bags filled with books

- prerecording lessons to be accessed from iPads or computers

- creating how-to videos and guides for using technology

- setting up office hours for both students and parents/guardians

IMAGINE

Imagine being a teacher in Ms. Savage's district or Ms. Ortega-Miller's school.

What do you consider most positive in their response to the pandemic?

_____

_____

_____

_____

_____

_____

How have the crises changed the landscape of your school or district?

_____

_____

_____

_____

_____

Have you been able to transition from panic mode to seeking best practices for virtual teaching? If so, what steps did you take to initiate this change?

_____

_____

[blank boxed note area with writing lines]

 Available for download from **resources.corwin.com/BeyondCrises**.

We are about to confront some of the constraints that have negatively impacted classrooms, teachers, and multilingual learners (and their families) during these most recent crises. In examining some of the challenges we face and proposing how we might tackle them, we encounter the following:

✓ federal and state laws that impact schools and classrooms

✓ district and school policies that are not inclusive of students and families

✓ curriculum that doesn't reflect our families and students

✓ high-stakes assessment

✓ systemic racism and linguicism that pervade society

The Challenge of Federal and State Laws That Impact Schools and Classrooms

Educators are challenged by competing priorities and policies; together they must go on the offensive to defend what is just for students and families.

The passage of national educational legislation often spurs state statues and rules, which in turn are interpreted by state educational agencies through guidance documents. These major policy-making bodies exemplify a hierarchical relationship that directly affects every school district. However, here is where federal and state policy meets local contexts, for it is districts that have the direct connections with their communities, schools, and classrooms.

Figure 8.1 illustrates the relationship among policy-making bodies where federal legislation and litigation heavily influence states and their educational agencies. Districts, schools, and classrooms, being somewhat removed from national educational policy, have some latitude in deciding how best to educate their students. Notice how the power of classrooms and schools is helping to reverse dependence on the federal government in order to help equalize power and influence in the educational system.

A recent case study discloses the reliance of states on federal law and their subsequent impact on the types of language education models that are enacted in districts and schools. Analysis of language education policy across the United States reveals that while 60 percent of states have produced substantive guidance for districts

Figure 8.1 • Inverse Relationship Among Top-Down and Bottom-Up Educational Policy-Making Bodies

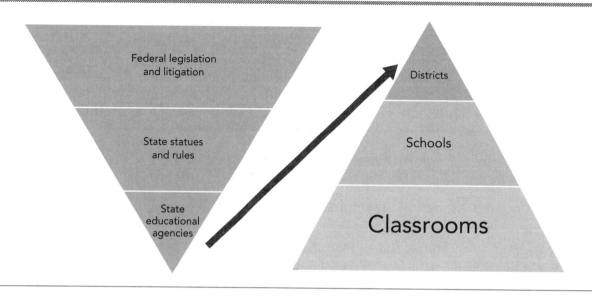

based on specific statutory mandates and regulations, close to 40 percent of states tend to rely exclusively on federal guidance (Gottlieb, Hilliard, Sánchez-López, Díaz-Pollack, & Salto, 2020).

The Historical Roots of District and School Accountability

A brief history of educational accountability at the federal level shows origins in equity that, to some extent, were stinted long ago. Ever since 1965, with passage of the Elementary and Secondary Education Act (ESEA), states have been beholden to federal legislation. This law and its subsequent iterations have been crafted in the name of equity, originally touted as a cornerstone for President Lyndon Johnson's War on Poverty and a landmark commitment to equal access to quality education. From it was born the Bilingual Education Act of 1968, which signaled recognition of the growing presence of multilingual learners, albeit as a problem rather than a resource. Thus, the legitimacy of bilingualism as an educational approach has always seemed to be tainted by being seen through a deficit lens.

Two decades later, the priorities of Title 1 under ESEA shifted from financial regulation to student achievement. In 1994, the Improving America's Schools Act mandated math and reading/language arts standards along with standardized testing. In 2002, the No Child Left Behind Act (NCLB) required increased accountability from schools for both teachers and students, with sanctions attached. NCLB stripped all references to bilingual education while introducing English language proficiency standards and assessment. Required disaggregation of achievement data by student subgroups under NCLB increased visibility of English learners and students with disabilities, on one level, but state reliance on a single data set for accountability only exacerbated inequity of minoritized students.

Continuing the tradition of ESEA, in 2015 with the passage of the Every Student Succeeds Act (ESSA), it became obligatory for states to implement schoolwide accountability systems along with continued standardized testing. In addition, ESSA stipulated that states must "identify languages other than English that are present to a significant extent in their participating student populations," and for the languages for which annual achievement tests are not available, "make every effort to develop such assessments." What appears as a move toward equity actually has stalled, as few states have made the effort to develop or administer achievement tests in languages other than English for accountability purposes.

On one hand, accountability has been beneficial to schools, multilingual learners, and other minoritized students. Back in the 1990s English learners were exempt from federal requirements, while now there is a requirement for the disaggregation and reporting of data by student groups, including English learners, English learners with disabilities, long-term English learners, and students of poverty. To some extent, this information is useful for classrooms so that teachers can scaffold content and language learning. On the other hand, the labels or classification schemes attached to these students are not neutral, negatively affecting their identities and carrying lifelong consequences (Kibler & Valdés, 2016). Although there is now some acknowledgment, visibility, and transparency for minoritized students in our larger educational system, we still are a long way from educational equity.

REFLECTION

Many states tend to adopt federal legislation as de facto compliance when it comes to educational policy, especially for multilingual learners.

Examine your state's website to ascertain whether there are specific statutes that protect or extend the rights of your minoritized students. What do you find?

_____

_____

_____

_____

_____

Based on the results of your search, to what extent do you feel that your students are protected under the law? What evidence do you have?

_____

_____

(Continued)

(Continued)

_____

_____

_____

_____

If not, what school or district policy might you suggest?

_____

_____

_____

_____

_____

_____

online resources ▶ Available for download from **resources.corwin.com/BeyondCrises**.

The Challenge of District Policies That Are Not Inclusive of Students and Families

Today there are extraordinary challenges in education that are also front and center in all our lives. The duo pandemics of COVID-19 and systemic racism are just as much educational issues as societal ones. These circumstances bring additional burdens and responsibilities to schools and classrooms. Notwithstanding, there are policies at district and school levels that are just not sensitive to communities, families, and students. The following are some highlights from this list of inequities.

Provision for Technology and Internet Connections

The digital and technology divide is not a new equity issue facing minoritized students, but COVID-19 has exacerbated its impact and has brought it into sharper focus. The overnight expanded role of technology, when education became instantaneously converted into distance online learning, left minority communities literally out in the cold. It is suggested that state and district policy makers "initiate public-private partnerships to incentivize broadband, technology, and digital providers to provide additional services to students and families in high need communities" (Ed Trust-West, 2020); however, the effectiveness of doing so has yet to be measured.

Many schools and districts have scurried to provide laptops or other devices to all students. Without access to broadband in poorer communities, this act of generosity is often to no avail. For students not experienced in digital technology, the benefit of having a computer is still negligible. When hotspots are on school buses in parking lots, how are students supposed to reach them? When connectivity isn't speedy or is always being interrupted, how are students expected to interact with their teachers and peers or conduct research? Online education can be effective only if it is reliable, supported by schools, embedded in instruction, and reinforced by teachers. The following voice from the field reiterates the challenge that teachers, students, and families face in trying to communicate through technology.

In Her Own Words

Jennifer Hunter, English Language Acquisition Coach, Brockton, Massachusetts

Ms. Hunter, what major teaching challenges have you faced this school year?

The preparations through the summer did not fully prepare us for the complications that would happen at home with an insurmountable amount of technical difficulties, from families not understanding where the power button is to not knowing how to charge the tablet. For some of our families, the language of technology is not something they have been exposed to. Even something as simple as having a conversation with a student is now limited due to technology issues. It has been a struggle for many educators because everything takes so much more time.

We are quite sure Ms. Hunter's experiences resonate with many of you. Indeed, technology can facilitate or impede learning in K–12 settings. Figure 8.2 is a checklist for evaluating the circumstances under which minoritized students, especially those in poverty, are trying to use technology to learn that might be applied to a classroom, multiple classrooms, or a school.

Figure 8.2 • A Technology Checklist for Students

DO YOUR STUDENTS HAVE . . .	ABSOLUTELY	NOT YET
1. Up-to-date technology of their own?		
2. Affordable or free access to technology?		
3. A reliable internet connection?		
4. A buddy to assist or tutor them (e.g., peer, older student, sibling, teacher, family member, IT person)?		
5. A quiet or dedicated place to use technology?		
6. A sense of digital literacy (e.g., computer basics)?		
7. Keyboarding skills?		
8. Time to become acquainted with and practice different features (e.g., labels, downloading/uploading, attaching photos/drawings, video recording, creating folders, organizing documents)?		

(Continued)

Figure 8.2 • (Continued)

DO YOUR STUDENTS HAVE . . .	ABSOLUTELY	NOT YET
9. Exposure to and understanding of programs and apps that require critical thinking and creativity?		
10. A daily schedule or routine to use technology (especially if needed to be shared with siblings)?		
11. A desk or work area of their own?		
12. Additional stress caused by not feeling secure with technology?		

Teachers everywhere have had to quickly figure out how to maximize opportunities for language development for their multilingual learners through technology. Ms. Hunter, who serves multiple grades, goes on to say how she has been able to overcome some of these challenges.

In Her Own Words

Jennifer Hunter, English Language Acquisition Coach, Brockton, Massachusetts

Ms. Hunter, what changes have you had to make in your classroom?

The chat feature in video calls may be helpful for older students or those who have used a keyboard before, but for some of our younger students this may be too complicated. Instead of using the chat feature in calls or asking students to type, it may be beneficial to utilize technology that allows for audio and video recordings. I am currently working with teachers in language-based classrooms who have assigned their students to respond to a question using Flipgrid. This was assigned only after modeling by the teacher and opportunities to practice. While new technology can be new and exciting for some, it can be very overwhelming for others. Therefore, I also feel it is important to continue to allow student choice.

If the use of technology is not going well for some students, another option for practicing language could be an at home "talking buddy." I will be sending home designated talking buddies to students in Kindergarten through Grade 2. . . . My hope is that my students will use these talking buddies during times I would like them to turn and talk. This will allow them to practice the target language or vocabulary we are focusing on. Once they have had a chance to turn and talk with their talking buddies, some students will be called on to share with their peers on the video call.

Speaking of technology, Álvaro is very excited as Mrs. Pérez has trusted him in using the family mobile phone, a lifeline to stay in touch with relatives back in Guatemala. Being a middle schooler, he soon becomes adept at manipulating many of the phone's features, and one day he decides to show his little sister some of the study tips that he has learned. First, Álvaro teaches Inés how to use the alarm clock for dedicated study time. Then he demonstrates how he thinks through problems and orally records his ideas in Spanish. Later he returns and, sometimes with the assistance of translation from a search engine, he transcribes his recording and translates or paraphrases it into English. At times, Álvaro asks his ESL teacher, Ms. Rozier, to check what he has done. Álvaro enjoys teaching his little sister how to use technology. It creates a bond among family members and connects the family to school.

Ensuring Accessibility and Opportunity for All Students

Accessibility to grade-level content coupled with opportunities to learn is a huge issue confronting minoritized students, especially those with named disabilities. It turns out that for English learners, there is disproportionate representation in special education—with the tendency to underrepresent these students in lower grades (Samson & Lesaux, 2009) and overrepresent them in higher grades (Linn & Hemmer, 2011). While there has been an urgent call for additional research, this systemic problem of misidentification among ELs and subsequent lack of policy guidance has to be rectified (Park, Magee, Martinez, Willner, & Paul, 2016).

To some extent, Universal Design for Learning, a framework for improving teaching and learning, should extend the protection of all students and increase their accessibility to rich and rigorous learning experiences (Meyer, Rose, & Gordon, 2014). The application of its three basic principles—insistence on availability of and access to multiple means of engagement, multiple means of representation, and multiple means of expression—helps ensure that all students potentially benefit from schooling. Families are to be assured that there are high expectations in every classroom so that all students become expert learners.

The challenge of accessibility has been exacerbated by the pandemic as teachers confront a whole new set of classroom configurations and formats. The following account is from a second-grade teacher who is desperately trying to continue momentum and growth of his class under difficult circumstances. The angst of teaching effectively is quite remarkable, especially when there are constantly changing face-to-face combinations of students while simultaneously reaching out to a remaining group of students who stay remote.

In His Own Words

Michael Silverstone, Second-Grade Teacher, Amherst, Massachusetts

Mr. Silverstone, what has been the greatest challenge teaching this year?

Maintaining engagement with lessons while maintaining distance has been at times like juggling while surfing. On a typical day I might try to meet with a scheduled group in one of four spaces: an acoustically challenging hallway, an alternate classroom, the library, or

(Continued)

PART III • CLASSROOMS

(Continued)

an outdoor canopy. In addition to having to bring all the materials needed for the lesson, including a portable easel and a basket of markers, scissors, sticky notes, whiteboard markers, and other materials, I also have to have a laptop open so that remote learners can take part, which comes with its own additional landscape of challenges. The remote learners need to be related to and visually oriented and involved with their classmates on site. I need a vantage point for the computer in these different locations so that the sight lines are adequate and visuals meaningful—and of course, we are masked, and it's difficult for children to hear each other's responses, and mine are often delivered in elevated volume. We maintain distance, which while increasing safety makes engagement for some learners more problematic.

A Language Policy for Classrooms With Multilingual Learners

As an extension of accessibility and opportunity for multilingual learners, there should be a coordinated set of district, school, and classroom language policies that help shape students' identities and enable them to optimize opportunities for building emotional strength and academic success. A schoolwide language policy for multilingual learners helps establish coherent language programming across grades that, in many cases, supports the languages of the community. A classroom language policy should be a personalized pact between a teacher and students. Even if the teacher is not bilingual, students who are should be able to communicate in the language of their choice during agreed-upon times or circumstances. Figure 8.3 is a list of students' everyday activities that can be used as a survey. The information from this list can help teachers determine language practices of individual classrooms in one or multiple languages. It is also an effective tool for designing a schoolwide language policy that might be useful across the K–12 spectrum.

Figure 8.3 • Formulating a Classroom Language Policy Based on Multilingual Learners' Language Use

GIVEN THE LANGUAGES OF OUR CLASSROOM, WE CAN . . .	USING ENGLISH	USING ANOTHER LANGUAGE	USING BOTH LANGUAGES
1. Ask and answer questions			
2. Research a topic			
3. Discuss the topic and exchange ideas with my peers			
4. Clarify misunderstandings			
5. Takes notes			

GIVEN THE LANGUAGES OF OUR CLASSROOM, WE CAN . . .	USING ENGLISH	USING ANOTHER LANGUAGE	USING BOTH LANGUAGES
6. Use digital resources or explore internet references			
7. Write a first draft of a paper			
8. Prepare for presentations			
9. Join in conversations			
10. Think through issues			

The Appropriateness of Grading

Grading policies were all but abandoned with the onset of COVID-19 and the disruption of education as we knew it. Much has changed since then that gives us pause and time for reflection on our pedagogical practice, hopefully resulting in the realization that we cannot return to the same inequities, student anxiety, and teacher fluctuation around grading. Here are some suggestions for altering grading policies, starting with the convening of a task force, committee, or professional learning community:

- Create individual, personalized learning goals, based on dialogue with each student, as the basis for evaluation.

- In designing lessons for shortened instructional periods, select only the most essential standards to create "I can" statements with students and match them to different kinds of evidence for learning.

- Substitute standards-referenced performance tasks that are agreed upon with students for traditional quizzes or tests so that teachers can give descriptive, actionable feedback.

- Increase student input in grading through self-reflection on their learning.

- Emphasize student progress toward goals or standards rather than numbers or letters.

- Design a student or class portfolio, and have a dialogue with students to negotiate grades, if applicable.

Grading is a time-honored tradition that needs to be revisited and revised in light of the ongoing presence of educational inequities.

Central to policy making that will make a difference in the education of minoritized students is cultivating and maintaining relationships among teachers, students, and families. After all, it is the relationship building at the heart of fostering trust that leads to empowerment (Gerzon-Kessler, 2019/2020).

PART III • CLASSROOMS

IMAGINE

Imagine that you are chairing a leadership team to revisit school policy, particularly grading policy.

Why is it important to change or revise what is currently in place?

_____

_____

_____

_____

_____

_____

What steps might you take to initiate change?

_____

_____

_____

_____

_____

_____

---

online resources ▶ Available for download from **resources.corwin.com/BeyondCrises**.

The Challenge of Curriculum That Doesn't Reflect Our Students and Families

One of the most pervasive challenges facing classrooms with minoritized students is how to deal with curriculum that does not mirror the multicultural faces that teachers encounter every day. In other words, what can teachers do with curriculum that is based on monolingual ideologies that reflect anglocentric middle-class values? It is the classroom context, although influenced by standards and texts, that should shape curriculum (Graves, 2008). Simply stated, when the student population is multilingual and multicultural, our curriculum should reflect that reality. Multilingual learners should be given ample and diverse opportunities to access their full linguistic and cultural repertoires from lesson to lesson, and those assets should be embedded in classroom assessment (Gottlieb, 2021).

Culturally responsive teaching, an approach that leverages students' strengths to make learning more relevant and effective, should reflect culturally responsive curriculum. Ms. Ortega-Miller, for example, carefully selects multicultural stories from authors around the world; as she reads each one to the class, students relate them to their lives and investigate where the author is from. On occasion, the class is even able to contact the author via Zoom to ask questions!

New America (Muñiz, 2019) has developed a set of research-based teacher competencies on culturally relevant, responsive, and sustainable practices. What the competencies reveal, in essence, is ripe for curriculum design that indeed is inclusive of students, their families, and their histories. To summarize, in applying these competencies to curriculum, educators should

- recognize and counteract bias by presenting multiple perspectives;
- draw on students' culture, historical roots, and experiences;
- incorporate real-world issues of interest to students;
- include high expectations for all students with built-in scaffolds for learning;
- promote respect for student differences and identities;
- invite collaboration with families and the local community;
- encourage discussion of varying views, with students assuming different roles;
- incorporate principles of Universal Design for Learning;
- be sensitive to students' experiences (e.g., exposure to hardship and trauma), along with linguistic and cultural nuances; and
- allow students to express themselves in multimodal ways.

IMAGINE

Imagine that you have a linguistically and culturally sustainable curriculum that is a match for your students.

Which characteristics named above are present in your curriculum?

_____

_____

_____

_____

_____

_____

(Continued)

(Continued)

What steps might you take to adapt your current curriculum to make it more linguistically and culturally sustainable?

_____

_____

_____

_____

_____

_____

online resources ⟋ Available for download from **resources.corwin.com/BeyondCrises**.

Ms. Ortega-Miller and her second-grade team are sensitive to the research-based teacher competencies associated with culturally sustainability practices. The teachers deliberately choose thought-provoking multicultural materials for their students that represent curricular themes. One of the more recent books the team discovered that they know would appeal to all their students is *What We Believe: A Black Lives Matter Principles Activity Book* (Garcia, 2021). Written and illustrated by two teachers, the informational text highlights the principles behind the movement—empathy, loving engagement, and just action—that have had wide applicability across their classrooms, school, and local community.

To stimulate discussion about this very sensitive topic, one day Ms. Ortega-Miller creates a sign around the classroom clock (Figure 8.4). She waits to see if anyone notices. The students immediately recognize this multimodal symbol. Ms. Ortega-Miller takes the opportunity to weave social justice into social-emotional learning through student interaction. She says to student partners, "Look at the wall at the clock. What does it say? What does it mean to you?" The second-grade teacher wants to determine students' depth understanding of this very simple but powerful phrase.

Figure 8.4 • You Matter Sign

The Challenge of High-Stakes Assessment

In some sense, federal legislation pertaining to K–12 education has historically been a paradox for multilingual learners and other minoritized students as its vision for social reform and equity remains elusive. The reason federal legislation has been a challenge is that many states, districts, and subsequently schools are driven by the necessity for high-stakes testing. However, when standardized testing is the sole source of accountability, it often has negative consequences for our diverse student populations. Ever since the 1990s there has been a call for equitable assessment policies for English learners (LaCelle-Peterson & Rivera, 1994), but in large part it remains unheeded.

The pandemic has introduced much turmoil and uncertainty into large-scale assessment and accountability. Luckily, Ms. Ortega-Miller and her class fall under the radar because, traditionally, federal accountability for student achievement is not initiated until Grade 3. However, for older students in the school and across the district, it remains a dilemma. Here are some suggestions that have been considered this past year to lessen the ill effects of large-scale achievement testing:

✓ Collect contextual data to better interpret the results from any interim or annual measure. Mixed conditions for instruction—from full-time remote, to hybrid, to in-class—have disrupted the flow of learning and warrant an expanded indicator system.

✓ Focus on designing and implementing opportunity-to-learn (e.g., access to instructional materials, technology, and safe learning conditions) data collection efforts.

✓ Insist on gathering student learning data at multiple levels, including state, local (district/school), and classroom with parent input (Marion, Gonzalez, Wiener, & Peltzman, 2020).

Additionally, as a result of recent crises and the reinvention of education, we have witnessed how growth goals have not been realized for the majority of students and, in fact, have been disadvantageous for students of poverty. There are two reasons for this. Results from diagnostic measures have been inappropriately interpreted given that students' circumstances have not been factored into the reporting, and interim tests relate normative data, which compare students to their peers (in a sample) rather than their movement toward grade-level expectations (Huff, 2020).

Heavy reliance on these forms of assessment *of* learning (or summative assessment) that are generally standardized and externally imposed on schools and classrooms simply does not give us an assets-based account of student performance or growth. It is only through a balanced assessment system that is learner-centered, taking place in everyday classroom activities and tasks, that we have a true sense of what students can do. Thus, schools need to endorse assessment *as* learning (student-driven) and assessment *for* learning (teachers facilitating students) as companions to assessment *of* learning and as pathways to equity (Gottlieb & Katz, 2020).

PART III • CLASSROOMS

> *Together, assessment as, for, and of learning offers opportunities for students to provide a full complement of evidence of learning.*

How might we elevate the status of classroom assessment so that includes student voice? An effective strategy for classroom teachers is to seamlessly integrate student self-reflection and peer assessment into the classroom routine. For multilingual learners there is no reason why self-assessment cannot occur in languages other than English, as more than likely these students are thinking in those languages. Thus, assessment *as* learning becomes an opportunity for students to gain confidence on their road to empowerment.

Figure 8.5 is an example of a checklist that Ms. Ortega-Miller uses with her second graders when they are working with partners or in small groups. She has recorded it in Spanish for her Latinx students to play, if they so choose, and some family members have translated the checklist into other languages. A couple students have even ventured to attach emojis to the questions so that they will remember what they are.

Figure 8.5 • Student Self-Assessment in Small-Group Participation

What do you do in your group? Put an X in the box if the answer is yes.

IN MY GROUP, I . . .	YES, I DO!	IN MY GROUP, I . . .	YES, I DO!
Ask questions		Answer questions	
Ask for help		Give help	
Ask others' opinions		Give my opinion	
Work with others		Work by myself	
Know what to do		Show others what to do	
Check my work with others		Check my work all by myself	

IMAGINE

Imagine that you could craft a linguistically and culturally relevant plan that accounts for assessment *as, for,* and *of* learning.

How might you and your grade-level team or department counteract the ill effects of annual achievement testing, especially for minoritized students?

_____

_____

_____

_____

_____

_____

What opportunity-to-learn factors are important to consider for your classroom or school?

_____

_____

_____

_____

_____

_____

online resources ☞ Available for download from **resources.corwin.com/BeyondCrises**.

The Challenge of Systemic Racism and Linguicism That Pervade Society

Admittedly, systemic racism (discrimination based on race) and linguicism (discrimination based on language and dialect) are well-established patterns of oppression that are not going to be eradicated in the near future. Nevertheless, schools and classrooms can definitely be starting points for alleviating prejudice and evoking reform. Whereas racism has been equated with U.S. history since the birth of our nation, linguicism, although it has always existed, is a rather newly defined construct. In 1986, Phillipson and Skutnabb-Kangas introduced linguicism in education as a worldwide phenomenon that has brought attention to the disparity in power and resources between groups based on language. Today the two concepts have merged somewhat as several scholars have adopted raciolinguistic ideologies that underscore the intersection between race and language (see bodies of work by Rosa and Flores [e.g., 2017, 'Do you hear what I hear? Raciolinguistic ideologies and culturally sustaining pedagogies']).

Chipping away at racism and linguicism should be a whole-school effort that is visible in every classroom. Here are some small steps to counteract unfair treatment of minoritized students based on race and language:

- Make a commitment to linguistic and cultural sustainability.

- Accentuate the assets of every student in every classroom.

- Facilitate courageous conversations on language, race, social justice, and equity in grade-level teams and school leadership teams.

- Include students helping students to solve microaggressions, such as cyberbullying or racial slurs.

- Ensure that curriculum and assessment are equitable and representative of teacher and student voice.

- Involve families in all important school decisions that affect policies touching on language, ethnicity, and race.

- Take advantage of professional learning opportunities around teaching tolerance, confronting discrimination, and minimizing bias.

Classrooms, like schools, should be creative and dynamic learning environments where all students thrive. According to Quaglia and Lande (2017), "Listening to, valuing, and incorporating teacher voice is the heart of meaningful transformation of schools" (p. 30). Teacher voice translates into collaboration with others and direct engagement in the design and enactment of innovation.

To sustain momentum and growth, however, it is our contention that teacher voice must be coupled with voices from the community, school leadership, and students to represent the three intersecting and interconnected spheres of influence. Only then can we begin to right some of the entrenched educational inequalities. For it is the interactions among family members, teachers, and students, such as those that that we've seen with Mrs. Pérez, Ms. Ortega-Miller, and Inés, that ultimately drive reform and make a difference in students' lives.

Extending Opportunities for Engagement

"Beyond crises" signals a new beginning for classrooms and schools, with opportunities to think about teaching and learning in innovative ways. The educational community, as the world, has been rocked and subsequently bound by a common hardship. As a result of this experience, educators can more readily relate to one another and extend that understanding and empathy to students and families. Given this unexpected opportunity for professional renewal, what can we do differently to improve our educational system? Here are some goals we may wish to strive toward:

- ✓ more collegiality, respect, and trust among educators
- ✓ more collaboration among stakeholders
- ✓ more modes of communication
- ✓ more empathy and compassion to contextualize learning
- ✓ more student ownership of data

The Opportunity for More Collegiality, Respect, and Trust Among Educators

No one has escaped the ravages of COVID-19 or been immune to the systemic racism that has become so visible and continues to permeate our collective souls. More than any other segment of society, our minoritized students have been directly and disproportionately impacted by these twin pandemics, and they are hurting. As educators we must unify in offering solace and support for our students and their families. We cannot accomplish this mission unless we begin by understanding ourselves and each other.

Ms. Ortega-Miller, being Latinx, realizes that she carries an additional burden of social injustice; at times, she has been criticized for speaking Spanish in public. In kinship, she reaches out to her second-grade team, and together they share personal stories of how horrendous events like this have affected their lives. It is comforting to realize that her fellow educators have more common ground than not; together they contemplate becoming a pod. Their bonding over tragedy has motivated the team to continue to be compassionate and share a piece of themselves each month. As a result, the teachers tend to reach out to one another more often for advice and Ms. Ortega-Miller senses the lessening of discrimination.

The Opportunity for More Collaboration Among Teachers, Students, and Family Members

Decades ago, Henry Giroux (1983) stated that we "must provide the conditions that give students the opportunity to speak with their own voices to authenticate their own experiences" (p. 203). By creating classroom environments that promote purposeful student collaboration and discussion, teachers enable students to begin seeing themselves as valued contributors to learning. Additionally, in classrooms where students engage in quality interactions that foster conceptual, social-emotional, and language development, they are able to learn in authentic ways and then apply that knowledge to new situations.

Promoting collaboration is the next step after establishing student interaction. Imagine how teachers might plan for increasing collaboration in their classrooms. Think about how these suggestions can be applied to in-person or virtual settings. Figure 8.6 offers some tips that have been converted into a checklist to get you started.

Figure 8.6 • Ideas for Promoting Student Collaboration

IN MY CLASSROOM, I . . .	ABSOLUTELY!
1. Ask open-ended questions for students to discuss with each other	
2. Give students choices in topics to pursue	
3. Design tasks with students that call for inquiry and engagement	
4. Invite multiple personal, historical, or cultural perspectives	
5. Ensure that all students can participate and have access to content	
6. Make sure students partake in creative and deep thinking	
7. Extend student learning by having them question each other	
8. Challenge students to problem solve together	
9. Urge students to elaborate, clarify, and reply in more than one way	
10. Encourage students to reach consensus on issues and make decisions	

Source: Adapted from Billings & Mueller (n.d.).

PART III • CLASSROOMS

One of the more positive side effects of COVID-19 on classrooms and schools is that it has created circumstances that call for increased communication among teachers, students, and family members. Historically, students of immigrants or from non-standard-English-speaking homes have been perceived as not having equal status, and their cultural practices have been devalued. Traditionally, schools have not been structured for true partnership with parents and other family members. Although these inequities have not been rectified, they have been recognized, which is the first step in addressing this pervasive issue.

One of the consequences of living through a pandemic is that the world has been turned upside down, which is one of the reasons we have inverted the traditional triad of classroom, school, and community and have introduced communities as the place to begin our exploration of educational equity. In Ms. Ortega-Miller's class, for example, circle time for the whole-class morning meeting has been converted into conversing with small groups of students in virtual breakout rooms. Additionally, she sets up one-on-one time with each student for a special exchange.

Increased collaboration among teachers, students, and families during the crisis has stimulated innovative literacy practices that include multimodalities. In the Pérez household, the two siblings, at times with their mother, enjoy co-authoring books. Inés likes to record and then illustrate oral folklore and songs from Guatemala recounted and sung by her mamá. Since Álvaro is literate in Spanish, he transcribes the stories and lyrics and translates them into English. Sometimes the children even dance to Latin rhythms that they incorporate into their narratives. It is an empowering experience for the entire family that Inés shares with her teacher and class.

IMAGINE

Imagine how you might reach out to families.

How might you embed students' home lives and experiences into linguistically and culturally relevant themes? What steps might you take to extend collaboration to families?

_____

_____

_____

_____

_____

online resources ☝ Available for download from **resources.corwin.com/BeyondCrises**.

Lastly, collaboration goes beyond classroom activities among students. It also entails generating a trusting environment where families and we, as educators, feel safe, a sense of belonging, value, and competence in working together. In that sense, it is as mutually rewarding as it is a place where we truly understand each other and are inspired to work together.

The Opportunity for Using More Modes of Communication

We express our inner thoughts, feelings, and ideas in large part through language; for many multilingual families, that means in a language other than English. The notion of communication, however, is no longer exclusively associated with language—it has expanded beyond oral and written text to include additional modalities. Teachers realize how multimodal communication, such as through visual, spoken, written, and gestural means, enhances their reach and messaging to students, families, and the community. Multilingual learners and their families can readily engage with a range of multimodal texts, including picture books, graphic novels, comics, murals, posters, web pages, videos, even texting with emojis, and they may use one, two, or a combination of languages to make meaning from them all.

Staying in touch has been critical during the pandemic, and at no previous time has worldwide communication been more important. It has been remarkable what communities have mustered to help each other out. In turn, schools have offered helping hands to families; many, in fact, have become community centers by graciously donating supplies, computers, clothing, and food. The use of multimodalities has helped spread the message to the community at large. Think, for example, how signage has played a critical role during the pandemic, reminding us where to line up and how far to stay apart, mask wearing requirements, information on availability for testing, and posters on the warning signs of the virus. As we approach a better normal, we will undoubtedly continue to rely on multimodal means to communicate with each other.

IMAGINE

Imagine that you have surveyed students about their multimodal preferences for learning.

Which multimodal means of expression do you think your students prefer, and to what extent are these incorporated into your classroom use?

_____

_____

_____

(Continued)

(Continued)

_____

_____

_____

How does the use of multimodal communication enrich the learning experience for your students?

_____

_____

_____

_____

_____

_____

online resources Available for download from **resources.corwin.com/BeyondCrises**.

The Opportunity for More Empathy and Compassion to Contextualize Learning

Empathy is the ability to relate to others with acceptance and to share their feelings, whether in agreement with you or not. It is being sensitive to and aware of the situation of others. At no other time, with literally millions of people hurting, has being empathetic been so essential to our nation's ultimate restoration of emotional health. In school, social-emotional learning informed by an equity lens provides a vehicle for teaching kindness, compassion, and understanding without judgment. Having these traits, coupled with acceptance of cultural differences, is useful in relationship building, solving problems, and adapting to the pressures of everyday life.

At this juncture, historical empathy as part of social studies curriculum takes on new meaning and application as it directly relates to helping undo the evils of racism. It involves understanding how people from the past thought, felt, made decisions, acted, and faced consequences. Through cognitive and affective engagement with historical figures, students are able to better understand and contextualize their own lived experiences, decisions, and actions (Endacott & Brooks, 2013). These empathetic ways of being have direct application to today's classrooms and provide an ideal way to connect the present to the past.

The Opportunity for More Student Ownership of Data

In data-informed instruction there is always a learning target and accompanying evidence, where interaction among students fosters engagement in and documentation of learning. Students are aware of their learning targets because they helped formulate them, and they are receiving, giving, and acting on concrete actionable feedback as part of the classroom routine. Their contributions to the assessment process should not stop there.

In assessment *as* learning, students are directly involved in the process of planning, gathering, and interpreting data. Assessment *as* learning calls on our students to become leaders of their own learning by assessing their own progress toward mutually agreed-upon learning goals. Additionally, students have opportunities to provide feedback to peers based on success criteria that have been crafted as a classroom community (Gottlieb, 2016, 2021).

If educators are to give students more decision-making power, then students should become intimately familiar with their own data. Figure 8.7 is a summary of characteristics of a data-rich, student-centered classroom presented as a checklist. It might contribute to determining students' role in driving instruction and assessment. As you answer the questions, think about how you might be more sensitive to students as keepers of their own data.

Figure 8.7 • Features of Student-Centered Data-Rich Classrooms

AS A STUDENT-CENTERED DATA-RICH CLASSROOM, IS/ARE THERE . . .	YES	NOT YET
1. Shared goals or targets for learning with evidence to match?		
2. Representations of multiple data sources for decision making?		
3. A balance of different approaches to assessment that are inclusive of students?		
4. Student self-assessment and reflection?		
5. Peer assessment and feedback?		
6. Student choice for representing what they know and can do?		
7. Mutually agreed-upon criteria for success to interpret student products, projects, or performances?		
8. Student-annotated evidence for learning?		
9. Students as decision makers and assessment leaders?		
10. Student voice in grading or evaluation?		

Crises ebb and flow in our personal and educational lives, but when it comes to classrooms, we have to remember that our students are our most important treasures. For them, we must maintain the drive and momentum to ensure that each and every one continues to grow emotionally, linguistically, and academically. We realize there seems to be a steady stream of obstacles in our way and challenges we face, but at all costs, we cannot fail our students.

We have witnessed how Ms. Ortega-Miller and her students have turned many of the challenges they face individually and collectively into opportunities. As a classroom, the camaraderie of the group is able to sustain the momentum of learning and growing together. The positivity that prevails among these young learners and the personnel of Sally Ride Elementary carries through to the last chapter of this book, where they are joined by families and the community to work toward overcoming linguistic and cultural inequities.

Striving for Interconnections Among Communities, Schools, and Classrooms

9

Schools are not islands in themselves; they are connected to communities.

—Robert Redfield, Director of the Centers
for Disease Control and Prevention (2020)

In the intertwining and interconnecting ecosystems that we address—communities, schools, and classrooms—we view learning as a recurring element within and across all these sectors. A school's mission, vision, and values that commit to an assets-based philosophy of educational equity and excellence foster these interconnections. As shown in Figure 9.1, minoritized students, particularly multilingual learners, and their families—the most important stakeholders in any educational system—crosscut these three ecosystems.

In this final chapter, we move beyond crises as we strive to reconnect and interconnect with others as we return to relationship building. Although injustices persist and most likely will always exist on some level, we are beginning to make strides in moving the needle toward more equitable educational practices through the collective voice of communities, schools, and classrooms. In particular, we envision how classrooms might take center stage with teachers and students joining forces to further educational partnerships. With agency and empowerment as central themes, we see examples of how our multilingual learners can be bolstered by their linguistic and cultural strengths. We close our book with hope for the future, where reason prevails and educational inequity becomes a phenomenon of the past.

Figure 9.1 • Multilingual Learners and Their Families as Central Players in Communities, Schools, and Classrooms

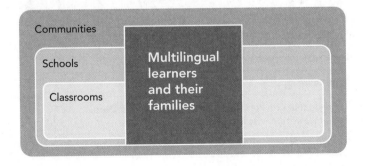

Advancing Teaching and Learning

In restructuring schools to meet today's academic demands and ever-changing demographics, along with dealing with current educational, health, and even societal injustices, we have come to the realization that educational decision making must be a schoolwide process that includes students, family members, and communities. We also believe that school should be a place where linguistic and cultural sustainability should prevail no matter what the circumstances and school population (Miramontes, Nadeau, & Commins, 2011).

So far in this third part of the book, we have examined classrooms and their teachers. In addition, we have posed challenges and countered them with opportunities for communities, families, and multilingual learners. In order to sustain momentum and continue growing, we now turn to advancing teaching and learning by giving students more direction and support so that they can increasingly take on responsibility. In particular, we highlight these student-driven classroom practices:

- ✓ promoting agency
- ✓ building students' metacognitive, metalinguistic, and metacultural awareness
- ✓ emphasizing collaboration
- ✓ envisioning efficacy in education

Advancing Teaching and Learning by Promoting Agency

To advance the teaching and learning of multilingual learners, indeed all students, we have stressed the importance of building and maintaining positive relationships in classrooms and throughout school. Having a safe and secure environment and feeling valued as a person are prerequisites for students to become risk takers. Only then can students develop agency, the capacity and desire to take purposeful initiative. Figure 9.2 is a checklist that identifies signs of student agency as enacted in classrooms; you may wish to make a mental note of all those that apply in your context.

Figure 9.2 • Promoting Student Agency in the Classroom

AS AGENTS OF LEARNING, STUDENTS . . .	ABSOLUTELY!
1. Are contributors to personal and classroom decision making	
2. Have choice in selecting partners to work with	
3. Offer ideas for learning targets, activities, and tasks	
4. Choose the mode that provides the best evidence for their learning (e.g., oral, graphic, written, visual, digital)	
5. Feel secure participating in class (in one or more languages)	
6. Have time to reflect on their learning	

AS AGENTS OF LEARNING, STUDENTS . . .	ABSOLUTELY!
7. Engage in school or community outreach and social action	
8. Are liaisons and representative of their families, languages, and cultures	
9. Contribute to classroom and school websites, newsletters, displays, and murals	
10. Show empathy for others and appreciate varying perspectives	

Source: Adapted from Gottlieb & Castro (2017, p. 154).

IMAGINE

Imagine your students as agents of their own learning.

Guided by Figure 9.2, which signs of student agency do you see in your classroom?

_____

_____

_____

_____

_____

Which features of agency might you push your students to pursue? How might you do this?

_____

_____

_____

_____

_____

 Available for download from **resources.corwin.com/BeyondCrises**.

When learning is characterized by student agency, students engage in the design of classroom experiences, contribute to goals and learning targets, and have opportunities to self-assess their learning in relation to mutually agreed-upon criteria for success. As such, learners have choice and voice in their educational experiences.

> *The goal of developing agency is for students to become lifelong learners and advocates for their own learning.*

Harnessing their own intrinsic motivation to learn, students strive to ultimately participate in and take ownership of learning (Cooper, 2017). In linguistically and culturally sustainable classrooms where multilingual learners feel at home and connected to community, they can more readily take steps to become agents of their own learning.

Analogously, ongoing professional learning that is conceptualized and directed by teachers, especially when it deals with topics directly related to student and community issues, leads to teacher agency, the capacity of teachers to purposefully direct their professional growth and enrichment. In turn, multilingual families who are connected to school; feel that their presence, languages, cultures, and views are represented; and have a sense of belonging become agentic. Figure 9.3 illustrates how linguistically and culturally sustainable school and classroom environments can lead to family, teacher, and student voice and agency.

Figure 9.3 • Voice and Agency in Linguistically and Culturally Sustainable Environments

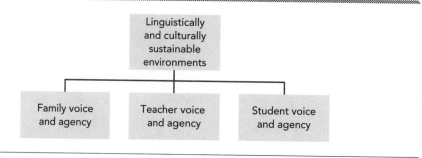

Source: Adapted from Gottlieb & Ernst-Slavit (2019).

Advancing Teaching and Learning by Building Students' Metacognitive, Metalinguistic, and Metacultural Awareness

Multilingual learners need to see themselves in the curriculum, and teachers have to ensure the curriculum's relevance, accessibility, and careful interweaving of content and language. Having a classroom filled with multilingual-multicultural students, Ms. Ortega-Miller is keen on building students' metacognitive, metalinguistic, and metacultural awareness. She wants to ensure that these young children gain a sense of the value of and have pride in possessing multiple languages and cultures.

Several times a week, Ms. Ortega-Miller devotes time to having students explore cross-linguistic and cross-cultural connections derived directly from the curriculum. She always relies on examples from the languages and cultures of her students so that they can relate to the learning experience. She is aware of the advantages of her students becoming sensitive to and knowledgeable of multiple cultural traditions and perspectives. She also realizes that boosting students' metalinguistic awareness has significant positive effects on their reading comprehension (Zipke, 2007).

Multilingual learners' identities are wrapped around their languages and cultures.

Currently, the second-grade class is investigating domestic and wild animals, so today Ms. Ortega-Miller writes two sentences in Spanish on the whiteboard: "El elefante es enorme. El león es feroz." She divides students into small groups, making sure that Spanish speakers are evenly distributed, and asks them to figure out (1) what the sentences say, (2) which words they can identify, and (3) how the words (the cognates) are the same or different from those in English. The students become excited in making their own linguistic discovery; they don't find it in a textbook, their teacher doesn't tell them—they rely on each other's comparative language expertise.

Metacognitive awareness (being mindful of how you think and the strategies you use), metalinguistic awareness (your conscious reflection on the nature of language), and metacultural awareness (being familiar with and being able to navigate across cultures) are unique to multilinguals. Together, this trio of awareness building helps students gain self-assurance and tackle new challenges, take linguistic risks, and make sense of the world. Through their analysis and reflection, students gain insight into and expand their world of multilingualism and multiculturalism. As shown in Figure 9.4, these three competencies contribute to shaping multilingual learners' multilingual identities.

Figure 9.4 • Blending Metacognitive, Metalinguistic, and Metacultural Awareness in Shaping the Identity Formation of Multilinguals

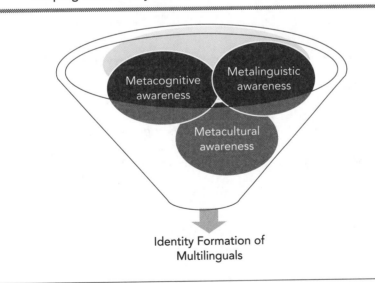

Advancing Teaching and Learning by Emphasizing Collaboration

Learning is a social activity that involves interaction among individuals and the exchange of ideas, feelings, and opinions. For teaching and learning, collaboration and cooperation are at the heart of forming relationships and can be powerful tools in shaping student performance. In schools, collaboration that involves teachers revolves around an array of partnerships:

- content (subject area, classroom) and language (English language development [ELD], bilingual) teachers

- dual-language (in immersion classrooms) and language (ELD) teachers

- dual-language, ELD, or content teachers and special education teachers

- teachers of "specials" and content, dual-language, or ELD teachers

- media specialists or technology teachers and content, dual-language, or ELD teachers

- leadership or instructional teams and teachers

- coaches and teachers

- grade-level or department teacher teams

- school administrators, leadership teams, and teachers

- school staff (such as lunchroom, custodian, security) and teachers

- community partners and teachers

- family members and teachers

- students and teachers

- students

IMAGINE

Imagine collaboration at its finest in your classroom and across your school.

Which partnerships are most important to you? Why?

_____

_____

_____

_____

_____

Which relationships would you like to pursue or would like to improve? Why?

_____

_____

_____

_____

_____

_____

What are some ideas (from Figure 9.5) that you may wish to try out in your classroom?

_____

_____

_____

_____

_____

_____

online resources 🔗 Available for download from **resources.corwin.com/BeyondCrises**.

Collaboration is especially important for multilingual learners as their educational success is dependent on meaningful integration of content and language throughout their classroom experiences. When multilingual learners share a language and they can use it with each other, those benefits are reinforced. Many classroom activities, such as the following, naturally promote student interaction:

- turn-taking
- asking and answering questions
- conversing about topics of interest
- giving oral feedback to each other
- providing written feedback based on common criteria or descriptors
- practicing (and revising) presentations
- exchanging information
- clarifying misunderstandings
- summarizing or paraphrasing narrative or informational text

PART III • CLASSROOMS

The goal of collaboration among teachers in educational settings is for members of a learning community to work together to improve their practice and further learning. Among those relationships, teacher partnerships are essential to ensure the flow, coherence, and continuity of instruction. They foster a collaborative culture where teachers gain appreciation and respect for each other. Even when instruction is virtual, teachers are able to access each other's work, share ideas, and spread news across their network. Figure 9.5 is a checklist of ideas for teacher collaboration in classrooms with multilingual learners along with space for generating examples.

Figure 9.5 • Forging Collaborative Partnerships Between Teachers

TOGETHER WE . . .	YES, WE DO! HERE ARE SOME EXAMPLES TO SHARE.
1. Ensure linguistic and cultural sustainability in our classrooms	
2. Leverage the knowledge of our students (their linguistic and cultural assets, interests, experiences) in planning instruction and assessment	
3. Embed students' strengths within and across lessons	
4. Provide opportunities for students to build community and interact with each other	
5. Offer multimodal ways (oral, written, graphic, digital, visual) for students to demonstrate their learning	
6. Encourage student interaction in their partner language whether teachers are proficient in the language or not	
7. Support the integration of content and language learning	
8. Make provisions for scaffolding learning to maximize students' opportunities to reach their learning targets and goals	
9. Provide time for students to inquire, practice, and reflect on their learning	
10. Set clear, attainable learning targets with students	
11. Use common language to offer feedback to students	
12. Rely on student input in crafting end-of-unit projects, products, or performances	
13. Craft criteria for success or provide descriptors for self- and peer assessment	
14. Think about how to reteach or extend teaching in new, innovative and personal ways, as necessary	
15. Challenge and encourage students to push their learning forward	

Advancing Teaching and Learning by Envisioning Efficacy in Education

Self-efficacy of teachers has to do with their individual positive impact on a student or class. Collective teacher efficacy, however, is more powerful as it examines the potentially positive change in student performance at a school level that is strongly correlated with student achievement (Hattie, 2009). Furthermore, Donohoo (2017) suggests that efficacy is about evidence-based conversations. She attributes collective efficacy to school leadership that

- creates opportunities for meaningful collaboration;
- empowers teachers through participatory decision making;
- sets clear, reachable goals and high expectations; and
- interprets results by examining student data and providing feedback.

Educational efficacy, or the measure of effectiveness in improving student performance, also extends to families and community. To empower every family, instructional practices must be inclusive of students' experiences and interests outside of school, such as when family members are invited to share their expertise (e.g., when Mrs. Pérez demonstrated how to sew simple patterns to her daughter's second-grade class). When families can relate to a curriculum that is linguistically and culturally sustainable, they become more immersed in learning that occurs at school. Additionally, linguistic and cultural relevance can extend to enhance and support learning at home (Constantino, 2016).

Figure 9.6 • Envisioning Efficacy Across Communities, Schools, and Classrooms

In Part I, we witnessed how solid school–community partnerships coupled with family engagement can result in strong efficacy efforts and highlight the strengths of minoritized student populations. In Part II, we saw how ongoing whole-school professional learning can lead to a shared sense of efficacy among faculty who are bound by their high expectations for all students. In this last part, we envision efficacy stemming from a collaborative effort between classroom teachers who believe in students as agents of their own learning, forge strong ties with families and the community, and have substantial decision-making power in co-planning and enacting instruction. Figure 9.6 shows the interconnected relationships that we have described in establishing efficacy among communities, schools, and classrooms.

Overcoming Educational Inequities

We have illustrated through the Pérez family how communities, schools, and classrooms are indeed interrelated and codependent. In forming a symbiotic relationship, each is reliant on the other as we see the richness of multilingualism and multiculturalism permeate the three ecosystems. In essence, as shown in the photograph of the heart-shaped bread (Figure 9.7), we are all family.

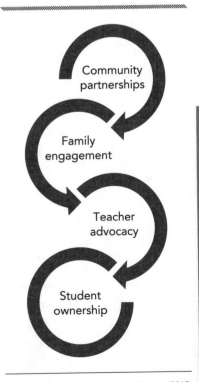

Source: Adapted from Gottlieb & Castro (2017, p. 176).

PART III • CLASSROOMS

Figure 9.7 • Poster in a Bakery in Bogotá, Colombia

SOMOS UNA EMPRESA DE

FAMILIA

*Creemos en la **familia** como la responsable de todas las cosas buenas que pasan en la vida.*

Translation: We believe in family as responsible for all good things that happen in life.

By forming a strong alliance among the three ecosystems that we have interwoven throughout the book, we can potentially offset and mitigate the pervasive inequities that are gnawing away at our educational principles, beliefs, and ideologies. Whatever the outcome, we must remain hopeful at all costs, as it is hope that is fundamental to our well-being and a robust predictor of our mental health. In this last section, we strive for interconnections among communities, schools, and classrooms, remaining confident that all stakeholders commit to

- ✓ coordinating education of promise, not compromise;
- ✓ coming together of communities, schools, and classrooms;
- ✓ co-constructing a future for schooling through the lens of equity;
- ✓ optimizing conditions for fostering teaching and learning; and
- ✓ overcoming linguistic and cultural disparities.

Coordinating Education of Promise, Not Compromise

No doubt about it, we have all lived through the most difficult and demanding of times that have caused emotional upheaval and hardship for so many. In the end we will have redefined education and life as we know it. To fulfill the promise of overcoming inequity, every classroom, school, district, and community organization must make a concerted and coordinated effort to preserve the language, history, and culture among minoritized groups through curriculum and action in school and community-based programs.

What specifically can teachers do in their classrooms to promote equity? Let's reiterate some of the major themes we have touched on that hold promise:

- The assets of students, not their deficits, are the focus of teaching and learning.

- Learning is scaffolded for students based on where they are and where they are to go next (a Vygotskyan principle), not as a whole group but as individuals.

- All students can meet high expectations, and teachers challenge students to do so.

- Students and their families have agency and are empowered to make decisions.

- An inclusive learning environment fosters student interaction and discussion.

- Curriculum, instruction, and classroom assessment invite a variety of perspectives.

- Students' linguistic and cultural identities are preserved and enhanced.

The promise of education rests with providing each and every student with access to learning. We have stressed the importance of teachers adhering to principles of Universal Design for Learning. In the heterogeneous second-grade classroom where there are students of multiple languages and cultures, with and without disabilities, recent arrivals or newcomers to the United States, Ms. Ortega-Miller takes special care in extending opportunities for learning to each and every student by following the checklist in Figure 9.8.

Figure 9.8 • Checklist for Optimizing Student Opportunities for Learning

TEACHERS . . .	SURE DO!
1. Present information in multimodal ways (through visual, aural, and graphic means)	
2. Use a variety of media (e.g., PowerPoints, audiobooks, videos)	
3. Include transcripts for multimedia materials, as available	
4. Provide supplemental materials and resources (e.g., websites, books in languages other than English, books on tape, glossaries, illustrations)	
5. Adjust features of technology, as needed (e.g., increase text size, adjust brightness) for individual students	
6. Allow students of shared languages to interact in those languages to further their learning	
7. Read instructions aloud, even if they appear in print	
8. Make materials and resources available to family members	
9. Are compassionate, empathic, understanding, and sensitive to student and family trauma, distress, and other issues that affect learning	
10. Connect students and families to school and community services	

PART III • CLASSROOMS

IMAGINE

Imagine what your classroom would look like if you adhered to the principles of Universal Design for Learning for every student. Consider making a chart where, by each student's name, you note their unique qualities and best approach to learning.

What are some ideas (from Figure 9.8) that you might use in your classroom to further equity of opportunity for your students?

_____

_____

_____

_____

_____

_____

online resources   Available for download from **resources.corwin.com/BeyondCrises**.

> *Multilingualism and multiculturalism facilitate connections among communities, schools, and classrooms and enrich the learning of all students.*

The Coming Together of Communities, Schools, and Classrooms

The making of community–school–classroom partnerships is not easy or spontaneous. Epstein's (2001) research-based framework, for example, notes different types of involvement of families through partnerships that focus on goals for school improvement. Included in this initiative is an action team dedicated to leading the partnership efforts, an action plan, an evaluation to assess its effectiveness, and goals for continual improvement. In addition, Epstein suggests forming school learning communities composed of educators, students, parents, and community partners who work together to enhance students' learning opportunities that can lead to academic success.

Learning partnerships with schools can bolster and support communities by

- connecting students and families to local services,

- improving the quality of educational programs,

- fostering a shared vision for learning through coordinated programs for students,

- maximizing use of resources, and

- strengthening relationships between schools and communities.

Learning partnerships can benefit schools by

- complementing the curriculum with a variety of supplemental services and activities,
- supporting transitions from elementary school to middle school to high school,
- extending family and student experiences by reinforcing concepts learned in school,
- bolstering school and community culture through exhibitions and performances, and
- providing access to mentors and other resources to enhance in-school learning.

Finally, learning partnerships are advantageous for students and their families because they

- ✓ provide continuity of resources throughout the year,
- ✓ ease transitions with before- and after-school activities,
- ✓ facilitate access to a range of services,
- ✓ encourage information sharing (in multiple languages) with families, and
- ✓ provide multiple entry points to support personalized student learning.

As communities, schools, and classrooms coalesce, we must instill hope as we chip away at dismantling prevailing injustices. Incorporating the information on the productivity and usefulness of partnerships, Figure 9.9 is a planning sheet for initiating or identifying different types of partnerships or collaborations across communities, schools, and classrooms.

Figure 9.9 • Planning Learning Partnerships Across Communities, Schools, and Classrooms

	TYPE OF PARTNERSHIPS OR COLLABORATIONS	POTENTIAL CONTACTS AND ACTIONS	PERCEIVED BENEFITS
Families and communities			
Educators and schools			
Students and classrooms			

PART III • CLASSROOMS

Fast-forward to sometime in the future. In one sense, the idea of the partnering of communities and schools seems elusive as educational and societal inequities have become so entrenched in our society. On the other hand, the context of social distancing has brought teachers and family members closer together in community building. In some small ways, it might be easier to collaborate as communities, schools, and classrooms share concerns over the pandemic and pose problem-solving strategies. Additionally, as many students are spending more time at home than at school, family members may be more accessible to discuss issues and seek solutions.

Let's admit it: the crises that we have endured will have prolonged effects and will alter our communities, schools, and classrooms for years to come. If we had a crystal ball, it might be easy to prepare for our future. The following account is a glimpse at one teacher's sentiments and prediction about teaching in a post-COVID world. Like Ms. Ortega-Miller, he is optimistic that education will be in a better place and that students as well as teachers will appreciate restored freedom and their ability to engage once more in learning as a social activity.

In His Own Words

Michael Silverstone, Second-Grade Teacher, Massachusetts

Mr. Silverstone, if you could imagine your classroom post-COVID, what would it look like?

I imagine students having an even greater degree of focus and gratitude for the opportunity to come together freely and socialize and learn. It's only human nature for many students to push against the limits of school and regard necessary regimentation needed for efficient delivery of lessons and transitions and movements as a restraint on their freedom. There's a lot of "have-tos" that can sometimes be overwhelming and make for a general feeling of "Yay, it's Friday." What the pandemic has highlighted is the overarching reality that it is in fact a gift to be in a place devoted to learning and the development of human potential and the acquisition of tools for living and working with others.

In the past when I heard or thought, "We're lucky to have this opportunity to be in school," I suspected that on some level this was simply rhetoric—someone's idea of what we should think. For many of us—teachers, students, and parents—these words have taken on a vivid and living meaning, a meaning that I for one intend to never forget and that will no doubt influence my gratitude for postpandemic teaching going forward, as the Great Depression influenced the values of the post–World War II generation.

We have emphasized throughout our book how communities, schools, and classrooms are ecosystems unto themselves yet are interconnected to form an interlocking and codependent system. In Figure 9.10 we revisit the three overlapping circles that represent their interconnected relationship. This time we center our attention on the contributions of the classroom in forming and supporting educational ecosystems.

Figure 9.10 • Building a Cohesive Classroom Community

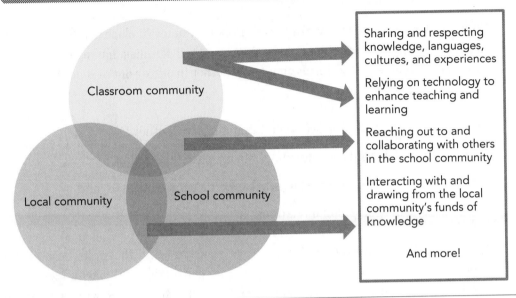

Co-constructing a Future for
Schooling Through the Lens of Equity

Schools have historically thought that students in poverty, English learners, students with disabilities, those of different sexual orientation, those with certain religious beliefs, and those who have undergone significant trauma seem compromised and remain at risk no matter what the circumstances (Fisher, Frey, & Hattie, 2021). Presently, it is difficult to fathom the future of school in times of a better normal when equity will have more of a presence. We have seen how the Pérez family has navigated the educational system with assistance from a family–school liaison, devoted and caring teachers, and schools that offer sustained professional learning. However, in these unsettling educational times, that may be the exception rather than the rule.

Restrictive educational policies of the past have limited educators from developing a humanistic approach to education, one that prides itself in caring about the whole person so that ultimately each student's full potential can be reached. A humanistic educational stance is student centered, with learners encouraged to set realistic goals, become self-motivated, and gradually take on more responsibility. Teachers are role models who give students freedom to choose tasks and encourage collaborative group work. By becoming empowered, learners ultimately gain more control over their own learning. Humanism and humanistic education are inclusive of equity, individual rights, and social justice to bring about social change.

By co-constructing interdependent and interconnected partnerships with various sectors of the community, parents/guardians in collaboration with teachers can strive to ensure students' physical, social-emotional, and intellectual growth.

Different partnerships can begin to reverse challenges that children and families face to let their assets shine through.

Students, families, and teachers all need support systems in place to advance teaching and learning. For multilingual students and their families, having services and resources available in multiple languages, whether inside or out of school, is essential for them to be able to

- feel comfortable and secure in interacting with others,
- fully understand the information in order to take action,
- have confidence in knowing what is being communicated, and
- establish interpersonal relations.

Ms. Ortega-Miller and the family liaison are able to fulfill that role, becoming a support system for Inés and Mrs. Pérez. By co-constructing a plan with Mrs. Pérez and creating a schedule for the seamstress mom to share her sewing acumen in the primary grade classrooms, everyone is feeling good about setting a course of action for the family. The liaison already contacted a local dry goods store, which was happy to donate its extra yardage on a regular basis. With that in mind, Ms. Ortega-Miller shared the idea with Mrs. Pérez of starting a sewing club of local family members. Feeling empowered, Mrs. Pérez was thrilled at the invitation as she was hoping that it would lead to opening a co-op for the neighborhood where women would sell their homemade goods.

Now let's return to the quote at the beginning of this chapter: "Schools are not islands in themselves; they are connected to communities." What we have tried to depict in our narrative is the strength of interconnections, relationships, and partnerships among communities, schools, and classrooms in overcoming inequities. In this day and age, we feel that the success of schooling, no matter what the educational landscape, is contingent on humanism, where we extend community outreach, maintain viable communication networks, and believe in each other. A literacy coach expresses these exact sentiments as a vision for her classroom post-COVID in the following account.

In Her Own Words

Jennifer Iamele Savage, Literacy Coach, Charleston County Public Schools, Charleston, South Carolina

Ms. Savage, if you could imagine your classroom post-COVID, what would it look like?

I think [the pandemic] has spotlighted the role of schools as being pillars in our communities—not just for education but for community and the teaching of social-emotional skills and values.

In the post-COVID classroom, I envision a lot more time and space for reflection and integration of feelings and experiences. This time has reminded me of what is truly important and that we are raising human beings over anything else, so giving them the space to process their own thoughts, feelings, emotions, and learning is critical.

I believe that many shadows and injustices in our society have been brought to light during this time, and I have made a commitment to make sure that I am always examining and reexamining my own biases and listening and learning so that I can do better for my students and for myself.

Therefore, my post-COVID classroom will be one that feels more diverse, inclusive, and equitable. And even if I cannot control the diversity of the learners in my classroom, I can certainly control the diversity of the content that I present and the way in which I present it. My post-COVID classroom will be intrapersonally reflective and culturally responsive and a place where no human's life or lived experience is taken for granted.

Optimizing Conditions for Fostering Teaching and Learning

We close our story on an optimistic note. Whether in person or remote, students, teachers, and other school leaders deserve nothing short of being able to create and participate in educational experiences that are meaningful and fair. In that process, families are to be engaged, respected, and supported as they, too, juggle the untenable demands that have been placed on them. In partnership, we look forward to the day when we can truly declare that we have overcome what historically has been unjust for communities, schools, and classrooms.

In optimizing conditions for teaching and learning, we envision communities that work in tandem with schools and classrooms to

- expand learning outside of school walls or computer screens,

- form strong and enduring partnerships,

- extend their offerings of services and resources, and

- improve educational access and opportunities for students and their families.

In optimizing conditions for teaching and learning, we envision schools that

✓ exceed the parameters set by state and district policy;

✓ engage in collaboration and cooperation to form community partnerships;

✓ involve students and family members on a deep level;

✓ leverage the presence and use of multiple languages, dialects, and cultures; and

✓ give voice and decision-making power to families, teachers, and students.

In optimizing conditions for teaching and learning, we envision classrooms that are

✓ noisy, interactive places where students engage in purposeful discussion;

✓ student-centered empowerment zones where students are agents of their own learning;

✓ happy, inviting, and motivating spaces for exploring and investigating; and

✓ linguistically and culturally enriching, as are curriculum, instruction, and assessment.

Overcoming educational inequities requires relationship building through interconnections among communities, schools, and classrooms.

It is our hope that the strengths of communities, with all their linguistic and cultural capital, are absorbed into schools and that those assets permeate each and every classroom. We leave you with a vision of an alliance where equity reigns for families, educators, and students (see Figure 9.11).

Figure 9.11 • In Partnership: Overcoming Linguistic and Cultural Inequities Across Communities, Schools, and Classrooms

COMMUNITIES
- Designing strengths-based partnerships
- Building interdependent and interconnected relationships
- Contributing to schools and classrooms

SCHOOLS
- Honoring multiple perspectives and views
- Supporting teachers through professional learning
- Collaborating with communities

CLASSROOMS
- Leveraging linguistic and cultural sustainability
- Ensuring student agency and voice
- Sharing community and family expertise

Overcoming Linguistic and Cultural Disparities

We imagine how the pervasive inequities that have plagued minoritized students and families can be ameliorated, in part, through interconnected classrooms, schools, and communities. We see how classrooms have become laboratories for learning, not only for content and disciplinary practices, but also where students are members of a productive and collaborative community that seeks equity and social justice. We imagine how every student is well equipped to strive for excellence, where each one has access and opportunity to pursue learning from a multicultural lens and gain deep knowledge, insight, and perspectives of the interconnected world in which we live.

The Pérez family and their interconnections with their schools and community illustrate a strengths-based approach to improving educational opportunities for minoritized students. Through Álvaro, Inés, and Mrs. Pérez, we have imagined how partnerships among educators, families, and community services grow trust and respect. As a result, the children's schools have become responsive by creating a linguistically and culturally sustainable climate that showcases students' assets in school and beyond. Additionally, school leadership teams have collaborated in creating a professional development plan that ensures enactment of student-driven learning throughout the school year. Through teacher voices and actions, we have highlighted how crises have been able to stimulate postcrises excellence for our students and their families.

It is with firm conviction that we believe one day educational inequities of the past, especially those that emanate from linguistic and cultural disparities and discrimination, will dissolve (or be resolved). Additionally, we sincerely hope that the idealism we have imagined for transforming education for communities, schools, and classrooms postcrises will become reality for our students, their families, and the nation.

References

August, D., Beck, I. L., Calderón, M., Francis, D.J., Lesaux, N. K., & Shanahan, T. (2008). Instruction and professional development. In D. August & T. Shanahan (Eds.), *Developing reading and writing in second language learners: Lessons from the Report of the National Literacy Panel on Language-Minority Children and Youth* (pp. 131–250). New York, NY: Routledge.

Baltimore City Board of School Commissioners. (2016, October). *Community school strategy.* Retrieved from https://www.boarddocs.com/mabe/bcpss/Board.nsf/files/AEXQ2G672538/$file/ADH-%20Community%20School%20Strategy.2nd%20Reader%20CLEAN.pdf

Belway, S., Durán, M., & Spielberg, L. (2015). *State laws on family engagement in education: National PTA reference guide.* Retrieved from https://s3.amazonaws.com/rdcms-pta/files/production/public/State_Laws_Report.pdf

Bethell, C. D., Davis, M. B., Gombojav, N., Stumbo, S., & Powers, K. (2017, October). *A national and across-state profile on adverse childhood experiences among children and possibilities to heal and thrive.* Baltimore, MD: Johns Hopkins Bloomberg School of Public Health. Retrieved from https://www.greatcircle.org/images/pdfs/aces-brief-101717.pdf

Billings, E., & Mueller, P. (n.d.). *Quality student interactions: Why are they crucial to language learning and how can we support them?* Albany: New York State Education Department, Office of Bilingual Education and World Languages. Retrieved from http://www.nysed.gov/common/nysed/files/programs/bilingual-ed/quality_student_interactions-2.pdf

Biswas-Dienera, R., Kashdan, T. B., & Gurpal, M. (2011). A dynamic approach to psychological strength development and intervention. *Journal of Positive Psychology, 6*(2), 106–118.

Brockton Public Schools. (2020). *FAQs.* Retrieved from https://www.bpsma.org/schools/health-services/faqs

Brockton Public Schools. (n.d.). BPS social emotional services call center. https://resources.finalsite.net/images/v1585838014/brockton/foi2nsdigprxv4pxguqy/Socialemotionalservicescallcenter.pdf

Burns, M. (2016, November 22). 5 strategies to deepen student collaboration. *Edutopia.* Retrieved from https://www.edutopia.org/article/5-strategies-deepen-student-collaboration-mary-burns

Calderón, M. (1984) *Training bilingual trainers: A quantitative and ethnographic study of coaching and its impact on the transfer of training* (Unpublished doctoral dissertation). Claremont Graduate School/San Diego State University.

Calderón, M. E. (1999). Teachers learning communities for cooperation in diverse settings. *Theory Into Practice, 38*(2), 94–99.

Calderón, M. E. (2007). *Teaching reading to English language learners, grades 6–12: A framework for improving achievement in the content areas.* Thousand Oaks, CA: Corwin.

Calderón, M. E. (2017) *Expediting comprehension for English language learners: Administrators manual.* Washington, DC: Margarita Calderón & Associates.

Calderón, M. E., Dove, M., Fenner, D. S., Gottlieb, M., Honigsfeld, A., Singer T. W., . . . Zacarian, D. (Eds.). (2020). *Breaking down the wall: Essential shifts for English learners' success.* Thousand Oaks, CA: Corwin.

Calderón, M. E., Espino, G., & S. Slakk. (2019). *Integrando lenguaje, lectura, escritura y contenidos en español e inglés. Integrating Language, Reading, Writing and Content in English and in Spanish.* Los Angeles: Velazquez Press.

Calderón, M. E., Hertz-Lazarowitz, R., & Slavin, R. E. (1998). Effects of bilingual cooperative integrated reading and composition on students making the transition from Spanish to English reading. *Elementary School Journal, 99*(2), 153–165.

Calderón, M. E., & Minaya-Rowe, L. (2011). *Preventing long-term ELs: Transforming schools to meet core standards.* Thousand Oaks, CA: Corwin.

Calderón M. E., & Montenegro, H. (2021). *Empowering LTEL with social emotional learning, language, literacy and content.* El Monte, CA: Velázquez Press.

Calderón, M. E., Trejo, M., Montenegro, H., Carreón, A., Peyton, J. K., Marino, J., & D'Emilio, T. (2015). *Literacy strategies for English learners in core content secondary classrooms.* Indianapolis, IN: Solution Tree Press.

Carnegie Council on Advancing Adolescent Literacy. (2010). *Time to act: An agenda for advancing adolescent literacy for college and career success.* New York: Carnegie Corporation of New York.

Carver-Thomas, D. (2018). *Diversifying the teaching profession: How to recruit and retain teachers of color.* Washington, DC: Learning Policy Institute.

CASEL. (2020). *SEL: What are the core competence areas and where are they promoted?* Retrieved from https://casel.org/core-competencies/

Center for Collaborative Education. (2016–2020). *Thought leadership*. Retrieved from https://www.cce.org/thought-leadership

Centers for Disease Control and Prevention. (2020, July 24). *Health equity considerations and racial and ethnic minority groups*. Retrieved from https://www.cdc.gov/coronavirus/2019-ncov/community/health-equity/race-ethnicity.html

The Center for Reaching and Teaching the Whole Child. http://crtwc.org/strategic-plan-2/mission-and-vision/

Child and Adolescent Health Measurement Initiative. (2013). *Overview of adverse child and family experiences among US children*. Retrieved from https://www.childhealthdata.org/docs/drc/aces-data-brief_version-1-0.pdf

Communities in Schools. (2020). *Our model*. Retrieved from https://communitiesinschools.org/our-model/

Constantino, S. M. (2016). *Engage every family: Five simple principles*. Thousand Oaks, CA: Corwin.

Cooper, R. (2017, November 6). *How can educators best promote student agency?* Retrieved from https://www.educationdive.com/news/how-can-educators-best-promote-student-agency/508050/

C-SPAN. (2020, April 9). *User Clip: Fauci: Coronavirus "is shining a bright light" on health disparities*. Retrieved from https://www.c-span.org/video/?c4867412/user-clip-fauci-coronavirus-is-shining-bright-light-health-disparities

Donohoo, J. (2017). *Collective efficacy: How teacher beliefs impact student learning*. Thousand Oaks, CA: Corwin.

Drummond-Forrester, K. (2020, August 2). The role social-emotional learning plays in teaching white children about race. *EdSurge*. https://www.edsurge.com/news/2020-08-02-the-role-social-emotional-learning-plays-in-teaching-white-children-about-race?fbclid=IwAR0IXUF4DGRz02TGo-z6PUC_EjRtRq4aVuxE_zLpo9SxSOUrScuKOR6pBa28

Ed Trust-West. (2020, April 7). *Education equity in crisis: The digital divide*. Retrieved from https://west.edtrust.org/resource/education-equity-in-crisis-the-digital-divide/

Edwards, P. A., Domke. L., & White, K. (2017). Closing the parent gap in changing school districts. In S. B. Wepner & D. W. Gomez (Eds.), *Challenges facing suburban schools: Promising responses to changing student populations* (pp. 109–123). Lanham, MD: Rowman & Littlefield.

Edwards, P. A., & White, K. L. (2018). Working with racially, culturally, and linguistically diverse students, families, and communities: Strategies for preparing pre-service teachers. *Journal of Family Diversity in Education, 3*(1), 6–7.

Endacott, J., & Brooks, S. (2013). An updated theoretical and practical model for promoting historical empathy. *Social Studies Research and Practice, 8*, 41–58.

Epstein, J. L. (2001). *School, family, and community partnerships: Preparing educators and improving schools*. Boulder, CO: Westview Press.

Epstein, J. L. (2009). *School family and community partnerships, caring the children we share*. In J. L. Epstein & Associates (Eds.), *School, family, and community partnerships: Your handbook in action* (3rd ed., pp. 9–30). Thousand Oaks, CA: Corwin.

Epstein, J., & Associates. (2009). *School, family, and community partnerships: Your handbook in action* (3rd ed.). Thousand Oaks, CA: Corwin.

Every Student Succeeds Act of 2015, Pub. L. No. 114-95, §114 Stat. 1177 (2015–2016).

Families in Schools. (n.d.). *Ready or not: How California school districts are reimagining parent engagement in the era of local control funding formula*. Retrieved from https://www.scusd.edu/sites/main/files/file-attachments/families_in_schools_lcap_report.pdf?1491522608

Ferlazzo, L. (2020). Q & A Collections: Professional Development. [Opinion Blog.] *Education Week*. https://www.edweek.org/education/opinion-q-a-collections-professional-development/2020/08

Fisher, D., Frey, N., & Hattie, J. (2021). *The distance learning playbook, grades K–12: Teaching for engagement and impact in any setting*. Thousand Oaks, CA: Corwin.

Fisher, D., Frey, N., & Nelson, J. (2012). Literacy achievement through sustained professional development. *The Reading Teacher. 65*(8): 551–563.

Flannery, T. (2016). Foreword. In P. Wohlleben *The hidden life of trees: What they feel, how they communicate: discoveries from a secret world*. Vancouver, British Columbia, Canada: Greystone Books.

Flannery, M. E. (2019, March). The epidemic of anxiety among today's students. *NEA Today*. Retrieved from http://neatoday.org/2018/03/28/the-epidemic-of-student-anxiety/

France, P. E. (2018). A healthy ecosystem for classroom management. *Educational Leadership, 76*(1).

Garcia, L. (2021). *What we believe: A Black Lives Matter principles activity book*. New York, NY: Lee & Low Books.

García, O., Ibarra Johnson, S., & Seltzer, K. (2017). *The translanguaging classroom: Leveraging student bilingualism for learning*. Philadelphia, PA: Caslon.

Gauvain, M. (2001). *The social context of cognitive development*. New York, NY: Guilford Press.

Gauvain, M. (2013). Sociocultural contexts in development. In P. D. Zelazo (Ed.), *Oxford handbook of developmental psychology: Vol. 2., self and other* (pp. 425–451). New York, NY: Oxford University Press.

Gerzon-Kessler, A. (2019/2020). Involving families: A relationship-centered approach. *Educational Leadership, 77*(4).

Giroux, H. (1983). *Theory and resistance in education: Towards a pedagogy for the opposition*. Westport, CT: Bergin & Garvey.

Gonzalez, N., Moll, L. C., & Amanti, C. (Eds.). (2005). *Funds of knowledge: Theorizing practices in households, communities, and classrooms*. Mahwah, NJ: Lawrence Erlbaum.

Gottlieb, M. (2016). *Assessing English language learners: Bridges to educational equity: Connecting academic language proficiency to student achievement* (2nd ed.). Thousand Oaks, CA: Corwin.

Gottlieb, M. (2021). *Classroom assessment in multiple languages: A handbook for teachers*. Thousand Oaks, CA: Corwin.

Gottlieb, M., & Castro, M. (2017). *Language power: Key uses for accessing content*. Thousand Oaks, CA: Corwin.

Gottlieb, M., & Ernst-Slavit, G. (2019). Promoting educational equity in assessment practices. In L. C. de Oliveira (Ed.). *The handbook of TESOL in K–12* (pp. 129–148). Hoboken, NJ: John Wiley.

Gottlieb, M., Hilliard, J., Sánchez-López, C., Díaz-Pollack, B., & Salto, D. (2020). *Language education policy in the United States: A promising outlook: A state and district analysis of language development models and programs with support of national professional organizations.* Chicago, IL: Paridad Education Consulting.

Gottlieb, M., & Katz, A. (2020). Assessment in the classroom. In C. Chappelle (Ed.). *The concise encyclopedia of applied linguistics.* Hoboken, NJ: John Wiley.

Graham, S., & Perin, D. (2007). *Writing next: Effective strategies to improve writing of adolescents in middle and high schools.* Washington, DC: Alliance for Excellent Education.

Grant, R. (2018, March). Do trees talk to each other? *Smithsonian.* Retrieved from https://www.smithsonianmag.com/science-nature/the-whispering-trees-180968084/

Grantmakers for Education. (2013). *Educating English language learners: Grantmaking strategies for closing America's other achievement gap.* Portland, OR: Author. Retrieved from https://edfunders.org/sites/default/files/Educating%20English%20Language%20Learners_April%202013.pdf

Graves, K. (2008). The language curriculum: A social contextual perspective. *Language Teaching, 41*(2), 147–181.

Hattie, J. (2009). *Visible learning: A synthesis of over 800 meta-analyses relating to achievement.* New York, NY: Routledge.

Hattie, J. A. C. (2012). *Visible learning for teachers. Maximizing impact on achievement.* Oxford, UK: Routledge.

Hattie, J. (2017). *Visible Learning for teachers: Maximizing impact for learning.* Thousand Oaks, CA: Corwin.

Hofstede, G. (2011). Dimensionalizing cultures: The Hofstede model in context. *Online Readings in Psychology and Culture, 2*(1).

Hofstede, G., & Hofstede, G. J. (2005). *Cultures and organizations: Software of the mind (2nd ed.).* New York, NY: McGraw-Hill.

Huff, K. (2020, August 30). How "growth" goals actually hold students back. *EdSurge.* Retrieved from https://www.edsurge.com/news/2020-08-30-how-growth-goals-actually-hold-students-back

Ibarra, H., & Scoular, A (2019, November-December). The leader as coach. *Harvard Business Review.* Retrieved from https://hbr.org/2019/11/the-leader-as-coach

Improving America's Schools Act of 1994, Pub. L. No. 103-382 (1994).

Jagers, R.J., Rivas-Drake, D., Borowski, T. (2018). Equity & Social and Emotional Learning: A Cultural Analysis. CASEL. Measuring SEL Using Data to Inspire Practice. https://measuringsel.casel.org/wp-content/uploads/2018/11/Frameworks-Equity.pdf

Joyce, B., & Showers, B. (1982). The coaching of teaching. *Educational Leadership, 40*(1), 4–10.

Kibler, A., & Valdés, G. (2016). Conceptualizing language learners: Socioinstitutional mechanisms and their consequences. *Modern Language Journal, 100*(S1), 96–116.

Kotok, S., & Frankenberg, E. (2017). Demography and educational politics in the changing suburbs. In S. B. Wepner & D. W. Gomez (Eds.), *Challenges facing public schools: Promising responses to changing student populations* (pp. 1–14). Lanham, MD: Rowman and Littlefield.

LaCelle-Peterson, M. W., & Rivera, C. (1994). Is it real for all kids? A framework for equitable assessment policies for English language learners. *Harvard Education Review, 64*(1), 55–73.

Ladson-Billings, G. (1994). *The dreamkeepers.* San Francisco, CA: Jossey-Bass.

Lau v. Nichols, 414 U.S. 563 (1974); 42 U.S.C. § 2000d to d-7.

Lave, J., & Wenger, E. (1991). *Situated learning: Legitimate peripheral participation.* Cambridge, UK: Cambridge University Press.

Lebeaux, D. (2020). *Building for equity: A guide for inclusive school design.* Boston, MA: Center for Collaborative Education. Retrieved from https://www.cce.org/uploads/files/CCE-BuildingforEquity.pdf

Lewis, J. (2017). *Across that bridge: A vision for change and the future of America.* New York, NY: Hachette Books.

Linn, D., & Hemmer, L. (2011). English language learner disproportionality in special education: Implications for the scholar-practitioner. *Journal of Educational Research and Practice, 1*(1), 70–80.

Marion, S. F., Gonzales, D., Wiener, R., & Peltzman, A. (2020). *This is not a test, this is an emergency: Special considerations for assessing and advancing equity in school-year 2020–21.* Dover, NH: Center for Assessment.

Maslow, A. H. (1987). *Motivation and Personality* (3rd ed.). Delhi, India: Pearson Education.

Maslow, A. H. (1999). *Toward a psychology of being* (3rd ed.). New York, NY: John Wiley & Sons.

Meyer, A., Rose, D. H., & Gordon, D. (2014). *Universal design for learning: theory and practice.* Wakefield, MA: CAST.

Miramontes, O. B., Nadeau, A., & Commins, N. L. (2011). *Restructuring schools for linguistic diversity: Linking decision making to effective programs* (2nd ed.). New York, NY: Teachers College Press.

Moats, L. (2020). *Teaching reading is rocket science, 2020.* Washington, DC: American Federation of Teachers.

Muñiz, J. (2019). *Culturally responsive teaching: A 50-state survey of teaching standards.* Washington, DC: New America. Retrieved from https://www.newamerica.org/education-policy/reports/culturally-responsive-teaching/

National Center for Education Statistics. (2019). Table 219.46. Public high school 4-year adjusted cohort graduation rate (ACGR), by selected student characteristics and state: 2010–11 through 2017–18. Retrieved from https://nces.ed.gov/programs/digest/d19/tables/dt19_219.46.asp

New York City Department of Education. (2020). *Teaching and learning.* Retrieved from https://www.schools.nyc.gov/school-year-20-21/return-to-school-2020/teaching-and-learning

Oluo, I. (2019). *So you want to talk about race.* Seal Press.

No Child Left Behind Act of 2001, Pub. L. No. 107-110, § 115, Stat. 1425-2094 (2002).

Paris, D. (2012). Culturally sustaining pedagogy: A needed change in stance, terminology, and practice. *Educational Research, 41*(3), 93–97.

Park, S., Magee, J., Martinez, M. I., Willner, L. S., & Paul, J. (2016). *English language learners with disabilities: A call for additional research and policy guidance.* Washington, DC: Council of Chief State School Officers.

Phillipson, R., & Skutnabb-Kangas, T. (1986). *Linguicism rules in education, Parts 1–3*. Roskilde, Denmark: Roskilde University Centre.

Quaglia, R. J., & Lande, L. L. (2017). *Teacher voice: Amplifying success*. Thousand Oaks, CA: Corwin.

Ramirez, J. D. (2010). *Building family support for student achievement: CABE Project Inspire Parent Leadership Development Program*. Retrieved from: http://ww2.acoe.org/acoe/files/edservices/projectinspire/me-2010-pirc.pdf

Randolph, L. J., Jr., &, and Johnson, S. M. (2017). Social justice in the language classroom. *Dimension*, pp 9–31. Southern Conference on Language Teaching. Retrieved from https://www.scolt.org/wp-content/uploads/2019/08/1_Social-Justice_Randolph_2.pdf.

Rosas, J., & Flores, N. (2017). Unsettling race and language: Toward a raciolinguistic perspective. *Language in Society, 46* (5) 621–647. Cambridge, UK: Cambridge University Press.

Saifer, S., Edwards, K., Ellis, D., Ko, L., & Stuczynski, A. (2011). *Culturally responsive standards-based teaching: Classroom to community and back* (2nd ed.). Thousand Oaks, CA: Corwin.

Samson, J. F., & Lesaux, N. K. (2009). Language-minority learners in special education: Rates and predictors of identification for services. *Journal of Learning Disabilities, 42*(2), 148–162.

Saphier, J. (2017). *High expectations teaching: How we persuade students to believe and act on "smart is something we can get."* Thousand Oaks, CA: Corwin.

Short, D., & Fitzsimmons, S. (2007). *Double the work: Challenges and solutions to acquiring language and academic literacy for adolescent English language learners*. New York, NY: Alliance for Excellent Education.

Slavin, R. E., & Calderón, M. (Eds.). (2001). *Effective programs for Latino students*. Mahwah, NJ: Lawrence Erlbaum.

Soto, I., & Ward Singer, T. (2020). From silence to conversation. In M. E. Calderón, M. Dove, D. S. Fenner, M. Gottlieb, A. Honigsfeld, T. W. Singer, S. Slakk, I. Soto, & D. Zacarian (Eds.), *Breaking down the wall: Essential shifts for English learners' success* (pp. 89–110). Thousand Oak, CA: Corwin.

Southern Education Foundation. (2020). *New majority series*. Retrieved from https://www.southerneducation.org/what-we-do/research/newmajorityreportseries/

Steele, C. M. (2010). *Whistling Vivaldi and other clues to how stereotypes affect us*. New York: W.W. Norton.

Swain, M. (2006). Languaging, agency and collaboration in advanced language proficiency. In H. Byrnes (Ed.), *Advanced language learning: The contribution of Halliday and Vygotsky* (pp. 95–108). London, UK: Continuum.

Takanishi, R., & Le Menestrel, S. (Eds.). (2017). *Promoting the educational success of children and youth learning English: Promising futures*. Washington, DC: National Academies of Science Press.

Taketa, K. (2017, February 5). International students find refuge, opportunity in Ritenour's English school. *St. Louis Post Dispatch*. Retrieved from https://www.stltoday.com/news/local/education/international-students-find-refuge-opportunity-in-ritenours-english-school/article_4c7dfc73-4ee6-5259-b4b9-ade2948ce867.html

U.S. Department of Education. (1995). *Helping teachers teach well: Transforming professional development*. Retrieved from https://www2.ed.gov/pubs/CPRE/t61/t61c.html

U.S. Department of Education. (2016). *The state of racial diversity in the educator workforce*. Retrieved from https://www2.ed.gov/rschstat/eval/highered/racial-diversity/state-racial-diversity-workforce.pdf

U.S. Department of Education. (n.d.). *Title III—Language instruction for limited English proficient English learners and immigrant students*. Retrieved from https://www2.ed.gov/policy/elsec/leg/essa/legislation/title-iii.pdf

U.S. Department of Education & U.S. Department of Justice. (2015, January 7). *Dear colleague*. Retrieved from https://www2.ed.gov/about/offices/list/ocr/letters/colleague-el-201501.pdf

U.S. Department of Education, Office of Civil Rights. (2020). *Schools' civil rights obligations to English learner students and limited English proficient parents*. Retrieved from https://www2.ed.gov/about/offices/list/ocr/ellresources.html

van der Heijden, H. R. M. A., Geldens, J. J. M., Beijaard, D., & Popeijus, H. L. (2014). Characteristics of teachers as change agents. *Teachers and Teaching, 21*, 681–699.

van Lier, L. (2007). Action-based teaching, autonomy and identity. *Innovation in Language Learning and Teaching, 1*(1), 46–65.

Watkins, C. (2005). Classrooms as learning communities: A review of research. *London Review of Education, 3*(1), 47–64.

Wilcox, L. (2018, June 4). *Top 5 strategies for motivating students*. Retrieved from https://www.nbpts.org/top-5-strategies-for-motivating-students/

Wolpert-Gawron, H. (2016). The many roles of an instructional coach. *Educational Leadership, 73*, 56–60.

Yoshikawa, H. (2011). *Immigrants raising citizens: Undocumented parents and their young children*. New York, NY: Russell Sage Foundation.

Zacarian, D., Alvarez-Ortiz, L., & Haynes, J. (2017). *Teaching to strengths: Supporting students living with trauma, violence and chronic stress*. Alexandria, VA: ASCD.

Zacarian, D., & Silverstone, M. A. (2015). *In it together: How student, family, and community partnerships advance engagement and achievement in diverse classrooms*. Thousand Oaks, CA: Corwin.

Zacarian, D., & Silverstone, M. A. (2020). *Teaching to empower: Taking action to foster student agency, self-confidence, and collaboration*. Alexandria, VA: ASCD.

Zacarian, D., & Soto, I. (2020). *Responsive schooling for culturally and linguistically diverse students*. New York, NY: W. W. Norton.

Zipke, M. (2007). The role of metalinguistic awareness in the reading comprehension of sixth and seventh graders. *Reading Psychology, 28*, 375–396.

Index

A SAGE Publishing Company

Helping educators make the greatest impact

CORWIN HAS ONE MISSION: to enhance education through intentional professional learning.

We build long-term relationships with our authors, educators, clients, and associations who partner with us to develop and continuously improve the best evidence-based practices that establish and support lifelong learning.